Eco Kiwi

GREEN SOLUTIONS FOR EVERYDAY LIFE

Simon & Jane
COTTER

National Library of New Zealand Cataloguing-in-Publication Data

Cotter, Simon.
Eco kiwi: green solutions for everyday life / Simon and Jane Cotter.
Includes index.
ISBN 1-86941-594-9
1. Home economics—New Zealand. 2. Dwellings—Environmental aspects—New Zealand.
3. Dwellings—Environmental engineering—New Zealand. 4. Environmental protection—
New Zealand.
I. Cotter, Jane. II. Title.
640—dc 21

A RANDOM HOUSE BOOK
published by
Random House New Zealand
18 Poland Road, Glenfield, Auckland, New Zealand

www.randomhouse.co.nz

First published 2003

© 2003 Simon and Jane Cotter

The moral rights of the authors have been asserted

ISBN 1 86941 594 9

The authors would like to thank the many individuals who, in either a private capacity or as representatives of government and non-government agencies and organisations, provided information, encouragement and feedback.

Cover design: Matthew Trbuhovic, The Bureau
Cover photographs: Getty Images and Natural Science Image Library of New Zealand
Illustrations: Martin Northcott
Eco logo design: Jill Godwin

Printed by Griffin Press, Australia

No chlorine chemicals were used in the production or bleaching of the paper used to print this book. The environmental matters at the paper mill are based on the EMAS Regulation (EC Eco Management and Audit Scheme) and on the ISO 14001 environmental standard, and both these systems have been certified.

Contents

Part Four: Resources

Introduction

This is a book for all eco Kiwis: eco zealots, eco cynics, eco slobs, eco sentimentalists, but especially it is a book for down-to-earth, eco-sympathetic Kiwis.

It aims to provide a framework for eco living in New Zealand homes: a framework that is accessible, local, current, useful, healthy and informative. It aims to bring eco living out of the clouds and into the home.

The main focus is on making eco choices for the environment and living systems. The implications for human health are also considered. Emphasis is placed on eco living rather than eco building. The idea of living in a brand-new eco home is not a realistic option for most people, whereas changing the way we live in our present home is. Therefore, we suggest the gradual introduction of eco-friendly living solutions into daily routines in existing homes and look at some of the eco choices around buying, building or altering a home. It aims at eco *evolution* rather than eco *revolution*.

Topics range from the mundane to the exotic. Eco living has no parameters but of necessity some subjects are explored in detail while others are given less attention. Priority has been given to areas which lend themselves to practical solutions or where misconception is common. Whether you are buying products for use in the home, putting more sustainable systems into place, renovating a room or creating an organic garden, having access to good information is a valuable first step.

This book presents little that is new; rather, it is a distillation of material from many sources, including government agencies, environmental groups, scientific organisations and passionate individuals. In putting it together we have tried to present a balanced view. Hopefully, this practical and inclusive approach will make it easier for Kiwis to live eco-friendly lives in eco-friendly environments.

If anyone has information they would like to submit for possible use in future editions, please feel free to contact us.

Simon and Jane Cotter
E-mail: sico@ihug.co.nz

The Eco Wheel

Every decision, purchase, daily routine or practice has an ecological implication. The eco wheel is a relatively simple way of assessing your options. Use the eco wheel to see how ecosystems measure up and to identify specific weaknesses, which can then be explored and perhaps corrected.

~ *Easy* Eco living must be easy to understand, easy to implement and easy to sustain. Like the wheel it needs to be a simple, self-propelling system that, with a little initial effort, provides its own momentum.

~ *Effective*   If it is to work, an eco cycle has to be practical, adaptable and inexpensive.

~ *Ethical*   In eco living all must benefit. The eco cycle must work for all living systems. It must serve the animate and inanimate. It must serve cynics, slobs, sentimentalists and zealots. It must serve the individual and it must serve the masses. Like a cogged wheel, an eco cycle should aid and not impede other eco cycles.

~ *Enduring*   If eco living is easy, effective and ethical, it will create its own momentum, meet little resistance and so be self-sustaining.

Bearing in mind that often there are eco wheels within wheels, eco wheels that drive other wheels, and eco wheels that impede other wheels, it is possible to identify a number of major eco cycles which contribute differently to a healthy and eco-friendly lifestyle in the home. These can be loosely grouped as:

➤ The shelter cycle

➤ The elements

➤ The life cycle

These major eco cycles each have one part of the book devoted to them.

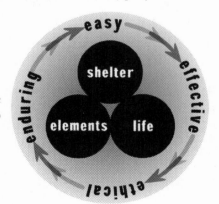

Part One

The
Shelter
Cycle

Chapter 1

Location and design

CHOOSING A HOME

There is no ideal place in which to be eco friendly – it is a matter of doing what you can, where you can. No matter where you live there'll be something you can to do to make your lifestyle greener. If you live in an inner-city apartment, other residents may not be keen on the idea of keeping a worm farm in the lobby but will be none the wiser if you use eco-friendly cleansers in your kitchen. If you live in a well-insulated suburban house, the pros and cons of installing insulation may be irrelevant, but you may like to install a solar panel for hot water.

Check out the local environment

Carefully considering eco issues when buying or moving home makes it easier to maintain an eco-friendly lifestyle. Location is the one thing you can't change (unless you pick up your house and move it), so check out the local environment before you decide to move in or buy. If you are considering a specific property, a Land Information Memorandum (LIM – see panel on the next page) report, obtained from the local territorial authority, is a good place to start. But go one step further and ask the neighbours what they can tell you about an area and whether they know of any drawbacks.

Think through the implications of the local economy. A quiet rural area may look idyllic but be subject to intensive horticultural spraying; a nearby piggery may not be visible or audible, but you'll know about it when the wind blows your way; commercial forests are eventually clear-felled and even small rivers dammed.

Closer to town, assess the possibility of air, noise, industrial and visual pollution. Look at the possible effect on your chosen location of motorways,

> ## What is a LIM report?
>
> For a fee, territorial councils will prepare a LIM (Land Information Memorandum) report. A LIM report provides information on special land characteristics such as potential erosion, subsidence, slippage and flooding. It will indicate the presence of hazardous contaminants, if known to the local council, and provide information on private and public stormwater drains and sewerage, as shown in the council's records.
>
> A LIM report will outline the allowed use of land and buildings and show any previous dealings with the council, including consents relating to building or site works. Prospective buyers often use a LIM report to uncover building work that is incomplete, or that doesn't have a building permit. Potential problems can be exposed. ('Did the council issue a building consent for construction of that leaky basement?') This alone makes getting a LIM report a good idea before finalising a purchase, but it is also useful in assessing the property's value, checking it is free from restrictions and deciding whether your intended use of the land is feasible.

industrial zones, airports and flight paths, railways and freight yards, overhead power pylons, and infrastructure facilities such as landfills and sewage works. Check out the availability of public transport, parks, recycling services and organic food supplies.

The history of an area, its topology and climate all hold clues to what you can expect if you choose to live there. Much of what is mysteriously referred to as Feng Shui, the Chinese art of placement, is little more than a commonsensical assessment of the influences of the natural elements on a site. We are entering an era of pronounced climate change. It will be characterised by higher rainfalls, stronger and more frequent winds, inland flooding, rising sea levels and coastal erosion. When buying or building, think how these factors could affect your site.

Spiritual concerns about a particular place can be dealt with according to personal belief; a tohunga can be asked to clear or lift a tapu from sites with indigenous significance. Other beliefs and faiths have similar procedures for dealing with unsettling atmospheres.

ORIENTATION AND PASSIVE SOLAR DESIGN

On a cold winter day, where would you rather sit — in the shade or the sun? It has been suggested that many of the homes first built in this country were built facing south because that's what was done in the northern hemisphere. In some instances, as in Dunedin, early subdivisions planned in Britain were designed and built with houses facing south. In rural locations, factors such as the sun, prevailing wind, access and view would have been given greater consideration, but in town, expediency ruled. Once surveyors had marked out the roads, houses were usually built to face the street. If the section was big enough, ridgelines ran parallel with the road but little thought was given to orientating living spaces towards the sun.

If you are building a sustainable, comfortable home you need to consider as many environmental features as possible at the design stage. If you are buying or moving into an existing dwelling, an assessment of the same features will give you an insight into how the home operates and how it can be made to work better.

Sun

The way a home is placed on a site has an impact on its seasonal and day-to-day comfort. Each site or dwelling should be viewed within the context of its own location but, as a rule, a northern aspect with the main axis of the building running east-west and areas that are lived in facing north, provides maximum sunlight and warmth in winter. The kitchen is perhaps better placed facing east, to catch the early morning sun. Rooms facing west will catch the late evening glare. The colder and darker southern quarter is best given over to garages, workshops, bathrooms and laundries.

Topography and air movement

Factors such as ease of access, visibility and exposure to prevailing winds need to be considered in light of landforms, vegetation and site drainage (which encompasses the movement of both water and air). A home on a hill will experience stronger winds than a home on the flat, making it harder to heat in winter. In the summer, however, it is more likely to be blessed with a breeze, as the warm air moves up the hill.

A beachfront home will enjoy a sea breeze during the day as the land warms up and pulls the breeze inshore. At night, with the land cooling more rapidly than the sea, the breeze reverses.

A home in a valley will be hit by cool night air travelling down the hill, collecting in the valley and forming frost. Try to work out how windbreaks, other vegetation and natural features close to the home will affect the comfort of your home in winter and summer.

Thermal efficiency

At little extra cost, homes can be designed to be naturally warm in winter and cool in summer using the right combination of glass, insulation and building mass. A thermally efficient home is not only more comfortable and healthy to live in, it also reduces energy costs, preserves valuable natural energy resources and avoids the production of carbon dioxide associated with energy generation and consumption.

Any building with thermal mass has the ability to absorb, store and slowly release heat. Passive solar design works when free energy from the sun passes through glazing, is absorbed by the mass of the building, retained within the building by good insulation and only released when the indoor temperature cools to a point where it slowly flows out again. Heavy mass is not, however, a recipe in itself for energy efficiency. For optimum performance it needs to be combined with effective insulation.

Concrete, masonry and earth are good examples of building materials that capture the free energy of the sun through the windows. This cycling of thermal energy, of steady absorption and release, has the effect of moderating indoor temperatures — extremes are evened out. Without any mechanical assistance thermal mass cools the air on warm days and warms it on cool days.

Low-mass buildings, on the other hand, experience greater seasonal extremes of temperature — you will feel colder on cold days and hotter on warm days — and will need to make greater use of artificial heating and cooling to be comfortable.

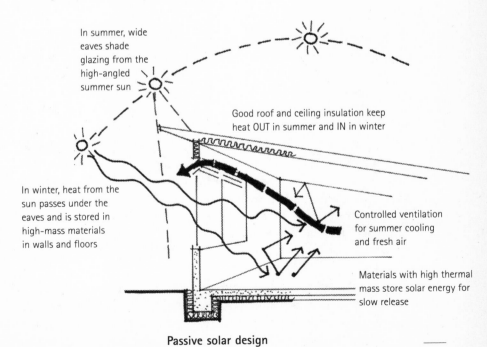

In summer, wide eaves shade glazing from the high-angled summer sun

Good roof and ceiling insulation keep heat OUT in summer and IN in winter

In winter, heat from the sun passes under the eaves and is stored in high-mass materials in walls and floors

Controlled ventilation for summer cooling and fresh air

Materials with high thermal mass store solar energy for slow release

Passive solar design

BUILDING MATERIALS

Wood, straw or stone? As the three little pigs discovered, building materials play a major part in personal health. Their extraction, manufacture, use and disposal also play a part in the health of the environment.

Ideally, an eco home uses durable materials from sustainable resources, whose production and disposal have no adverse impact on the environment, whose toxicity is minimal and whose level of recyclability is high. In reality, anyone designing, building or renovating a home based on eco principles faces a considerable challenge locating suitable materials, evaluating their viability and understanding the implications of their use. In practical terms, eco solutions often involve a degree of compromise.

Sustainability

Choice of material plays a part in the sustainability of earth's resources.

A sustainable material is one that can be endlessly replenished at the same rate or more quickly than it is being used. Rainforests are a renewable resource, but not at a rate which supports their unsustainable use. Plantation timber is a good example of a sustainable resource: it can be harvested, used and recycled while new plantation timber is growing to replace it. The growing tree is an essential component of the carbon cycle (see page 26) and the harvested tree avoids the need to fell old-growth indigenous rainforests.

Few building materials are truly sustainable; most come from resources that, once depleted, will not be replaceable. However, some, such as the clay used in earth building and for brick making, are so abundant they are unlikely to ever run out.

Durability

The proverbial 'brick and tile' homes abundant throughout New Zealand are held in high regard for a simple reason: they are solid, durable and require minimal maintenance. An eco home, while it might choose a different aesthetic, should copy these proven characteristics.

A durable material is efficient: less of it needs to be used over time, conserving the resource and the energy needed to exploit it. However, its durability should not be an impediment to the breakdown of the material once it returns to nature.

Once installed, a naturally durable material requires less maintenance.

If it is not naturally durable (straw bale, for example, is not naturally durable), then it must be either treated or used in such a way that it gains durability. A broad hat (wide roof overhang) and dry feet (raised foundation) are two basic design features which help a building resist deterioration by protecting it from weathering.

As a general rule, durability by design is preferable to durability by treatment. Materials that need to be treated to gain durability usually entail some health risk to people and the environment.

THE EMBODIED ENERGY EQUATION

A large amount of the energy we use goes into the construction of housing, its daily running and its maintenance. Just as we aim to reduce our energy use as householders, we should be looking to reduce the energy needed to create the structure.

For the eco zealots, there is a branch of environmental science which looks at the energy efficiency of different construction materials throughout their life cycle and gives them an appropriate embodied energy rating. The rating is a measure of the energy used — calculated in megajoules (mJ) — to extract, process, transport, use and eventually dispose of different materials. The rating is not absolute but it gives an idea of the comparative amounts of energy needed to transform different raw materials into building materials and construction systems.

At the low end of the spectrum, air-dried hardwood has an embodied energy rating of 0.5 mJ/kg. At the other end, aluminium has an embodied energy rating of 170 mJ/kg. (A figure has been allocated to most building materials in between.) By adding up the figures a picture can be gained of the overall impact a completed house has on the environment over its expected lifetime.

The 'total embodied energy' of various building elements can also be weighed against the likely cost of heating and cooling a building over its lifetime. A house with a concrete floor, for example, may have a higher embodied energy total than one with a suspended timber floor. However, if the concrete floor contributes to the capture and storage of heat in the winter, the reduced cost of heating that home will eventually make it a sizeable energy saver compared to the timber-floored home.

TOP TIPS
FOR MOVING AND BUILDING NEW

✓ Check out the local environment.

✓ Request a LIM report.

✓ Favour passive solar design.

✓ Favour durable materials from a sustainable resource.

Chapter 2

Building health

HEALTH PROBLEMS BUILT IN

Health problems are often built into a house through ignorance or through disregard for the toxicity of some materials. The materials used to build New Zealand's older housing stock (pre-1950s) contained fewer of the volatile organic compounds (VOCs) associated with sick building syndrome (see below), than those in use today. Many of them, however, contained other contaminants that are now known to present serious health risks. These include the lead and cadmium used in household paints, the asbestos fibres used in asbestos cladding and insulation, and a number of highly toxic pesticides used in timber treatment.

The manufacture and sale of building materials containing these contaminants is now prohibited. But the houses remain and they continue to release harmful particles into the environment, particularly when disturbed during renovations.

Sick building syndrome

Sick building syndrome was first diagnosed in modern commercial and public buildings, where a mixture of air pollution, poorly modulated air conditioning and fluorescent lighting was believed to cause headaches, nausea, and irritations of the eye, nose and throat. The possibility of excess exposure to radon, electromagnetic radiation, asbestos, bacteria and mould spores have since been added to the list.

The main source of air pollution in a modern building is usually the 'off-gassing' of the VOCs found in timber panel products, plastics, glues, vinyls, foam rubber furnishings, carpets, paint and other finishes. New homes built and furnished in a similar way to commercial buildings may exhibit the same symptoms, though not everyone will react to them in the same way.

The syndrome is essentially an individual intolerance or 'sensitivity' to the toxic materials in a confined environment. Individuals vary in susceptibility, depending on factors such as stress, lack of sleep or hereditary disposition. As a person becomes sensitised (allergic) to a chemical, it often takes less and less exposure to produce a reaction. But the body can mask this reaction — a person may have a physiological reaction yet remain unaware of it. With the symptoms masked and the immune systems activated, the body continues to do its best to adapt to the contaminant. After long exposure, the immune system is depleted and illness is likely to follow.

Maintain adequate ventilation

Ventilation is important to the removal of VOCs and other pollutants from buildings. Window joinery can be designed to incorporate a screened ventilation system within the window frame, allowing discrete ventilation to occur when the house is closed up. These ventilation units can be retro-fitted.

Lead poisoning

Lead-based paint was once widely used in New Zealand. Other than in special-purpose paints, which must be clearly labelled, the use of lead in paint has been prohibited since 1965. Before that time, children who chewed on painted cots and toys were at risk of lead poisoning. So too was anyone who was exposed to the dust that was released when painted surfaces were sanded during redecoration. Buildings that pre-date the 1970s may have layers of lead-based paint beneath coats of more modern paint. The removal of this old paint presents the danger of lead poisoning to both the person doing the job and the occupants. In addition, airborne lead dust from exterior renovations may settle in garden soil, contaminating vegetables and fruit and the gardener's hands when working the soil.

Lead is absorbed into the body through the lungs or the mouth and is a cumulative poison, being stored in the bone tissue. Early symptoms of lead poisoning are tiredness, headache, aching bones and muscles, forgetfulness, loss of appetite and sleep disturbance. One tell-tale sign is a blue line on the gums. This is followed by constipation and attacks of intense pain in the abdomen, called lead colic.

Young and unborn children are especially at risk of suffering brain damage over a period of time and pets will often show symptoms before people. Diagnosis is confirmed through checking blood lead levels.

It isn't possible to tell lead-based paint from appearance. Unless proven otherwise, assume that the paint on buildings which pre-date the 1970s is lead based. Finishes that are painted over and left undisturbed pose little immediate risk to health.

Asbestos

In terms of the impact of a single building material on the health of a nation, asbestos has no rivals. Asbestos is a fibrous mineral mined from rock that was widely used to add heat resistance and strength to building materials. Since its introduction in 1940, New Zealand has used hundreds of thousands of tonnes of raw asbestos in insulating and heat-resistant products, water mains, drainpipes, claddings and coatings.

Although these products are no longer manufactured in New Zealand, deteriorating asbestos building products still present a significant human health hazard. A dangerous level of contamination of soil and air from haphazard mining, manufacturing and disposal has also occurred, mainly in the South Auckland area from Onehunga to Papakura, where residential subdivisions are built on heavily contaminated sites.

Asbestos is classified as an A1 human carcinogen. All asbestos breaks down into microscopic particles that enter the lungs and either remain there or migrate to other parts of the body. There is no known safe level of exposure and the deadly effects of inhaling fibres may remain latent for 15 to 50 years. There is a suggestion that children may be more susceptible. There is no known cure for asbestos-related diseases, which include lung cancer, mesothelioma and asbestosis.

In residential situations, asbestos is most often found in asbestos cement products manufactured before the 1980s such as wall and roof claddings, textured ceiling coatings and vinyl floor coverings. In some cases, the only sure method of determining the presence of asbestos is to have material tested by an accredited laboratory. Exposure is most likely to occur when materials containing asbestos are broken, sawn, sanded, drilled or demolished.

If asbestos in a building is in a stable condition it doesn't necessarily have to be removed. If it is painted (encapsulated) and kept in good condition free of lichen, the fibre and dust hazard is significantly reduced. Haphazard removal,

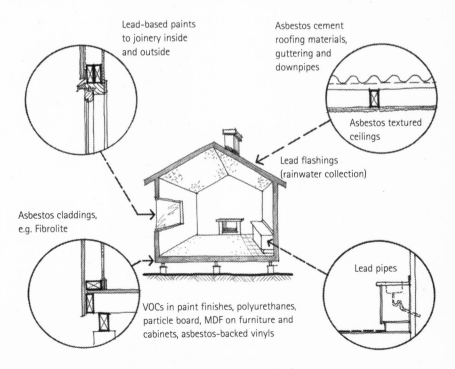

Hazardous building materials in the home

however, can turn a relatively harmless situation into a dangerous one. If a hazard does exist, removal or encapsulation falls into an area categorised by Occupational Safety and Health (OSH) as 'restricted work' and should be carried out by a registered person (consult your Yellow Pages under 'Asbestos').

~ *Asbestos cement claddings* Asbestos cement, the most common form of asbestos in New Zealand, was used to make products such as Fibrolite wall claddings (these include flat sheets, shingles and a range of boards with wood-grained finishes); Super 6 and Coverline corrugated roofing; and a range of roofing accessories including guttering and downpipes.

Some early housing companies made extensive use of Fibrolite claddings, as did many bach owners. Consequently, Fibrolite sheds, garages, baseboards, eaves and gable walls and corrugated asbestos roofing are widespread.

~ *Textured ceilings* Textured ceilings are unmistakable with their porridge-like texture. They are usually light in colour and sometimes flecked with glittery metal flakes. Under names such as Glamatex, textured coatings were sprayed onto ceilings as a popular alternative to conventionally 'stopped' plasterboard. Not all textured ceilings contained asbestos — some finishes used organic fibres.

~ *Vinyl floor coverings* Vinyl floors are often overlooked as a potential source of asbestos but were common in decors in the 1970s and 80s. Unlike other products phased out in the early 1980s, asbestos-backed vinyls continued to be imported and laid into the 1990s. The distinctive geometric,

---

TOP TIPS FOR DEALING WITH ASBESTOS

✓ If a building is no older than the mid-1980s, it is unlikely to contain asbestos claddings or textured ceiling materials.

✓ If vinyl flooring is less than 10 years old it is unlikely to contain asbestos.

✓ The only way to be certain whether a product contains asbestos is to have it tested by an accredited laboratory. There are two in New Zealand (listed in the Resources, see page 216).

✓ Asbestos removal is a specialised task. Correct personal protection, collection and disposal is vital and should only be carried out by registered persons.

✓ If you are renovating and encounter dust deposits that you suspect contain asbestos, don't attempt to clean them up with a household vacuum cleaner — it simply redistributes the most lethal, fine particles of asbestos through its exhaust system and back into the air.

mottled and tiled vinyls of that era are often backed with asbestos. Sometimes, a layer of asbestos-backed vinyl is found underneath a newer replacement vinyl.

Asbestos-backed vinyls, if left undisturbed or covered over with a different material, present little risk. Pulling the vinyl covering up and sanding the residual backing off a floor can release high concentrations of airborne dust and create a grave health risk. Most commercial floor-sanding companies refuse to sand such surfaces and some have been prosecuted for doing so.

AIM FOR LOW OR NO VOCS

Organic chemicals are widely used as ingredients in household products. Much of the timber used for indoor furniture, floor and wall panels, paints, varnishes and waxes all contain organic solvents, as do many cleaning, disinfecting and cosmetic products. All of these products release volatile organic compounds (VOCs) throughout their lifetime.

When selecting materials for green building, the fact that a product is 'sustainable' or of 'natural' origin, rather than synthetic, does not necessarily prevent it from contributing to high VOC levels in a building.

Some 'natural' building products emit high levels of VOCs that irritate susceptible inhabitants as much as those released by synthetic products. For example, softwoods such as pine can contain high levels of naturally occurring aldehydes and terpenes. Their emission might be considered less harmful than the formaldehyde found in glued boards, but both have an obvious odour and presence that could irritate sensitive individuals.

However, odours don't necessarily give a good indication of poor indoor air quality. While they may be noticed when first encountered, their intensity tends to wear off as people become accustomed to them. Conversely, some VOCs, which are nearly odourless at levels found in indoor air, may take time to sense and their irritative effect may grow worse with time.

> *TOP TIPS FOR BUILDING HEALTH*
>
> ✓ Don't use a sander or a blowtorch to remove lead-based paints.
>
> ✓ Leave asbestos alone or leave it to the experts.
>
> ✓ Maintain adequate ventilation.
>
> ✓ Avoid the use of materials containing VOCs.

Chapter 3

Timber

This is not a book on eco construction. But in recognising that most Kiwis enjoy improving their homes, Part One discusses some topics relevant to building, including the selection and use of timber.

There are two main things to consider when buying timber:

➤ the sustainability of the resource

➤ its reliance on chemical treatment for durability.

SUSTAINABILITY

Before the first Maori settlers arrived in the 11th century, at least 75% of New Zealand was covered with natural forest, the remainder being too high, wet or dry for forest growth. When the first Europeans arrived, natural forest cover had fallen to about half the land area and the settlers made it a priority to clear-fell and burn forests to develop the land for pastoral agriculture. Later, tree felling became a primary industry, supplying timber for building and the export trade. In the 1850s it provided one-third of all export income.

Now, our original forest cover is down to just under one-quarter, with most of it locked up in national and conservation parks. In recent years, as a result of persistent pressure from conservationists, timber production from state forests has been virtually halted. Less than 2% of the total privately owned native forest area is potentially available for wood production and as little as 0.5% of our total timber harvest comes from native forests.

Because our native timbers are so slow growing, it is possible they will never become a sustainable commercial resource other than for limited uses such as furniture.

The upshot of a reduced supply of native timber for furniture and building has been increased reliance on other sources of supply.

Sustainable timber supplies are either:

➤ Locally grown or imported plantation timbers: radiata pine, eucalypts and the like.

➤ Locally grown farm timbers: macrocarpa, Lawson cypress and the like.

Unsustainable timber supplies include:

➤ Imported timber from the world's tropical and temperate native forests: balau, kwila, western red cedar and the like.

➤ Recycled native timber and timber 'recovered' from buried or submerged native forests.

Imported eco timber

Some conservationists argue that the world's untouched forests of tropical and temperate timbers are now so few that for the sake of biodiversity they and the biota they support should be left alone and not harvested. In other words, any type of tropical or temperate old-growth timber, even that which is 'sustainably managed', should not be bought or used.

Another argument allows that tropical forests can be sustainably managed. By purchasing this timber, small communities, especially those in emerging economies, can be supported and the viability of the resource maintained.

~ *New Zealand Imported Tropical Timber Group*   New Zealand imports of unsustainably logged tropical hardwoods — much of it brought in as decking — has dropped in recent years in response to pressure from conservationists.

In a co-operative venture between environmental organisations and the New Zealand Imported Tropical Timber Group (NZITG), supplies of tropical timber for floors, decks and furniture have been imported from sustainably logged, community-managed 'eco forests' in the Solomon Islands and Papua New Guinea. The trees, mainly taun and vitex, are felled with as little intrusive damage to the forest as possible, milled where they fall with portable mills and carried out of the forest to a road or river by hand. The timber is certified by the NZITG to give purchasers an assurance of its sustainable origin. This policy ensures sustainable forest management but delivers only small volumes of limited types of tropical timber to the market.

The members of the NZITG refrain from purchasing timber from countries known to log unsustainably such as Malaysia and Brazil. It also promotes the use of sustainable, locally grown alternatives like macrocarpa and the eucalypts.

~ *Forest Stewardship Council*   The Forest Stewardship Council (FSC) is an international organisation consisting of representatives of environmental and social as well as forestry and timber industry groups, which provides a certification system to indicate sustainably managed forest operations. The FSC logo can be found on products manufactured from FSC-approved timber.

Under the auspices of the New Zealand Forest Industries Council, a forest industry working group (Forest Certification New Zealand Inc) is currently developing two certification standards to FSC requirements, one for indigenous and another for plantation forests. These will allow those forest companies whose operations are 'certified' to use the certifying agency's brand on their timber when it goes to market.

Local protectionists argue that while FSC certification is a good thing in some 'poorer' countries because it indicates forests are not being clear-felled, there is no justification for applying similar certification to our indigenous forests, as they should never be logged.

~ *Less eco-friendly imports*   The strong demand for other species of wood is met by importing temperate and tropical timber from plantation sources that are not certified as sustainably managed, such as from Australia and Fiji. As unsubstantiated claims are easily made, timber should not be accepted as 'sustainably managed' without certification.

Locally grown plantation timber

The commercially viable plantation timbers grown in New Zealand are fast-growing species such as radiata pine (90%) and Douglas fir (5%). The government in the 1920s made the fortuitous decision to plant forests on the North Island central plateau. The timber chosen to do the job was a native of California, where it is generally known as Monterey pine, and to us as radiata pine (*Pinus radiata*). It grows 10 times faster than our indigenous timbers and has proved to be a versatile commercial commodity, providing furniture and building timber, and pulp for papermaking.

The environmental drawbacks associated with monoculture pine forests are:

➤ their failure to support a biodiverse culture

➤ the pollution associated with pesticide use and pulp and paper production

➤ the need to treat the sawn timber with preservatives, for all but interior use.

Engineered timbers

Sheets of plywood, particleboard, medium-density fibreboard (MDF) and hardboard are all examples of panels that have been 'engineered' to specific requirements. They are consistent in size, thickness and strength. Glue-laminated beams and laminated veneer lumber (LVL) are examples of timber that has been milled and re-engineered into components with a specific end use — structural beams, posts, floor joists and the like.

All engineered panels and timbers rely on glue, many of which contain VOCs, including formaldehyde. Formaldehyde causes health concerns through off-gassing, even long after installation (see Sick building syndrome, Chapter 2). Panel products that release a much lower level of formaldehyde are becoming available as glue formulations change to meet environmental concerns.

A wide range of single and mixed species of timber are planted and grown in woodlots, both by the large timber companies and the smaller individual tree-farmers. These are a sustainable resource (as long as trees are replanted to replace those which are milled); they provide a variety of exotic timber for both building and furniture, much of it not dependent on chemical treatment.

Recycled timber

It is no surprise that native timbers such as kauri, rimu, totara, matai and kahikatea are limited in supply. As the early settlers discovered, they had the right properties to fulfil a number of basic roles, from fence posts to buildings and butter boxes; their versatility sealed their fate.

As ageing structures such as bridges, wharves, factories and warehouses are removed and demolished, old-growth timber beams once again become available for recycling into household furniture and building products.

TOP TIPS
FOR SAFEGUARDING TIMBER RESOURCES

✓ Choose naturally durable timbers from local plantations: radiata pine, Lawson cypress, Douglas fir, macrocarpa and eucalyptus — not old-growth indigenous forests. See the Good Wood Guide (1999) for millers and retailers in your area: www.converge.org.nz/gwg/survey.htm

✓ Use recycled timber — the more times you can make it go round, the better.

✓ Avoid hardwood garden furniture — little of it is sourced from sustainable forestry.

✓ Plant more trees!

The carbon cycle

Growing forests act as a carbon store, reducing the amount of carbon dioxide in the atmosphere and reducing global warming. Carbon is a basic building block common to all living organisms. There is a fixed total amount of carbon in the world but the amounts that are stored in each of the major natural carbon sinks — the land, oceans, biomass and atmosphere — change slowly over time. Most of the increase of atmospheric carbon dioxide in the last 150 years, which is held responsible for global warming, has occurred through burning fossil fuels and changes in land use.

Trees soak up atmospheric carbon (carbon dioxide) during photosynthesis and lock it into their cell structures. Some carbon dioxide is recycled through respiration and when individual trees die and begin to decay, their total carbon content is released. (If this process is delayed, the organic matter is turned into fossil fuels such as petroleum, coal and natural gas.) In a mature forest the carbon cycle is in balance, and the carbon dioxide absorbed by growing trees is roughly equal to the carbon dioxide released by dead and decaying trees. In a young, growing forest, carbon absorption is greater than carbon release, giving it the potential to reduce the rate of carbon dioxide build-up in the atmosphere — which is why it is important to keep planting trees.

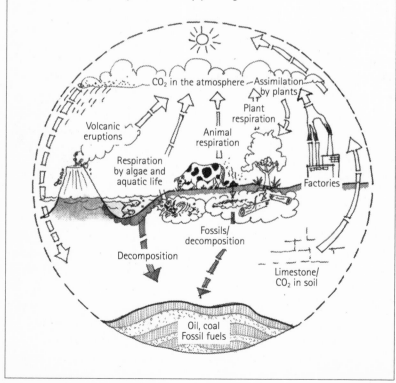

A small supply of recycled tongue-and-groove flooring, sarking and wall panelling trickles into the market, some remachined to look new. The premium attached to recycled timber, though it is often less than pristine in finish, reflects the sentimental value we have for a magnificent resource, now all but lost.

DURABILITY

The natural resistance of timbers to attack by insects and fungal decay is dependent mainly on resin deposits within the heartwood. For insect attack to occur, sapwood generally needs to be present. For fungal decay to occur moisture needs to be present. The ability of a timber species to withstand insect and fungal decay has, historically, helped determine its end use (see the table: Plantation timbers and their uses on page 28).

Timber in contact with the ground

~ *Native timbers* Totara and puriri are the two native timbers with the best-recognised decay resistance when in contact with the ground. They can last many decades, which explains their early use as foundation piles and fence posts. Black beech and silver pine are also durable. As there is no sustainable forestry or logging of native tree species, there are no readily available naturally durable timbers for use in situations where ground contact is required.

~ *Exotics* Before chemically treated pine became available, hardwoods were imported from Australia for use as railway sleepers, telegraph and power poles and wharf piles. Blackbutt, jarrah and ironbark have good natural durability in outdoor situations. Recycled piles, poles and sleepers, some still in good shape, can sometimes be found in landscape-supply outlets, second-hand timber yards, and railway and power utility maintenance yards.

Locally grown exotic timbers are attractive, versatile and sustainable but most lack durability when used in exterior locations. The heartwoods of macrocarpa, the eucalypts, cypresses and New Zealand redwoods have some natural durability (10–15 years) but are generally untreated and should not be used outdoors or in contact with the ground with any expectation of permanence.

Kiln-dried untreated pine is an ecologically sound, plantation-grown building timber, though it is likely to have been sprayed with an anti-sapstain chemical to limit discoloration. Without the protection of a preservative, kiln-dried pine should only be used in indoor applications where it is not going to get wet.

Timber treatments

The answer to a builder's prayer — timber preservative — is used to prevent fungal decay and insect attack in building timbers. Very simply, preservatives work by poisoning timber that would otherwise become a food source for insects and fungal organisms.

Early timber treatments involved dipping sawn timber in chemicals, then delivering it to the yard 'green' for use. This worked with limited success — the chemicals were prone to leaching — but later techniques made it possible to impregnate the timber under pressure, giving it greater durability. This breakthrough made it possible for radiata pine, a plantation timber with little natural durability in external situations, to be used for almost anything, from interior mouldings to ground-embedded piles.

PLANTATION TIMBERS AND THEIR USES

Function	Timber	Comments
Outdoor in contact with the ground, e.g. house piles, landscaping timbers	None	There is no (untreated) plantation timber with sufficient *natural* durability to resist decay when used in contact with the ground. Radiata pine and eucalypts with appropriate levels of treatment have a durability of up to 50 years
Outdoor above ground, e.g. decking, verandah posts, rafters, balustrades etc.	Eucalyptus: eastern blue gum, stringy bark	Heartwoods have a natural durability of 10–15 years
	Cedar	Use heartwoods only
	Cypress: Lawson, lusitanica, macrocarpa	Heartwoods have a durability of about 10 years
	Douglas fir New Zealand redwood	Not for in-ground use or where exposed to ground atmosphere where long-term structural integrity is vital, e.g. deck support beams
Indoor structural, e.g. framing, structural posts and beams	Radiata pine	Untreated kiln-dried H1 boric-treated timber on exterior walls is advisable
	Eucalyptus: eastern blue gum, stringy bark	
	Douglas fir	Douglas fir has little sapwood and is considered naturally resistant to borer
	Cypress: Lawson, lusitanica, macrocarpa	

Among the first commercially effective timber treatments were chemicals now known to be highly toxic to humans and persistent in their pollution of the environment. These included Dieldrin (used mostly in plywood glues); Chlordane (used mostly against borer and in glues); and PCP (used as a fungicide on freshly cut timber). As a consequence, there are scores of disused treatment sites and sawmills in New Zealand where ground pollution levels are still too high for safe use of the land.

Buildings built with treated timber between 1950 and 1990 are likely to contain timber treated with these chemicals. As the chemicals are highly stable, the residues persist and being volatile, they continue to off-gas for decades.

Current timber treatments can be classified according to the type of

Function	Timber	Comments
Decking and flooring	Eucalyptus	Must be correctly seasoned at time of installation. May move and fluctuate dimensionally with changes in moisture levels Professional advice on selection and installation is advisable
Interior framing	Radiata pine Douglas fir	Untreated kiln-dried. H1 boric-treated timber advisable on exterior walls to minimise fungal decay resulting from possible intermittent wetting
Furniture	All of the above species plus acacia, blackwood, black walnut, elm, oak, poplar, robinia	Limited availability and in some cases highly priced, e.g. black walnut
Veneer	Radiata pine, cypress, some eucalypts, blackwood, black walnut	Veneers used in plys may contain formaldehyde glues. Plys treated with light organic solvent preservatives (LOSPs) usually contain VOCs

liquid they are dissolved in: oil-borne (creosotes); waterborne (boric and copper chrome arsenic — CCA treatments), or solvent-borne (light organic solvent preservatives — LOSPs) liquids.

~ *Creosotes* Creosote is perhaps the earliest heavy-duty preservative. Made from coal tar, it was until recently used widely on farm buildings, bridge timbers, telephone and power poles, railway ties, backyard structures and suburban fences. In New Zealand, with the demise of coal-burning gas plants, creosote treatment has been almost completely replaced by CCA formulations but timber treated with creosote is still around. Creosoted railway ties and telegraph poles, for example, are often recycled as landscape items.

Coal tar creosote is an organic compound of the same family as petroleum. It contains hundreds of different chemicals including polycylic aromatic hydrocarbons, phenol and cresol. Creosote is sometimes mixed with heavy oil to aid its weathering characteristics. Creosote-treated timber exposed to soil, particularly moist soil, is at increased risk of leaching. It is toxic to plants and should not be used for landscaping or where there are food-bearing crops and vegetable gardens.

The International Agency for Research in Cancer (IARC) and the US Environmental Protection Agency (EPA) both regard coal tar creosote as probably carcinogenic to humans.

~ *Boric-treated timber* Boron is a naturally occurring mineral salt. It is used as a water-based treatment, mainly on framing timber, to prevent insect attack. It is considered the least noxious timber treatment but was largely discontinued in New Zealand in 1996 when it was realised that kiln-dried timber was not susceptible to insect or fungal attack as long as its 'in-use' moisture content remained lower than 18%.

Boron is not a recognised fungicide. However, at levels of treatment higher than those recommended by the Timber Preservative Authority (but often achieved in practice), boron has been shown to temporarily discourage fungal growth.

Recent controversy (the leaky house syndrome) over the expectation that framing timber in a residential dwelling would remain dry at all times, and so resist decay, has resulted in the reintroduction of boric-treated framing, with an added fungicide to discourage fungal decay.

Boron-treated wood should not be burnt in stoves or fireplaces — it rots out the grate.

~ *Copper chrome arsenic (CCA)* CCA formulations are the mainstay of the world's timber preservative regime. New Zealanders are the greatest users per head of population, treating more than one million cubic metres of timber (mostly radiata pine) every year, for use in exposed situations such as decking, weatherboards, structural posts, foundation piles, and landscape retaining walls.

In New Zealand, CCA-treated timber is commonly called 'tanalised' after the trademark CCA formulation Tanalith, but this is only one of a number of similar proprietary products on the market.

The compound is a mixture of metallic salts that are highly effective against insect and fungal decay. The copper acts as a fungicide, the arsenic as an insecticide and the chrome as a fixative to render the copper and arsenic insoluble.

CCA treatment is a waterborne treatment, applied using a vacuum pressure impregnation process. The timber is loaded into a sealed pressurisation chamber where its natural moisture is removed by vacuum and replaced with the treatment solution. The chamber is then pressurised, forcing the solution into the timber, and a vacuum is again applied to extract any excess solution.

Progressively heavier levels of chemical are applied depending on the end use of the timber; for example, H3 is for use outdoors but above ground, H4 and H5 for in-ground use, and H6 for marine applications.

CCA has been considered relatively 'safe' among timber treatments because, unlike timber which has been treated by diffusion methods (soaking), the vacuum pressure and the use of a fixative make it less likely to leach, a feature which assists durability.

A small amount of in-use leaching does occur, however, particularly in acidic ground conditions. There are health and environmental concerns associated with the treatment process and the disposal of CCA-treated sawdust, off-cuts and, at the end of its working life, the timber itself.

The environmental hazards are related to the high toxicity of copper, chromium and arsenic to non-target organisms in fresh-water, wetland and marine environments.

The United States timber industry has voluntarily withdrawn CCA from use in residential applications after December 2003, following concerns over exposure to arsenic in timber in the home and the build-up of arsenic in the environment. It will be replaced mainly by ammoniacal copper quaternary (ACQ) formulations.

A study released by the American Industrial Hygiene Association (*AIHA Journal* Vol. 63 No. 2, March 2002), found that workers sawing and sanding CCA-treated timber were consistently exposed to higher than recommended levels of the heavy metals commonly used in CCA-treated timber.

CCA-treated timber should not be burned in an open fireplace or barbecue, as the fumes emitted are toxic and chemically aggressive. It should be disposed of only in approved landfills — though even there, CCA leachate remains an environmental threat.

~ *Ammoniacal copper quaternary (ACQ)*   ACQ vacuum pressure timber treatments use copper, a commonly used pesticide, as a primary active ingredient. Quaternary ammonium compounds provide protection against copper-tolerant fungi and wood-destroying insects. (Quats, as they are called, are also commonly used in household cleansers and disinfectants.) ACQ has been in use for a decade and is marketed as a more environmentally safe compound than CCA preservative, but its long-term performance is still unknown.

~ *Copper azole (CuAZ)*   Copper azole is another copper-based preservative that is free of arsenic and chromium but is seldom used in New Zealand.

~ *Solvent-borne liquids: H1–H3 LOSP (light organic solvent preservative)*
H1 LOSP treatment uses an organic solvent — usually white spirits — to carry

HAZARD CLASSES AND TYPICAL USES FOR TREATED TIMBERS

Class	Hazard	Typical use	Treatment
H1	Above ground, protected from weather, insect risk (borer) only	Flooring, framing, panelling, interior mouldings, furniture	Boron (boron salts) H1 LOSP (Permethrin)
H3	Exterior, exposed to weather or intermittent wetting. Above-ground use only. Fungal and insect decay	Decking, weatherboards, floor and deck joists, joinery, fence rails, fence palings	H3 CCA (copper, chrome, arsenic) H3 LOSP (Tributyltin) ACQ (copper, ammonium compounds) CuAZ (copper)
H4	Exterior, in-ground use, non-structural, fungal and insect decay: 25 years	Landscape timbers, fence posts	H4 CCA ACQ
H5	Exterior, in-ground use, structural, fungal and insect decay: 50 years	Foundation piles and poles, retaining wall structural elements	H5 CCA ACQ
H6	Immersed in sea water, marine borer	Wharf and marina structural elements	H6 CCA

a low-level insecticide (usually the contact insecticide, Permethrin) into the timber. It is used on framing timber, internal flooring, interior joinery, panelling and furniture.

H3 LOSP treatment uses both an insecticide (Permethrin) and a fungicide (Tributyltin) to protect the timber. It is used on exterior timbers not in contact with the ground such as timber framing, decking, plywood cladding panels, exterior joinery and weatherboards.

The light organic solvent in freshly treated timber initially releases heavy concentrations of VOCs. Off-gassing continues at a lesser level for a considerable time and can be very noticeable in warm, closed environments.

The Tributyltin used in H3 LOSP formulations is a potent fungicide. Tributyltin is used as an active ingredient in anti-fouling marine paints to prevent marine creatures attaching themselves to ship hulls. Tributyltin marine paints are banned in New Zealand and in many other countries their use is restricted to boats larger than 25 m in length.

TOP TIPS FOR
TIMBER PRESERVATION

✓ Avoid preservatives if possible. Kiln-dried timber used indoors and kept dry is resistant to insect attack. Some timbers such as cedar contain resins and oils that extend their serviceable lifespan. Heartwood is more resistant than sapwood. A recently invented process that injects plant-based starch into radiata pine gives it a hardness and density more suitable for use in situations such as flooring.

✓ Instead of using heavily treated timber for outdoor applications look to use a more permanent material such as concrete, stone and masonry.

✓ Boron insecticide treatment is the most 'acceptable' commercial timber treatment, though it is toxic to plants. It has only limited fungicidal properties and should not be used on exterior applications or where the timber is exposed to moisture.

✓ A number of companies manufacture organically based products that offer protection rather than preservation. These include a range of paints, oils, stains, polishes and wax finishes. Advice from the manufacturer or supplier on their suitability for use with particular timbers and for different end uses is advisable.

✓ ACQ is currently viewed as the most acceptable timber preservative at hazard levels H3–H5, though its long-term impact is not fully known.

Chapter 4

Insulation

Historically, it has not been part of the national psyche to admit to being cold in winter. So it is no wonder that for 150 years we've built and lived in houses which behaved more like refrigerators in the cooler months of the year and hot boxes in the summer. Silly us: rather than looking askance at well-insulated homes, we should have seen them as a necessary comfort and an important tool in energy conservation.

It was not until the oil shocks of the 1970s that we began as a nation to think insulation made sense. Within months, the serious shortage of cheap oil for power generation acted as a trigger for legislation introducing minimum thermal insulation levels in new and refurbished residential housing. Even so, about 600,000 dwellings throughout the country still have little or no insulation.

The New Zealand Building Code now provides minimum insulation levels (listed as R-values) for new construction and renovations in three separate climate zones, depending on mean winter temperatures (see NZS 4218: 1996). A new Code of Practice (NZCP-4224, Specification guide for home insulation — roof, walls, windows and floors) goes one step further, defining *adequate*, *better* and *best* levels of insulation of the main housing elements, and explaining the economic benefits at each level.

The best time to insulate a home is when it is being built or renovated but existing homes can usually be retro-fitted without too much difficulty. Passive solar design, coupled with the use of high-mass building materials that have inherent insulation properties, is a more efficient, healthy and eco-friendly means of achieving the same effect.

HOW DOES INSULATION WORK?

Blanket or loose-fill bulk insulation works by trapping small pockets of still air within the insulating material (air is a poor conveyer of heat). Reflective insulation works by reflecting heat and trapping a layer of insulating air in an air pocket next to its shiny surface. The achieved insulation value (R-value) of bulk and blanket types depends on the material's ability to trap air and its thickness and density. (R-value is a measure of resistance to heat flow. The higher the R-value, the better the insulating value.)

INSULATION TYPES

Cellulose

Recycled, shredded paper can be sprayed or blown into wall and ceiling cavities. The paper sometimes contains a binder to help it remain in place. The addition of relatively harmless Borax (boracic acid) discourages insects and rodents, and acts as a fire retardant. Contracts should guarantee the compacted depth and minimum R-values.

Fibreglass

Fibreglass is the most widely used residential insulation. Made from silica sand and recycled glass, its dust causes short-term irritation to the skin, eyes and upper respiratory tract. The binding resins and oils used to stiffen and bond the fibres to prevent sag can also cause irritation. Fibreglass was for many years listed as a possible carcinogen by IARC, the International Agency for Research on Cancer. In 2002, the agency removed this classification.

Newer fibreglass insulation products use a larger minimum fibre size and 'biosoluble' fibres to reduce irritation. Fibreglass is chemically treated to resist rodent and insect attack. It doesn't burn but will melt under intense heat. It is available in blanket form.

Rockwool

Rockwool is a similar product to fibreglass but is spun out of basalt mineral rock rather than silica sand. It is denser than fibreglass and has better thermal and acoustic insulation properties. It is available in loose fill for vertical wall cavities and blanket form for ceilings and framed walls.

Wool insulation

As long as we keep breeding sheep, wool will be a renewable resource. Its insulating properties don't match those of fibreglass because it is less dense, and though dusty it is also a lot less irritating to install. The manufacturers make several ecological claims:

➤ It requires much less embodied energy to manufacture than fibreglass because it uses a resin rather than heat-bonding process to bind the fibres.

➤ It absorbs much of the formaldehyde present in new buildings.

➤ It absorbs and desorbs water vapour and so acts as a stabiliser to reduce peak humidity levels and condensation.

Wool does not ignite easily but will contribute to an established fire.

It is treated with relatively harmless boron compounds to discourage rodent and insect attack and may also be treated with fire retardants, sanitising agents and deodorants. It is available as loose fill and in blanket form. Wool/hemp and wool/polyester blends are also available.

Polyester

Polyester is a synthetic thermally bonded fibre manufactured from a non-renewable resource — petroleum oil. The same material is used in clothing, bedding and furnishings. It is dust free and non-allergenic (its free fibres are not of respirable size) and is therefore pleasant to handle. It is available in blanket form and once installed will not sag or lose its lift. It does not burn easily (though it does give off dense smoke when ignited) and insects do not eat it.

Wool/polyester blends combine the best physical characteristics of both materials.

Expanded polystyrene

Expanded polystyrene (EPS) is manufactured in rigid sheets by expanding and bonding petroleum-based polystyrene beads using (nowadays) a non-CFC expansion agent and heat. Used in floors, walls and ceilings, it has the best insulation value for thickness of all the insulating products but needs to be cut to an exact fit using a hot wire rather than a knife. EPS is moisture resistant, a characteristic that limits the free passage of air and vapour through the building element; it is not recyclable; and it doesn't readily break down in landfills when discarded. EPS is treated with flame retardant to prevent ignition but burns with intensity at high temperature and gives off dense smoke (as do many building products).

Reflective foil

Single- and double-sided reflective foils consist of a layer of aluminium foil laminated to paper and reinforced with strands of fibreglass. It is used beneath suspended floors, and under roofing materials where there is no provision for ceiling insulation. Sub-floor foil has pre-punched holes in it to minimise condensation build-up.

Foil reflects heat and visible and invisible light (ultraviolet — UV). It needs to be handled carefully when being installed: over-exposure to reflected UV rays could damage the eyes and cause sunburn, even on cloudy days. To gain maximum insulation value the reflective surface of the foil should inwardly face a framed cavity at least 25 mm deep.

Expandable glues and fillers

Expandable aerosol glues and foam fillers are used to either glue windows or doorjambs into place, or to eliminate air gaps between the framing and the jamb. Injected as a liquid, they quickly expand to form a solid insulating foam. The propellants, solvents and solids can contain harmful ingredients, including CFCs and HCFCs which degrade the ozone layer, formaldehyde which causes respiratory problems and isocyanates which are a known carcinogen. Newer polyurethane foams do not contain solvents but may still contain isocyanates.

INSTALLATION

To be effective, insulating materials must be correctly installed — near enough is not good enough. A tight fit is important. Even small gaps around the edge of an insulating material act as thermal holes and nullify R-value. Bulk insulation should be installed so that it doesn't sag with time, thereby lowering the R-value. In walls and under floors, a few well-placed staples will hold blanket insulation in place.

Protective clothing

When installing or handling insulation products which may emit dust or fibres, it is sensible to wear a protective mask, gloves, and clothing which is close-fitting at the wrists and neck. Goggles will prevent fibres irritating the eyes. Use cold or tepid water to wash irritating fibres from the skin — hot water opens the skin's pores and makes the irritation worse.

WHERE TO INSULATE

Ceilings

Most heat loss (about 40%) in an uninsulated house occurs through the ceiling. This is easily rectified with bulk or blanket insulation. Excessive air movement in a ceiling cavity or attic space can displace loose-fill insulation, removing it from some areas and piling it up in others. But don't be tempted to block off the ventilation grills installed in the eaves or gable ends: good ventilation reduces condensation in the roof space. Instead, use blanket insulation, making sure it is tightly fitted over or between the ceiling joists to prevent heat loss from the rooms below.

Walls

Cavity-type timber-framed walls account for about 25% of total heat loss, but are hard to insulate once built. When interior walls are being redecorated it is worth considering the replacement of existing interior linings to allow the installation of blanket insulation. In older timber-framed homes (villas, bungalows and the like) where the exterior walls contain vertical studs but not intermediate noggings, loose fill can be blown into the wall cavity through a hole drilled in the exterior or interior cladding (this is a job for an insulation contractor).

Floors

A warm floor is an excellent provider of comfort, as any warmth retained at floor level rises to warm the entire body. The space beneath suspended timber floors, though it might only cause a 15% heat loss, can usually be retro-fitted with blanket insulation, sisalation (single- or double-sided foil), or a combination of both.

In very cold climates a layer of compacted pumice (eco friendly) or expanded polystyrene sheeting (less eco friendly) placed beneath a concrete slab at the time of its construction will minimise heat loss through the slab into the ground and resist the penetration of cold from the ground to the interior.

Where underfloor heating is used it is important to insulate the perimeter of the floor and the juncture between the floor and the exterior walls, to minimise internal heat loss.

Cork flooring in all its forms is an excellent natural insulator. Wall-to-wall carpet has limited insulation value, though it does impart a sense of comfort and well-being.

Gaps

Air leakage through cracks in floorboards, poorly fitting windows, doors, skirtings and architraves is frowned upon by energy conservators but does guarantee a minimum exchange of air, albeit uncontrollable. Polyurethane aerosol foam is an effective way to fill small gaps, which would otherwise leak air and energy, but it is likely to contain diisocyanates, a chemical ingredient which is known to aggravate existing respiratory disorders and cause lung damage.

Windows

Windows are thermal holes — by far the biggest losers of heat in relation to their size. In the same way that windows allow solar energy to enter a building, they allow heat to escape. To maximise solar-collecting benefits and minimise energy losses, window type, size and orientation need to be carefully considered along with other design factors, such as view.

North-facing windows best capture winter sun and allow for eaves-shading in the summer months. East- and west-facing windows capture morning and evening sun but present problems with glare. South-facing windows capture little solar energy to compensate for the energy they allow to escape.

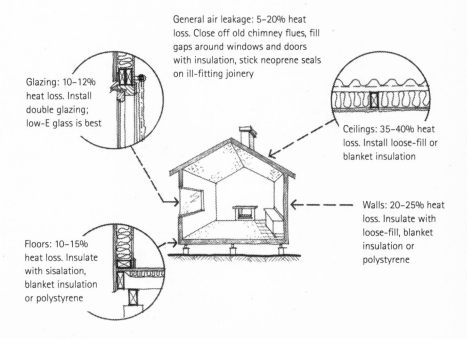

General air leakage: 5–20% heat loss. Close off old chimney flues, fill gaps around windows and doors with insulation, stick neoprene seals on ill-fitting joinery

Glazing: 10–12% heat loss. Install double glazing; low-E glass is best

Ceilings: 35–40% heat loss. Install loose-fill or blanket insulation

Walls: 20–25% heat loss. Insulate with loose-fill, blanket insulation or polystyrene

Floors: 10–15% heat loss. Insulate with sisalation, blanket insulation or polystyrene

Insulating your home

Heat loss through glazed windows

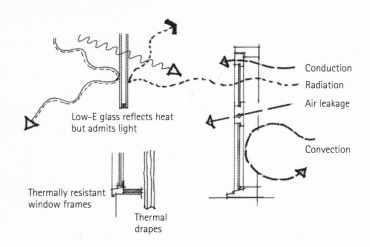

Conduction

Radiation

Air leakage

Low-E glass reflects heat
but admits light

Convection

Thermally resistant
window frames

Thermal
drapes

Windows lose heat in four ways:

Conduction — movement of heat through solid materials.
Problem Glass is a good conductor, so too are aluminium frames.
Solution Double glazing (especially with argon gas between the panes),
thermally resistant window frames and edge spacers.

Radiation — movement of heat through air from a warm medium to a cooler
one.
Problem In winter, warm radiant energy is absorbed by the glass, then re-
radiated to the cooler outdoors.
Solution Low-E coatings reflect heat but allow light to pass.

Convection — warm air rises, cool air sinks.
Problem In winter, warm interior air hits cold window glazing and sinks to
the floor. Warm air takes it place, setting up a thermal current, or draught.
Solution Heavy drapes interrupt this cycle, as do double glazing and thermally
resistant frames and edge spacers.

Air leakage — passage of heat through gaps in poorly designed windows.
Problem Controlled ventilation is good, uncontrolled air leakage is bad.
Solution Well-designed windows and window surrounds, durable weather
stripping and robust closing devices.

Ventilation

The more airtight the interior of a dwelling is made, the more important it is to provide an alternative and controllable source of ventilation, such as opening windows, to maintain oxygen supplies and minimise internal humidity and condensation. The use of 'breathable' exterior claddings and interior wall linings helps the free exchange of air between indoor and outdoor spaces.

Because New Zealand has a temperate climate, until recently more thought was given to style and colour than thermal efficiency in choosing windows. However, double glazing (which has the added benefit of minimising condensation), low-emissivity (low-E) glass, and window frames that are designed to break thermal conductivity, are now widely available. The Window Association of New Zealand's five-star efficiency-rating system allows participating suppliers to provide a certificate verifying the window efficiency rating (WERS) of each window type.

Hot-water systems

Hot-water cylinders, if not already rated 'AAA', will benefit from an insulation wrap. So too will all hot-water supply pipes, but especially those which run to areas of frequent use such as the kitchen. A split foam-rubber (neoprene) sleeve is marketed for just this purpose.

TOP TIPS FOR INSULATION

✓ Favour passive solar design.

✓ Insulate ceilings first.

✓ Replace standard glass with double glazing and low-E glass.

✓ Maintain adequate ventilation in tightly sealed rooms.

Chapter 5

Paints and finishes

The idea of treating the interior and exterior surfaces of our homes to reduce maintenance, improve durability and create more attractive surfaces is as old as ... well, paint. Very early paint recipes mixed natural products: beeswax, plant gums, earth pigments. Then came lime washes and, much later, mixtures of lead carbonate (an opaque, white pigment) and linseed oil. Not until the 1940s, with the advent of plastics and abundant supplies of petroleum, did paint technology and the DIY homeowner market develop rapidly.

The manufacture of products containing synthetic solvents, polymers, plasticisers, anti-foaming agents, fungicides and bactericides is now a multi-billion dollar industry. The technology has developed to the point where even chemists have difficulty making sense of paint formulae.

Many of the key ingredients in paints, varnishes and stains are unidentified, disguised by trade names, or assumed to be harmless. Yet many pose recognised risks to human health and the environment. In assessing the health and environmental risks associated with the paint industry, it would help if there were a clear-cut line between natural and synthetic paints. Unfortunately it is not as simple as that.

WHAT IS PAINT?

Paint products are complex but a typical paint consists of three essential components: a resin or binder; a solvent; and a pigment. A variety of additives are commonly used as thickeners, dispersing agents and preservatives.

Binders

The binder forms a durable skin when the paint dries. In water-based paints the binder is often an emulsion consisting of small particles of synthetic latex polymer dispersed in water. When the water dries, the latex polymers form a durable skin of paint.

Oil-based paints — sometimes called alkyd paints, or enamels — use an alkyd (enamel) binder made either from natural linseed oils or synthetic acids. Linseed oil, a vegetable oil derived from flax seeds, is the least toxic binder but is often combined with toxic metallic compounds to reduce its drying time. Conventional enamel paints contain high levels (50%) of solvent to make the binder easier to use and to quicken the drying time. Newer and 'safer' high-solid enamel paints contain 10–25% solvent and higher proportions of binders and pigments.

Solvents

The solvent keeps the paint liquid until it is applied. Paints are generally classified according to the type of solvent they contain. Oil-based paints typically use organic solvents. (The term 'organic solvents' refers to a large group of chemicals that come from petroleum-based products and incorporate molecules of carbon and hydrogen into their atomic structure. It doesn't refer to something produced on an 'organic' farm in the backblocks.) Many of these solvents are volatile; that is, they contain a relatively high percentage of VOCs (volatile organic compounds — see page 44).

Water-based paints — also referred to as latex, PVA, vinyl or acrylic paints — use water as the primary solvent, plus small amounts of organic solvents containing VOCs.

Pigments

Pigments give colour, opacity and consistency to paint, and help with durability. The earliest colouring materials in paints were of natural origin, such as the pale yellow, orange and red colours obtained from ochreous earth, or the plant pigments used for fabric dyeing.

A wider and more vibrant range of colour comes from metal oxides, which are formed through the interaction of naturally occurring metals, moisture and air. Oxides such as iron (first cousin to rust), copper and zinc have been used as paint colourants for a long time. However, many metal oxides are toxic and their production and use is hazardous: cadmium, chrome, lead and mercury fall into this category. Synthetic colouring agents are manufactured mainly from petrochemicals. Sometimes synthetic colourants replace the more toxic colourants derived from metal oxides but it is also common practice to mix colourants from both sources.

HEALTH HAZARDS OF HOUSEHOLD PAINTS

Solvents

The choice of solvent is the main cause for concern in natural and synthetic paint formulations. Not all natural solvents are harmless, not all synthetic solvents are bad. All solvents other than water should be treated with caution. Organic solvents in particular have a special but harmful affinity with the central nervous system. As many water-based paints contain small quantities of VOCs, skin contact with all solvent-based paints and inhalation of the aromatic fumes released by the paint as it dries should be avoided.

Synthetic organic paint solvents are derived from petroleum. Mineral turpentine is a good example. Besides containing relatively harmless aliphatic hydrocarbons, mineral turpentine typically contains up to 25% of the aromatic hydrocarbons benzene, toluene and xylene. Benzene is a carcinogen. Toluene is a neurotoxin and damages foetuses. Xylene causes poor concentration, disrupts the sense of balance and may damage foetuses.

Natural paint solvents, or terpenes, are derived from plant oils, mainly pine and citrus. Vegetable turpentine (oil of turpentine) is a good example. Natural terpenes, in spite of their pleasant smell, are potentially allergenic and can cause skin irritation, headaches and breathing difficulties in sensitive individuals. Balsamic terpene, made from Scandinavian and East European pine trees, is widely criticised for causing an allergic skin disease common among painters. Terpenes can also have a narcotic effect, irritate the eyes, nose and throat and damage kidney functioning.

VOCs

Both synthetic and natural paint solvents contain VOCs. Many water-based paints also contain small quantities of VOCs to boost paint performance; benzene, toluene and xylene are common examples. Paint is applied wet and must undergo a drying process (and sometimes a chemical reaction) to form a solid paint film. It is during this drying or chemical process that VOCs are given off. A wide range of health problems is attributed to VOCs.

All solvent-based paints, polyurethanes and varnishes continue to off-gas VOCs throughout their lifetime; a high percentage at first and decreasing amounts later. These fumes should be well ventilated during and after painting. When released into the atmosphere, VOCs are a prime cause of ground-level ozone (smog). Many countries now regulate the use of VOCs in manufactured products, particularly in paint. VOCs are also found in trace concentrations in groundwater.

NATURAL PAINTS

The common philosophy of makers of natural paints is that they contain ingredients from naturally renewable sources and are safer because they exclude the synthetic organic solvents and pigments derived from petroleum. It is argued that humans have had thousands of years in which to adapt to the effects of natural ingredients, unlike those of synthetic petrochemicals.

Another advantage of natural paints is that plant crops, from which vegetable resins and solvents are produced, consume the carbon dioxide created when aromatic hydrocarbons escape into the atmosphere.

Natural organic solvents break down in the environment more quickly than synthetic solvents and are not thought to cause long-term damage. This does not mean that they do not pose health risks. Natural solvents such as vegetable turpentine and citrus oil can be just as allergenic as synthetic organic solvents to those who are susceptible.

To confuse matters further, some paint manufacturers use non-toxic petrochemical solvents (isoaliphatic compounds) in natural paints because they are quicker drying than conventional natural solvents.

The slowness of drying, the limited range of applications and perceived higher cost are factors that have worked against natural paints in the professional market. However, they are becoming easier to use, contain fewer unfriendly additives, and can deliver a more durable finish than conventional synthetic water- and oil-based paints. Linseed oil paints, for example, have good adhesion and a high capacity to absorb moisture, which means they remain flexible and elastic. Natural paints have a limited shelf life. When considering the cost of natural paints versus synthetic organic paints, coverage rates need to be considered — the more natural options are not always more expensive.

Other pluses of natural paints include the following:

➤ In general, natural paints create a surface layer that breathes, providing a less humid and less electrostatically charged indoor climate.

➤ Natural paints don't use toxic additives, such as fungicides and preservatives, or heavy metals like chromium, copper or cadmium.

➤ Natural paints, when discarded, break down more readily in the environment.

➤ The manufacturers of natural paints make a point of listing the ingredients on the products, enabling allergic users to identify potential problems.

Milk paint

The best natural paint alternative to synthetic latex wall paints is traditional casein, or milk paints, sometimes called lime washes. As the name suggests, they use casein (milk protein) as a binder and lime as a pigment and filler (instead of titanium dioxide, which is a suspected carcinogen when inhaled as dust). They can be used indoors and outdoors on surfaces such as unfinished wood, plaster or masonry.

Milk paints breathe, have excellent diffusion properties and are very durable, particularly indoors: many ancient casein paint frescoes have lasted hundreds of years. They can be applied over the top of latex wall paints, or painted over with latex wall paints, but should be bought in powder, not liquid, form, and mixed with water directly before use.

Silicate paints

Silicate, or mineral paint, was developed in the late 19th century as a more durable substitute for lime wash on concrete, cement render, brick or stone surfaces. Silicate paints are open-pored, diffusive, and resistant to moisture, fungi and fire. Based on potassium silicate derived from quartz sand and inorganic colour pigments, silicate paints react with the mineral substrate on which they are painted — indoors or out — to form an insoluble and extremely long-lasting surface. A silicate paint effectively becomes a part of the surface, rather than just a film on top.

POLYURETHANE PAINTS

Polyurethane paints and varnishes are made from isocyanates, a family of organic chemicals used extensively to make materials including foams, adhesives, sealants, coatings and pressed-wood products. In conventional paints the film-forming component and pigment is deposited on the surface as the solvent dries. In polyurethane paint, the film is formed when the isocyanate reacts and becomes a plastic-like substance.

Polyurethane coatings are typically available in single- and two-part formulations. In single-part products the isocyanate reacts with moisture in the air; that is, the product is moisture-cured; in two-part products, a moisture-curing chemical is added.

Single-part polyurethanes such as polyurethane varnishes contain no free residues of isocyanates — they are already chemically reacted. However, because they use an oil- or alkyd-based solvent they present similar environmental and health hazards to conventional solvent-based paints in that they off-gas VOCs during and after application.

Two-part polyurethanes contain unreacted isocyanates and are much more hazardous to work with than single-part polyurethanes. Contamination typically occurs through skin contact or breathing in mist or dust from isocyanate evaporation. Occupational Safety and Health safeguards covering breathing apparatus and skin protection should be followed when polyurethane liquids are mixed or sprayed; when polyurethane coatings are burnt off during welding or torch cutting; or when polyurethane coatings that are not fully cured (24 hours at room temperature) are sanded.

The main effects of over-exposure are asthma and other lung problems, as well as irritation of the eyes, nose, throat, and skin. Symptoms can occur both soon after exposure or several hours later.

Isocyanates can also cause hypersensitivity pneumonitis, a lung disease whose symptoms include fever, body aches, shortness of breath, and cough with phlegm or sputum. It is possible, through exposure, to become sensitised to isocyanates so that any skin contact or breathing of isocyanate causes severe asthma, skin rashes, swelling, itching and hives. There is no way to predict who will or won't react to isocyanates.

EPOXY RESINS

Epoxy resin paints and surface coatings are used when a tough, durable coating or adhesive is needed. They consist of an epoxy resin and a curing agent and usually contain organic solvents. Some epoxies cure in a few minutes, others need additional time, or heat, to harden. Finished, or hardened epoxy products, are considered relatively harmless unless they are cut, sanded or burned. Exposure to uncured resins can be harmful. Single-part systems are less harmful than two-part systems, because the hazardous chemicals are already combined into less toxic polymers and do not evaporate as readily as the chemicals in two-part systems.

The most common effects of over-exposure are eye, nose, throat and skin irritation, skin allergies and asthma. The chemicals in some epoxy resin systems, such as methylene chloride, are suspected carcinogens. Solvent additives such as toluene, xylene and methanol are known to cause body irritation, headaches, dizziness and confusion in the short term. The longer-term effects include reproductive problems, central nervous system disorders and damage to the lungs, liver and kidneys.

WATER-BASED (ACRYLIC) ENAMEL PAINTS

Because they largely avoid the substantial use of organic solvents, acrylic paints are considered a better ecological choice than oil-based paints. Their development has encountered problems: unlike the hard 'enamelised' surfaces characteristic of conventional oil-based paints (alkyd enamels), the soft polymers used in acrylic paints have suffered a technical problem known as *blocking.* Blocking occurs when two surfaces painted with acrylic paint stick together under the influence of pressure and/or heat; this explains why many windows painted with acrylics haven't been opened in years. A recent development in the engineering of acrylic polymers has led to the development of paints that match the strong points of alkyd enamels. These new semi-gloss 'water-based enamels' are low-odour, quick drying, non-yellowing and have better weather resistance than alkyd enamels.

'Environmental Choice'

Many countries have introduced legislation to allow products that meet certified environmental criteria to use the term 'environmentally friendly' on labelling and in advertising. New Zealand operates 'Environmental Choice', a voluntary programme which aims to minimise damage to the environment in the production, distribution and disposal of products.

A large number of paint products now carry Environmental Choice classification. These characteristically contain low levels of VOCs; no formaldehyde or ethylene glycol; and minimal levels (0.1%) of heavy metals. They must be clearly labelled with information describing proper methods for disposing of leftover paint and cleaning paint equipment.

Any product made, used or disposed of in a way that reduces potential environmental harm can be considered a good environmental choice. However, the manufacturers of 'natural' paints are critical of the Environmental Choice certification system for three reasons:

➤ Obtaining and maintaining product certification can be costly.

➤ Certification merely requires the reduction, not elimination, of chemicals known to be toxic.

➤ Raw materials do not need to be sourced from renewable resources.

PAINTING AND CLEANING UP

Take the following precautions when painting:

➤ Wear a dust mask when sanding or removing old paint and make sure interior spaces are well ventilated when applying new paint.

➤ Avoid skin contact with the paint, solvent thinners and cleansers.

➤ Don't pour unwanted paint or solvents down the drain. City sewerage systems aren't equipped to deal with them. Avoid putting them into stormwater pipes that carry excess rainwater to the nearest natural watercourse.

➤ Clean water-based paints off brushes in a bucket of water. Allow the residue to settle, then tip the *diluted* solution onto a patch of lawn or garden — perhaps a patch of kikuyu — not down the drain. The residue in the bucket can be wiped out with paper and placed in the rubbish.

➤ Oil-based paints can be cleaned from brushes using solvents and the brushes wiped dry with a rag. The solvent can be left to settle, decanted and used again. The residue can be wiped out with a rag and put in the rubbish. *(Instead of using solvent-based cleansers to freshen a stiff and clogged paintbrush, try soaking it for an hour in hot vinegar.)*

➤ Leftover paint can be either recycled — some city councils organise collection points for hazardous household waste on a regular basis — or left with the lid off until it has solidified, then disposed of (still with the lid off) in the rubbish. If in doubt, check with your local council.

➤ Steel paint cans are recyclable when empty. Aerosol cans should be emptied by spraying into newspaper, then disposed of in household waste. Most plastic containers are recyclable if paint residues are dried and removed.

➤ For handling lead-based paints see page 18.

PAINT STRIPPER

Most commercial paint strippers are solvent based and work by dissolving the bond between the wood and the paint. Anything which strips paint shouldn't be used as a skin cleanser or tonic — most are capable of dissolving latex or rubber gloves used for protection.

Methylene chloride (DCM), a common active ingredient, is categorised by the US Environmental Protection Agency as a 'probable human carcinogen'. It evaporates quickly and is easily inhaled. Flammability is also an issue. Good personal protection and ventilation are necessary.

N-methylpyrrolidone (NMP) is a slower-working (and sometimes less effective) stripper based on citrus oils. It evaporates slowly, releasing VOCs. Good personal protection and ventilation are essential. It is combustible rather than flammable. Combined with dibasic esters (DBE) it forms a very powerful stripper.

Old-fashioned caustic strippers rely on the caustic action of caustic soda, or lye, to saponify and remove paint. Made from either sodium or potassium hydroxide they are effective on all but acrylic paints or delicate woods (it darkens timber surfaces). Caustic soda is not carcinogenic and doesn't contain VOCs but care still needs to be exercised when using it, particularly of the skin, eyes, and garden plants in the vicinity.

WHAT TO BUY

There is currently no regulatory body or set of standards for New Zealand paint manufacturers. Safety data sheets are demanded of the more toxic products but, by and large, paint choice is entirely in the customer's hands. Choosing the most environmentally friendly paint for a given application can be difficult.

TOP TIPS FOR PAINTS

✓ Look for paints that list their ingredients in full and carry the 'Environmental Choice' label.

✓ Natural paints that are free of organic solvents are best.

✓ Conventional water-based (acrylic and latex) paints, though they still contain small quantities of toxic substances, are preferable to oil-based (alkyd) paints.

✓ Oil-based enamels are preferable to epoxy resins and polyurethanes.

Chapter 6

Furnishings, fabric, furniture, utensils and materials

A web of eco issues surrounds our choice of furnishing and fabrics, floor coverings, appliances, utensils, clothing and paper. Whether products are 'natural' or 'unnatural', there are often hidden environmental and social costs.

NATURAL PRODUCTS FROM RENEWABLE SOURCES
Bamboo
Bamboo is used to make raffia for basketware, mats and sunhats. Bamboo is widely used in furniture, screen curtains and blinds. It grows prolifically so is a sustainable resource. The varnished finishes on bamboo are less eco friendly.

Coir
Coir is the fibrous outer coating of the coconut. Before use it is softened by soaking in estuaries and lagoons for up to a year, a process that can have an adverse effect on marine life. It is used in matting and in mattress stuffing. In mattressing it is firm and soft but packs down after a length of time. In matting, it is combined with sisal, another vegetable fibre, to reduce its sensitivity to changes in temperature and humidity. A latex backing makes coir matting more durable.

Cork
Cork bark is a renewable and sustainable resource with a long history of use. It is harvested in nine-year cycles from mature cork oak trees, which grow

mainly in the Mediterranean region and live up to 250 years. The unique cellular construction of cork — it contains approximately 40 million air-filled cells per cubic centimetre — makes it one of the best natural insulators. It is impermeable to gas and liquids (which is why it makes an excellent stopper in a wine bottle), does not absorb dust and is fire and insect resistant. Its long-lasting natural resilience makes it an excellent flooring material.

Cotton

It is believed that cotton has been used for up to 7000 years — we know Egyptians wore it earlier than 2500 BC.

Cotton is light, airy, soft, versatile and universal. It is used extensively in clothing and bedding but is seldom used in furnishing, as it is not durable. Kilims, or cotton rugs from Turkey, are lightweight but not long-lasting.

Cotton is part of the mallow family. It is a small shrub that grows only in hot climates but needs vast amounts of water, thereby depleting an often-scarce resource. It is a pest-prone monoculture with the inherent dangers of pesticide pollution and soil depletion. Synthetic dyes are used to create bright coloured fabrics and formaldehyde is used to produce non-iron finishes.

There is progress towards eco-friendly cotton production. Some growers are cross-breeding cotton strains to reduce the need for pesticides and to create a range of subtle natural colours including brown, green and red.

Down

Down is warm and light. It was traditionally gathered from the natural moult of waterbirds such as the eider duck, which yielded eiderdown. It now involves the farming and killing of caged birds. It is used in furnishings, pillows, beds, duvets and sleeping bags: the higher the proportion of down, the warmer the filling. Because the quills penetrate most fabrics, very closely woven coverings are needed to keep the feathers in. Recent research credits the tight weave of these coverings with keeping dust mites out and lessening the occurrence of asthma.

Flax

Flax has been used for over 7000 years. Fine linen (from flax) was used as burial shrouds for the Egyptian pharaohs.

Flax is second only to hemp in strength, versatility and antiquity. Linen is derived from flax straw, which grows in subtle creams, greys and tans. It is absorbent, colourfast, textured and durable. It is used in clothing and furnishings but tends to be expensive. Flax was used by Maori to make baskets, food containers, clothing and fishnets.

Hemp

Following a 50-year ban on production in the Western world because of its association with drug use, hemp has recently been rediscovered.

Hemp has been used as a valuable source of fibre for clothing and textiles for thousands of years. It may be the most ancient of textiles — a scrap of hemp fabric from about 8000 BC was found recently in what was ancient Mesopotamia (now Iraq).

Hemp is made from the *Cannabis sativa* (marijuana) plant and is very durable, airy, colourfast, washable, versatile and resistant to mould, mildew, pilling and ultraviolet light (it filters 95% of UV rays). Production does not require pesticides or extensive watering. It produces twice as much fibre per acre as cotton and improves soil condition, rather than depleting it. Due to its rapid growth rate it is a great absorber of carbon dioxide — one of the main gases contributing to global warming. Its uses include rope and twine, textiles, paints and varnishes, medicine, soap, plastics, biomass fuel, construction materials, paper, cardboard, feed stock, human-grade foods and oils, biodegradable plastics and fibreglass substitute.

In modern strains of industrial hemp the psychoactive ingredient (THC) sought by smokers is present in extremely low levels. In 2001, the first legal hemp since 1948 was sown in New Zealand.

Fur

The hunting and farming of fur-bearing animals for their pelts is embroiled in concerns over animal welfare and population depletion. Fur production from animals already targeted for eradication, such as New Zealand possums, is viewed less critically. Possum fur is used in knitted garments and hats. It is very soft and comes in a range of natural colours.

Horsehair

Horsehair, from the mane or tail, was traditionally used in stuffing furniture and mattresses. It is strong, coarse and durable but now scarce and expensive. Horsehair items can still be sourced in second-hand shops and refurbished or recycled.

Jute

Jute derives from long-stemmed plants grown around the Ganges Delta. It is mainly used with hemp in the production of hessian and as a backing for linoleum. As a soft weave it is not long-lasting but, when impregnated with a layer of linseed oil, pine resin and wood flour, it becomes one of the most durable and long-lasting sheet flooring materials available — linoleum. It is also anti-static and completely biodegradable.

Kapok

Kapok comes from the seedpods of the tropical silk-cotton tree. Warm and waterproof, its once extensive use in bedding, padded clothing and lifejackets has been replaced by synthetic fibres. After prolonged use it can release allergenic dust.

Latex

Latex foam rubber is derived from the sap of the rubber tree. Used in furniture and mattresses, it is firm but soft, breathes well and is very durable. There are ethical concerns in the felling of rainforest to accommodate rubber plantations and in the dangers of 'latex allergy', a health complaint experienced by plantation workers.

Leather

Leather is a hard-wearing, long-lasting product made by cleaning, salting, stretching and oiling the inner layers of animal skin. We can guess that early humans wrapped themselves in animal skin and, with long use, their sweat and body oil preserved and softened the leather. We know that sea salt and human urine were common prehistoric leather-tanning agents until replaced by the sweeter-smelling boiled barks of trees, five or six thousand years ago.

In the early 19th century, chemical salts, chromes and alums were introduced into the tanning process. These are most often used in the production of soft leathers. Chromium metal in the wastewater is toxic to humans and aquatic life. There are alternative non-toxic tanning processes that use teas and natural oils.

Paper

Paper can be made from wood pulp, banana fibre, bamboo, cotton and hemp. It is easily recycled and from a renewable source but the sheer quantity used places pressure on forests and on recycling facilities. The chemical dyes and bleaches used in production are toxic. Unbleached and recycled paper is available, for a small premium.

Rice straw

Rice straw is densely packed and covered with a finely woven matting to make Japanese tatami mats. The mats stain easily, so coverings typically need replacing every three or four years.

Seagrass

Seagrass is grown in sea water in the paddy fields of China where it forms part of nature's tidal defences for mangroves and reefs. It is hand woven to form matting and furniture. It is naturally stain resistant so dyes are not an option. In use, it can be dusty, slippery and a fire hazard.

Silk

Silk was developed in China around 5000 years ago but the secrets of cultivation and fabric manufacturing were closely guarded by the Chinese for about 3000 years. It has been farmed since about 2000 BC.

Silk consists of long, elastic filaments spun by silk worms around their cocoons as they feed on mulberry leaves. The silk worms are destroyed during harvest.

Silk is very soft, strong, luxuriant and long-lasting. It is used in clothing, furnishings, bed linen and rugs. It is expensive so mostly confined to the production of small, luxurious items such as lingerie, cushions and wall hangings.

Sisal

Sisal is a natural fibre extracted from the fibrous leaves of the sisal plant. It is soft but hard-wearing and, besides being used for cordage and matting, is used in automotive friction parts (brakes, clutches) and in textured coatings. Sisal is sometimes blended with coir for matting.

Wood

Wood is a renewable resource and easily recycled but so universally in demand that wholesale felling is unsustainable. Most imported hardwood is unsustainably logged and widespread clearing of rainforest now threatens the environmental health of the planet. The eco-friendly option is to use recycled wood or fast-growing sustainable plantation timbers. Engineered timbers and plywoods often use glues that off-gas VOCs, such as formaldehyde (see Chapter 3).

Wool

Sources include sheep, Kashmir goats, angora rabbits, yaks, llamas, alpacas and goats. Wool is warm, soft, absorbent and airy, and it has a degree of natural fire resistance. It is widely used in clothing, furnishings, carpets, blankets and mattresses. Matting together woollen fibres makes felt.

~ *Sheep dips* The dipping of sheep in non-persistent organophosphate and synthetic pyrethroid pesticides to eliminate parasites is common practice among sheep farmers. (Persistent organochlorine pesticides (POPs) are no longer used: the Ministry for the Environment is currently studying the extent of POP contamination in New Zealand.) Synthetic pyrethroid chemicals pose little direct threat to human health but are damaging to aquatic systems, particularly the tiny invertebrates that are essential for any thriving waterway.

Organophosphates interfere with an enzyme essential to the nervous systems in humans, animals and insects. While these chemicals break down relatively rapidly in the environment they are easily absorbed through the skin and are considered harmful to anyone handling wool that has been recently dipped. The effects of low-level, long-term exposure are not well understood.

Environmental concerns include the difficulty of disposal of dip on the farm without contaminating the land or waterways, and the pollution of waterways downstream from wool-scouring plants.

The period between dipping and shearing is, at present, the responsibility of the registrants of products and the wool industry and there are tests that can detect chemical residue in the wool. There are sources of organic wool in New Zealand and natural dyes are available. Alternatively the 'home-spun' colours ranging from cream to black don't require dyes.

~ *Natural dyes*   Natural dyes can be made from plants, animals and minerals, although some of these are scarce. Indigenous bark dyes include the following:

➤ Boiled bark of the rata vine will give a fawn or brown dye.

➤ Early settlers boiled the bark of miro in a large amount of water to dye hessian a rich henna colour.

➤ Tanekaha bark will produce a red dye.

PLANT DYES

Use equal quantities of fabric and plant material,
and salt to fix the dye. Boil for one to two hours.

Yellow	Goldenrod, onion skins, old man's beard
Green	Lily of the valley, Queen Anne's lace, rhododendron, gorse, iris, broom
Purple/lavender/blue	Blackberries, indigo, elder
Brown	Acorns, walnut shell
Red	Lichen, foxglove

NATURAL PRODUCTS FROM NON-RENEWABLE SOURCES

FURNISHINGS,
FABRIC,
FURNITURE,
UTENSILS
AND
MATERIALS

Minerals

The planet's mineral reserves are a finite resource. Iron, aluminium and magnesium make up 99% of the earth's crust. The 90-odd elements that account for the remainder are relatively scarce. At present rates of extraction, and if it could be reached, there's enough copper, tin, lead, silver and zinc in the earth's crust to maintain supplies for around 600–700 years. However, the *viable life expectancy* of accessible reserves is much shorter: somewhere between 15 and 30 years.

Mining destroys natural habitats and consumes large amounts of energy. Metals should now be regarded as precious items to be treasured and recycled rather than as a bottomless resource.

~ *Copper*   Copper mining causes high levels of pollution. About half of the copper used is recycled. It is a good heat conductor so is often used in cooking utensils. Oxidation (greening) is toxic so copper is used only on the outside or base of a pot where it does not come into contact with food. Because of its durability it is also widely used for hot and cold water supplies.

~ *Iron and steel*   Iron ore supplies are plentiful and recyclable but in their finished state iron and steel rust readily. They need enamel, paint or galvanising to protect them from corrosion.

Stainless steel is steel that has been protected from corrosion by the addition of chromium. It is long-lasting, easy to clean and recyclable.

~ *Lead*   Lead was used in the past for roofing, plumbing and as a pigment in paint but is highly toxic. Extreme care is needed in removing and disposing of lead paint (see Chapter 2).

~ *Aluminium*   Aluminium is extracted from bauxite ore. Reserves are abundant but aluminium production requires massive inputs of electricity with inherent energy and environmental costs. The metal degrades in acidic rain so is often powder coated. It is lightweight, durable and, unless powder coated, recyclable.

~ *Glass*   Glass is non-toxic, airtight but fragile. Sea sand cannot be used for glass making and though silica resources are plentiful, the mining of silica sand causes environmental damage.

SYNTHETICS FROM NON-RENEWABLE SOURCES
— PLASTICS

Since its chance invention back in the 1920s plastic has become the bedrock of consumerism. Global consumption is measured at over 100 million tonnes a year and production is growing. So too are the ecological problems associated with its manufacture, use and disposal.

Plastics are traditionally made from polymers derived from petroleum, a non-sustainable resource (1 litre of oil out of every 10 produced is currently turned into plastics) but they can also be made from biopolymers. Biopolymers are generated from renewable natural sources, are often biodegradable, and not toxic to produce. They can be produced from biological systems (micro-organisms, plants and animals), or chemically synthesised from biological starting materials (such as sugars, starch, natural fats or oils, and the like).

The traditionally manufactured plastics are pervasive because they are cheap to manufacture and are adaptable to almost any product requirement. They exist in many of the materials with which we build houses and in almost all types of household commodity — from toothbrushes to refrigerators and shoes to computers. Safer, effective substitutes are available for most plastic uses. These include the traditional sustainable materials: wood, metals, fabrics, paper, leather, glass, cork and ceramics. As a last resort, consider chlorine-free plastics, in particular polyethylene and polypropylene.

Plastic types

The more problematic plastics are chlorine-based and contain a high percentage of additives designed to tailor the resin to a particular use.

Based on problems related to production, additives, emissions, disposal and fire, Greenpeace ranks polyvinyl chloride (PVC) as the most environmentally harmful plastic, and plastics made from biopolymers, which more readily break down in the waste stream, the least harmful. Between PVC and the biopolymers a raft of plastics is listed in descending order of harmful environmental effects: polyurethane (PU), polystyrene (PS), polycarbonate (PC), polyethylene-terephthalate (PET), polyethylene (PE) and polypropylene (PP).

~ *Polyvinyl chloride*   Polyvinyl chloride (PVC) is used mainly in 'long-life' products, meaning products with an average lifespan of 35 years. In effect, this means that products manufactured 35 years ago are only now entering the waste stream and will be followed by the tens of millions of tonnes of PVC products manufactured in the intervening years.

The primary drawback with PVC is that vinyl chloride, the monomer from which it is made, is a highly toxic human carcinogen. The production process combines chlorine gas with ethylene dichloride — both toxic — to make vinyl chloride, which is then polymerised to make PVC. The production waste contains dioxins and furans, which must be dumped or burned. Dioxin is a persistent pollutant — the ecosystem is unable to absorb it — and has been linked to cancer, reproductive failure, endocrine disruption and suppression of the immune system.

Up to 60% of a PVC product's weight is additives. Pthalates are added for flexibility, but these are known to migrate out of PVC and have been linked to health problems including damage to the liver, kidneys and reproductive system.

More than half of the PVC manufactured worldwide is used in construction. In its hard form it makes products such as guttering, window frames, weatherboards and waste pipes. In its softer form it makes electric cable sheathing, flooring coverings, shrink-wraps and wet-weather gear.

Less than 1% of the world's PVC consumption is currently recycled yet there are no environmentally sound disposal options for PVC waste.

Over 200 communities and major cities in Europe restrict or avoid the use of PVC in public construction projects; some have successfully built major new buildings without PVC.

~ *Polyurethane*   Polyurethane (PU) and polystyrene (PS) plastics are widely used in the building and furnishing of houses. Polyurethane is a source of paints, glues and soft foamed products like carpet underlay. It is a chlorine-based plastic, and its manufacture creates numerous hazardous by-products including phosgene, isocyanates, toluene, and ozone-depleting gases. When PU products are burned or degraded these hazardous chemicals are released either into the air or into landfill leachate.

Plastics and consumers

There is a trend among some manufacturers to use less PVC and fewer types of plastic to aid recycling efforts. Some major retailers have adopted a PVC phase-out policy — IKEA (furniture), Tarkett (floorings), The Body Shop (cosmetics). Until plastics production becomes more sustainable and less toxic, concerned consumers can do little other than choose to use as little as possible, select goods made from alternative materials and recycle where the option exists. (Disposal options are discussed in Chapter 17.)

PFCs

One of the 'wonder' materials of the 20th century is the stuff that keeps food from sticking to pots and pans, repels stains on furniture and rugs and makes water roll off raincoats and outdoor garments.

Perfluorocarbons, or PFCs as they are known, are a family of synthetic chemicals that were thought to be biologically inert and, therefore, harmless. Recent findings indicate that PFCs are extraordinarily persistent and toxic chemicals that pervasively contaminate human blood and wildlife.

Unlike other toxic and persistent organic contaminants such as DDT, PCB, and dioxin, PFC chemicals are resistant to environmental degradation. This is, in part, what makes them such 'wondrous' industrial chemicals. But the unexpected discoveries regarding the accumulation of some types of PFC chemicals in the food chain, and the fact that they do not break down or leave the body, has made them an investigative priority for scientists and officials at the US Environmental Protection Agency.

What can you do?

The Environmental Working Group, a non-profit science group that advocates greater regulation of chemicals, advises homeowners as follows:

➤ Phase out the use of non-stick cookware and other equipment that is heated in your home. If you can afford to replace it now, do so. When heated to high temperatures, products with non-stick PFC coatings emit fumes that can be harmful.

➤ Do not use non-stick cookware in your home if you have pet birds. Fumes from these materials heated to high temperature during use can quickly kill birds.

➤ When you purchase furniture or carpet, decline optional treatments for stain and dirt resistance. Most of these chemical treatments contain PFCs.

➤ When buying clothing coated for water, stain, or dirt repellence, be aware that many of these coatings are PFCs. By buying alternatives you will help shrink the PFC economy and the associated global contamination.

➤ Minimise packaged food and greasy fast foods in your diet. These can be held in containers that are coated with PFCs to keep grease from soaking through the packaging. PFCs are used in a wide variety of containers, including chip boxes, pizza boxes and microwave popcorn bags.

➤ Avoid buying cosmetics and other personal care products with the phrase 'fluoro' or 'perfluoro' on the ingredient list. Among products that might contain PFCs are lotions, pressed powders, nail polish, and shaving cream.

~ *Polystyrene*   Polystyrene (PS) is a brittle plastic used to make model toys, disposable eating utensils etc. It is also the basis for open-celled styrene foam — as in an absorbent kitchen sponge — and the closed-cell styrene used in packaging and insulation. PS requires fewer additives than PVC, and because it doesn't contain chlorine it is regarded as being safer than PVC, but its production involves the use of known and suspected carcinogens (benzene, styrene and 1,3-butadeine). It is a fire risk unless treated with fire retardants.

~ *Polyethylene-terephthalate*   Polyethylene-terephthalate (PET) is tough, flexible and shatterproof. It is used mainly in foodstuff packaging and bottles — the impermeability of PET to gases makes it ideal for carbonated drink bottles. Though it contains up to 30% additives and makes use of heavy metals during production, it is regarded as being more eco friendly to both workers and the environment than PVC. PET recycling is high compared to other plastics.

~ *Polyethylene and polypropylene*   Polyethylene (PE) and polypropylene (PP) are simpler, chlorine-free plastics. They make relatively little pollution in their manufacture and are easy to recycle, but because so many PE and PP products have little substance (such as plastic bags) recycling is uneconomic and they are now a major source of uncontrolled pollution, particularly in stormwater systems and natural waterways.

Polyethylene is also called polythene and is manufactured in a range of densities to suit different uses: high-density polyethylene (HDPE) is tough, flexible, translucent and used for clear plastic tubing, electric cabling and film. Low-density polyethylene (LDPE) is turned into thin wraps, rubbish bags, coatings and bottles.

Polypropylene (PP) is stiff, and heat- and chemical-resistant and is made into battery cases, screw caps, and food tubs.

~ *Vinyl*   Vinyl is manufactured from PVC. It is used in wallpapers and floor coverings. The health risks associated with the migration of the chemical additives in PVC, such as phthalates, is of particular concern if infants and toddlers are spending time on the floor. The glues used to fix vinyl flooring often contain VOCs.

~ *Nylon, polyester and acrylic*   Nylon, polyester and acrylic from petro-chemically derived fibres use high-energy processes and produce toxins in their manufacture. They are used for stuffing as well as fabrics. They don't breathe well and are prone to static electricity and pilling but are durable and dry quickly. They burn rapidly, releasing toxic fumes.

An eco-friendly bedroom

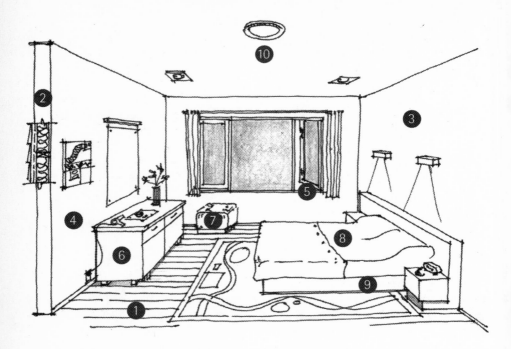

1   Flooring: solid concrete (uncovered to maximise passive solar heating); solid timber flooring, e.g. recycled T&G, *Eucalyptus saligna* finished with natural oils; low VOC particleboard. Flooring overlays — unglazed ceramic tiles (solar gain), T&G or parquet timber flooring, cork, linoleum, sisal/coir matting (light traffic), fitted wool carpets or throw rugs.

SYNTHETICS FROM RENEWABLE SOURCES

Rayon and acetate

Rayon and acetate are made from wood waste, mostly from the eucalyptus tree. They require chlorine in the early stages of production.

Rayon was the first artificial fibre. It is soft, limp and creases easily but is often blended with natural fibres. Viscose rayon is the most common.

Lyocell

Lyocell (trade name Tenecal) is produced from the wood pulp of trees grown specifically for this purpose. When mixed with cotton, it is very strong, soft and colourfast. It is processed using a solvent-spinning technique in which the dissolving agent is recycled, reducing environmental effluents.

2 Exterior walls — watertight but breathable e.g. brick cavity or weatherboard cladding; timber framing (boron-treated H1 Plus); wool/polyester insulation (hygroscopic); plasterboard lining.

3 Interior partitioning — timber framing (untreated), plasterboard lining, acoustic design or insulation where needed.

4 Interior wall finishes — 'Low VOC' acrylic paint finishes or natural paints, e.g. mineral, casein or lime-wash paints; wallpaper (not vinyl); timber panelling, e.g. Lawson cypress TG&V or natural fibres, e.g. hessian.

5 Window joinery — recycled timber joinery or aluminium frames with pine jamb liners and architraves; double glazing and/or low-E glass for thermal insulation, laminated glass for acoustic insulation; trickle ventilation built into joinery frame to provide ventilation when space is closed up.

6 Solid timber furniture — antique, pre-loved and restored items out of indigenous timbers; new furniture from reclaimed or recycled native timbers, and plantation timbers, e.g macrocarpa. Waxed or natural oil finishes.

7 Upholstered furniture — timber framing; natural latex, hemp/cotton or horsehair stuffing; leather, wool, hemp, linen covers.

8 Soft furnishings — natural fibres, organic cotton, linen, hemp (blends).

9 Bed — timber framing, timber slats, natural latex rubber mattress or cotton futon, hemp/cotton bed linen.

10 Domestic ventilation system — circulates warm, filtered air from attic space to living areas in winter.

FURNISHINGS AND MATERIALS OPTIONS

It is always a balancing act to find the most eco-friendly and effective options. Some relatively eco-friendly solutions are:

➤ beds — wooden slat beds with futons or mattresses made from wool, latex or coir (ideally, a combination of all three)

➤ pillows — feather, wool or, for a firmer option, latex

➤ bed coverings — wool blankets, patchwork quilts or feather/down duvet

➤ curtains and furniture fabrics — silk, hemp, linen, wool, undyed or natural dyes

➤ cushion and furniture padding – feather/down, latex, wool or a combination

➤ furniture frames – wood from a sustainable source or recycled

➤ floor coverings – vinyl flooring can be replaced with linoleum (made from the natural raw materials linseed oil, pine resin, wood flour and jute, and marketed under the trade names Marmoleum and Artoleum); cork flooring; ceramic floor tiles (unglazed earthenware); stone pavers (granite, marble and the like); timber (strip flooring, parquet etc.).

Natural fibre mats include wool, sisal/coir and jute. Hessian and felt underlays beneath fitted carpets avoid the VOCs released by synthetic underlays. Loose mats or carpets are easier to clean than fitted carpets and avoid the VOCs released by dry cleaning fluids.

> **TOP TIP FOR FURNISHINGS**
>
> ✓ Choose recyclable fabrics and materials from sustainable and renewable resources.

➤ utensils – stainless steel, ceramics and glass (preferably recycled)

➤ clothing – wool, linen, organic cotton, Lyocell, natural dyes.

Part Two

The Elements

Chapter 7

Energy

From the beginning of time, humans have played with fire. Harnessing the latent energy of the earth and the sun still forms the basis of our civilisation.

At present, three-quarters of the world's energy sources comes from fossil fuels — energy from ancient forests stored as oil, coal and natural gas. Not only are these resources finite but their use is causing global warming, air pollution, oil spills and acid rain. The most advanced alternative power generation technology is nuclear power. Nuclear power plants are an environmentally clean means of generating power. They release less radio-activity, carbon dioxide (the cause of global warming), sulphur dioxide and nitrogen dioxide (causes of acid rain) into the atmosphere than a coal-fired plant. But, historically, the mining and purifying of uranium has not been a clean process. The plants themselves are vulnerable to a catastrophic melt-down (such as at Chernobyl) unless designed and run properly, and the spent radioactive fuel and the retired plants present a disposal problem without equal: scientists are still trying to think of a safe way.

NEW ZEALAND'S ENERGY SOURCES

Until now, New Zealand has thought of itself as having abundant energy sources, other than oil. Our mainstay has been hydro power, a renewable, relatively 'clean' electricity-generation resource. It provides about two-thirds of our electricity; natural gas, coal, wind power and landfill gas provide just under a quarter and geothermal power less than a tenth. But even hydro resources are limited in number and size, and their exploitation dramatically alters the landscape, rivers and lake systems. Changing weather patterns make hydro power unpredictable in terms of consistent supply.

The potential for exploiting geothermal power is limited, and it is difficult to access. Natural gas supplies for power generation are not renewable, nor are they as big as first thought. As electricity demand increases the growth sector is likely to be coal — which is not good news for the environment. The most promising renewable alternatives at a commercial level are wind power and bioenergy.

Bioenergy is any form of energy released from biomass. Its sources include waste materials such as forestry residues, landfill waste and whey from the dairy industry, farming residues like straw, livestock slurry, chicken litter, and crops grown specifically for the purpose of producing energy. The fuel is available as a gas, a liquid and in solid form.

Bioenergy offers a large-scale alternative to fossil fuels — it is estimated that the biomass residues from New Zealand plantation forestry alone equate to roughly 10% of our total consumer energy demand. Some of our bigger primary producers already invest in biomass cogeneration — reusing waste materials from production processes to generate electricity.

THE ENERGY-EFFICIENT HOME

We need to think more about the way we use energy in the home, and explore safe and environmentally acceptable means of power generation at a localised level — in the local neighbourhoods — rather than at a national level. As householders, we do little other than purchase power at the gate, regardless of its source of generation. (We can't yet do as they are doing in some countries and specify, or pay a premium for, 'green' power.)

The householder's simplest remedy for unsustainable energy consumption is to reduce power consumption by installing solar water-heating panels (see Solar water heating, page 76), incorporating passive solar design principles in our construction (see Chapter 1) and making greater use of insulation (see Chapter 4).

In the meantime ... too many of us continue to use outdated and sometimes unsustainable energy technologies in our homes.

HOME HEATING

This section looks at both traditional and alternative means of home heating.

Space heating — warming the air around you — accounts for around 20% of home energy use, and is mostly done with heating appliances.

In choosing an energy-efficient appliance you need to consider not just its energy efficiency within the home but also the efficiency of its production. Flow-on benefits are also part of the energy equation; a coal range, or its wood-burning equivalent, will provide cooking, water heating, clothes drying and space heating — but only at the expense of contributing to air pollution.

Whatever form of heating you choose, it needs to be well maintained and thoughtfully utilised to gain maximum efficiency. Home insulation levels should also be considered — a good heating appliance can be rendered ineffective by too little home insulation.

Fireplaces and wood burners

All domestic fireplaces and solid-fuel burners must be installed according to building consent requirements, usually by approved installers. Free-standing burners require specific clearance distances and protective shields. An unpermitted fireplace may invalidate insurance claims for fire damage and jeopardise a potential house sale if the local territorial authority has no record of its installation.

~ *Open fireplaces*   Open fireplaces are the most romantic but least efficient type of indoor fire, losing as much as 90% of their heat up the chimney. Atmospheric pollution and thermal inefficiency have led to most open fireplaces being disused or fitted with more efficient inbuilt wood burners.

Solid-fuel burners are usually double-walled fireboxes, with a door for loading and dampers to control the rate of burn. They are mainly convection heaters: air is drawn through low vents, heated in the space between the firebox and the outer panel, and pushed out into the room through top vents, though the firebox and flue also heat up and radiate warmth. Burners can be free standing or inbuilt into existing open fireplaces with the flue installed in the chimney. Free-standing fireplaces are more fuel efficient than built-in fireplaces as heat is radiated into the room from the side panels and the flue.

_____   ~ *Solid-fuel burners*   These provide about twice the heat efficiency of an open fire but still waste heat through the flue. Innovative, low-emission wood burners have been developed in New Zealand. Some have a catalytic combustor, a honeycomb-shaped disc made of glass or ceramic with a rare-metal catalyst coating. They are usually located across the exhaust vent of stoves and burn off pollutants before they escape up the flue. One uses a liquid scrubbing process and particulate separator which is almost 100% efficient and emits only steam.

~ *Pellet fireplaces* These look very similar to solid-fuel burners and can be enclosed or free standing. Walnut-sized pellets, made from waste wood, are fed into the fire by an electronic feeder. They operate at about 95% heat efficiency — about six times the heat efficiency of some open fires — but are dependent on electricity to operate the feeder.

~ *Coal ranges* Coal ranges have all the advantages of free-standing fire-places with the added facility of cooking and water heating. Their major drawback, as with all fossil-fuel heaters, is that they contribute to carbon dioxide production (greenhouse gases), air pollution and smog.

~ *Fire efficiency* The greater the airflow, the faster the fire burns. Most stoves can be damped to control the rate of burn, either via a flue damper or through door vents. Slow-burning stoves tend to burn less efficiently — put out less heat and cause more smoke pollution — than when hot-burning. 'Double burning' stoves are designed to circulate the air twice through the firebox before releasing it into the room or up the flue, giving better combustion of the fuel and more warmth. However, double burning can amount to little more than inefficient combustion if the fire is damped to the extent that it cannot burn the fuel; that is, it smoulders, creating smoke pollution, instead of burning cleanly.

Heat output is rated in kilowatts per hour, but this only gives an indication of what a burner will do on a high setting when loaded with dry firewood. Most models of a size between 15 and 23 kW/hr will heat the average 150 square metre open-plan home. The ideal burner will have a long burn time on low output, with low emissions.

Conventional fires draw air from the room to feed the fire, in turn drawing cooler air into the room and lowering the room temperature. An innovative flue design has been developed which draws air to feed the fire from a source other than the space being heated. This improves heating efficiency by up to a third.

~ *Fireplace fuels* All fossil fuels pollute the atmosphere when burned. Coal is a particularly bad culprit, but firewood is close behind.

FIREWOOD is a renewable resource but strong demand for hot-burning timbers such as manuka/kanuka and even old-growth beech, rata and kamahi is having an adverse effect on our small, remaining native bush areas.

Plantation timber provides a more sustainable resource. Eucalypt, wattle and macrocarpa are excellent hot-burning alternatives; pine is also readily available but is not as hot or long burning. Willow and poplar are sometimes available but are of lesser quality as fuels.

Dry wood produces more heat and less smoke than green wood. Wood is best bought in spring or summer, split while still green and left to dry in a well-ventilated area. Wood which is dry (25% moisture content) usually displays radial cracking.

Start a fire with a light, dry, quick-burning wood and a high airflow to reduce pollution. As the fire burns down to an intense glow, slower-burning dense wood can be added.

COAL is a non-renewable resource and, as a fireplace fuel, is a substantive air pollutant. New Zealand has substantial coal reserves but makes little use of coal domestically (domestic use accounts for just 5% of production). It is very hot burning and has good burn duration, but stove fireboxes and fireplace grates must be designed to withstand the high heat coal engenders. Anthracite coal gives off the greatest heat and releases the least smoke. Bituminous — or brown — coal is most commonly used in homes.

PELLET FUEL is made from sawdust and wood scraps and provides a hot, clean heat.

COMPOSITION LOGS are often chemically treated to make them burn brighter.

CHARCOAL is not used for heating, but is the fuel of choice for summer barbecues. Charcoal is produced by heating wood to a point where it burns, but with insufficient air to allow complete combustion (which causes air pollution). In the process, water and volatile gases are released, leaving carbon residue or charcoal. When reignited, charcoal burns at 20–30% efficiency — three or four times the energy efficiency of wood. It produces heat without smoke, which makes it an excellent barbecue fuel. Charcoal production in many parts of the world has led to the deforestation of fragile environments. In New Zealand it is produced commercially from plantation offcuts.

Other types of heater

~ *Electric heaters* Electric heaters convert 100% of electricity entering the heater into energy, although the production of electricity may well be less than 100% efficient. Electric heaters range from bar and fan heaters, which

are good for a short, quick blast of heat, to oil-filled column heaters and heat
pumps which provide steady background warmth over a long period.

~ *Fuel oil and kerosene burners*   Fuel oil and kerosene burners have all but disappeared from New Zealand homes. They provide 50–75% energy efficiency but if not vented release pollutants and water vapour into the room. The fuel is not a renewable resource.

~ *Natural gas heaters*   Natural gas heaters (gas is piped in from the street) must be flued. Both natural gas and bottled LPG are environmentally unsustainable sources of energy — New Zealand has limited reserves.

~ *Portable LPG heaters*   Portable LPG heaters use natural gas supplies. These types of heater are an important source of heating for 33% of New Zealand households (2001 figures). They have the advantage of being moveable from room to room and their energy expenditure can be more readily controlled than with an electric heater. These heaters are more efficient than the flued models, giving 70–90% efficiency, but flueless gas heaters release water vapour, carbon dioxide and salts directly into the indoor atmosphere, encouraging respiratory complaints such as asthma and pneumonia. They are banned in some countries for these very health reasons. To avoid breathing the fumes good ventilation is essential when using flueless heaters — which somewhat defeats their purpose.

~ *Underfloor heating*   Underfloor heating provides a comfortable and even form of radiant heat. The type that uses a grid of electrically heated cables is expensive to operate. A better method draws hot water from a wetback and/or a solar panel, through pipes laid in a concrete slab.

~ *Column radiators*   Column radiators which draw on hot water supplied by a wetback and/or a solar panel are another efficent and comfortable form of radiant space heating.

~ *Nightstore electrical heaters*   Nightstore electrical heaters are suitable for people who are at home during the day. They use the cheaper electricity rate at night to store heat, which is released during the day. You need to be connected to a day and night electricity plan to take advantage of the cheaper night-rate electricity. Hot water cylinders and appliances such as washing machines and dishwashers can also be put on this cheaper night rate.

~ *Heat pumps*   A heat pump, as the name suggests, is an appliance which 'pumps' heat from one space to another. It is essentially an air conditioner working in reverse and, indeed, some are designed to work as air conditioners in the summer — cooling, filtering and dehumidifying the air — and as space heaters in the winter.

They work by extracting heat from outdoor air and releasing it indoors. Small models heat a single room, bigger models heat an entire house. A heat pump requires both a compressor and a fan to operate, components that are traditionally driven by fixed-speed motors. Newer models use electronic inverters to give quieter and more responsive speed control, with more accurate temperature control and improved energy efficiency.

Compared to standard portable electric and gas heaters a heat pump is a relatively expensive appliance to purchase and install, but it delivers two to three times the heat value of its consumption of electricity, which makes it an efficient, cheap to run form of heating.

Along with refrigerators and air conditioning units, heat pumps have traditionally used the chlorinated fluorocarbon (CFC) freon — which is destructive of the ozone layer — as a heat-transfer fluid. CFCs are no longer used in new appliances but residual amounts in older appliances are considerable. Newer 'eco-friendly' refrigerants are claimed to not have a damaging effect on the ozone layer.

COOLING

Air conditioning

In cooling mode, a heat pump operates as an air conditioner. Domestic refrigerators and air conditioning units both make use of heat pump technology to extract heat from air and provide a cool, conditioned atmosphere.

While New Zealand was quick to adopt household refrigeration in the mid-20th century, it has been comparatively slow to adopt residential air conditioning. Many town house and apartment developments are now being built with air conditioning options, and retro-fitting of compact units is increasing.

Air conditioners operate by extracting the heat from indoor air, expelling the heat outdoors, and recycling the cool air indoors. As the name suggests, 'conditioners' also allow air humidity and, in some cases, air pressure to be controlled.

Centralised air conditioning systems circulate air throughout the entire house via a system of ducts. Often, the same set of ducts is used for *central heating* in winter. Ducting is usually installed into floors, walls and ceilings at the time of construction and adds considerably to the overall expense of the system.

Centralised systems are designed either as a split-system unit or a packaged unit.

A split system places the warm (and possibly noisy) half of the unit containing a condenser and compressor outside the building, and the cool half of the unit containing an evaporator inside the building mounted on the floor, wall or ceiling. A cassette system is a split-system device mounted inside the ceiling space.

A packaged unit places the entire system outside the building, with the cool air being ducted to where it is needed.

Single-room air conditioners are compact units installed directly into a window or wall. Because they require no ducting they are cheaper to install and operate, but are less energy efficient than central units designed to heat an entire home. The proximity of the electrical fan and compressor to the living space also makes these units noisy.

Newer 'inverter' types allow more graduated control of the fan and compressor functions. They use eco-friendly refrigerants and are smaller, quieter and deliver better dehumidification and operational efficiency than fixed-speed types.

~ *Air conditioner energy efficiency*   Because warm air rises, even room heating is best achieved by vents placed near the floor. Conversely, cooling is best provided by vents near the ceiling.

Air conditioners that are designed to deliver warm air in winter and cool air in summer slightly compromise one function or the other depending on where the vents are placed. Directional louvres on vents help direct airflow.

For an air conditioner to operate efficiently it needs to be the sole source of incoming and outgoing air; doors and windows should remain closed (it is futile to try and air condition the entire neighbourhood) and air leaks within the system, and around windows and doors, should be minimised. Regular maintenance is important to maintain efficiency: this should involve routine replacement of air filters (monthly), cleaning of compressor coils and evaporator fins (annually), and occasional inspection by a service agent for general wear and tear, refrigerant leaks and air leaks in the ducting.

Factors that will affect the efficiency and performance, and therefore determine the appropriate size of a unit, include the amount of space to be cooled, the number of windows, the amount of shade that hits the building, the level of insulation within the walls and ceiling, and the amount of heat generated by occupants and appliances.

Because they recycle air rather than providing a complete air change, air conditioners and central heating units are also linked to the problem of sick building syndrome. Poorly maintained systems can become contaminated

> ## Air conditioning and energy use
>
> Like space heating, air conditioning is energy hungry. As an energy user, it places a much greater load on the generation capacity of the electricity network at a time (summer) when hydro lake levels are typically low. The failure of Auckland's inner city electricity distribution network in 1998 was, in part, caused by excessive, heavy demand for air conditioning services. This demand often triggers the use of substitute non-renewable sources of generation, including coal and natural gas.

breeding grounds for fungi and bacteria, which are then spread throughout the building. Air conditioning ducting is where Legionnaires' disease, a type of pneumonia, was first discovered.

Other ways to keep cool

The use of ceiling and portable fans does little to alter air temperature but by creating a breeze gives the impression of being cooler. Similarly, a window fan, or a portable fan placed on a window sill and blowing outward, can improve ventilation on hot, still nights.

Passive cooling of the home uses no energy and is a more eco-efficient solution. Here are a number of options:

➤ Plant shade trees to prevent sun strike.

➤ Use white, or other light and reflective colours and materials, on roof and wall surfaces to reflect the sun's heat.

➤ Provide roof space ventilation, preferably high in a gable end wall or through soffit vents in the eaves.

➤ Insulate roof spaces to limit the transference of heat to the living space below.

➤ Use energy-efficient appliances (particularly refrigeration) to reduce the generation of heat inside the living space.

➤ Open windows to take advantage of cross-ventilation; install high-level vents or windows (not skylights) to release heat build-up and to draw indoors a flow of cooler, outdoor air.

➤ Install window shades or retro-fit low-E films on problem windows to block infrared radiation (heat).

WATER HEATING

Water heating accounts for about 30–35% of a home's energy consumption (electricity and gas). Large reductions in hot water energy use are feasible by improving the thermal performance of the hot water system. Unless a cylinder is relatively new and has an 'AAA' sticker, it is likely to be under-insulated.

A cylinder wrap provides an easy, inexpensive solution with a one- to two-year payback period. (The use of a wrap precludes the traditional use of the hot-water cupboard as an airing cupboard. And while it is more energy efficient to use a clothes dryer for a few minutes than to allow a constant leakage of warmth from the cylinder, it is even more eco friendly to dry your clothes outdoors, or under shelter.)

Lagging the hot-water pipes with a neoprene sleeve also saves heat loss — wrap the entire pipe, not just the first metre out of the cylinder. Where possible, the cylinder should be close to utility areas such as the kitchen, laundry and bathroom to reduce the volume of standing hot water in the pipes.

Water temperature

The water stored in a hot-water cylinder needs to be hot enough that the cylinder doesn't become a breeding ground for Legionella bacteria (no less than 60°C), yet not so hot that it scalds the skin at the point of delivery. Water at 60°C takes about one second to scald the skin of a child.

For this reason, regulations require that hot water for personal hygiene in day-care centres, schools, nursing and retirement homes and similar institutions does not exceed 45°C at the point of delivery, such as shower, handbasin, bath.

For personal hygiene in other buildings, such as domestic residences, the water temperature at the point of delivery must not exceed 55°C (though it may be delivered to kitchen sinks and laundry facilities at between 55°C and 65°C).

If a tank thermostat is set to heat water to 60°C — hot enough to prevent Legionella propagation and for delivery to sinks and laundry fixtures — temperature regulation of the hot-water supply to the personal hygiene sanitary fixtures must be provided by way of an in-line tempering valve set to either 45°C or 55°C, depending on the use of the building.

~ *Tempering valves*   Hot-water cylinders heated by supplementary means such as solar panels or fireplace wetbacks can reach temperatures in excess of the safe levels normally controlled by thermostat devices. In these situations a tempering valve between the point of use and the tank reduces the risk of scalding at the point of delivery, but maximises the efficient storage of hot water in the cylinder.

Size plays a role here too: a 135-litre cylinder storing water at 75°C holds the same amount of heat energy as a 180-litre cylinder with water stored at 55°C. The bigger cylinder with its lower water temperature is a safer option for users.

Turning the cylinder off is an energy saving only if you are away for more than two weeks.

Demand or 'tankless' heaters

Instantaneous or 'demand' hot-water systems are modern versions of the old-fashioned (and rather scary) gas caliphont water-heating devices that perched over the cast-iron baths in many New Zealand homes and exploded into life when the hot tap was turned on.

By applying heat at the point of use demand heaters avoid the need for a hot-water tank. They have the ability to deliver an endless supply of hot water, but at a limited flow rate. Where the demand for hot water is extensive, or demand occurs at several fixtures simultaneously, more than one unit may need to be installed. Demand heaters can also promote lengthy showers, simply because the hot water doesn't run out.

Demand heaters can be electric or gas operated. Electronic ignition eliminates the need for a pilot light in gas models and digital remote controllers allow an exact water temperature to be selected without the addition of cold water. The units are compact and generally externally mounted. Gas models use natural or bottled LPG gas, both of which are an unsustainable source of energy.

Solar water heating

The solar water-heating movement has weathered bad press over the years, caused by the provision of government subsidies early in the 1980s for installations many of which failed prematurely because the industry was not fully fledged or experienced in the technology. There is no longer an incentive system to help homeowners install solar systems (though there is talk of bringing one back) and in the intervening 20 years the technology and the service has improved vastly.

The biggest hurdle to installing a solar hot-water system is the upfront cost. Once installed, it can provide 50–80% of the water-heating requirements for the average family without adverse effects on the environment.

Solar systems are reckoned to give at least 20 years' service with little maintenance. Financially, most break even in between eight and 12 years.

If solar water heating is used in conjunction with mains water heating it is advisable to check 'flat rate' versus 'controlled rate' mains supply options with your electricity supplier, as different electricity tariffs will affect savings.

A tempering valve must be included in the system to meet regulations governing water temperature at the point of supply.

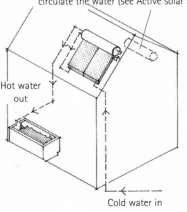

Alternative placement — in the roof space. But if the cylinder is placed at a level lower than the external solar panels, a pump is needed to circulate the water (see Active solar system)

Hot water out

Cold water in

Heated water rises naturally to the hot water cylinder mounted externally on the roof and positioned above the solar panels

Passive solar system

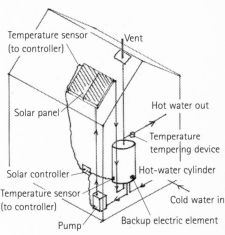

Temperature sensor (to controller)

Vent

Solar panel

Hot water out

Temperature tempering device

Solar controller

Hot-water cylinder

Temperature sensor (to controller)

Cold water in

Pump

Backup electric element

A pump to circulate the water allows the storage cylinder to be placed at a level lower than the solar panel. The pump turns on when the water in the solar panel is hotter than the water in the cylinder. The pump can be powered by a photovoltaic (PV) panel

Active solar system

~ *How do solar panels work?* Solar systems consist of a collector panel (1 sq m per person) connected by insulated water pipes to a storage cylinder. The collector panel is usually mounted on the north face of the roof and angled to catch the sun: higher angles collect more winter sun, lower angles more summer sun.

The storage cylinder (300 litres) can be mounted externally above the collector panel, in which case the water circulates naturally as it heats; or within the roof space or internal hot-water cupboard, with a temperature-sensitive electric pump (which requires a mains connection) controlling circulation.

Systems can use either low or mains pressure. Mains-pressure cylinders must be either stainless steel or ceramic-lined steel; low-pressure systems can be copper. Most modern cylinders are suitable; older models will need to be replaced.

Because sunshine is variable, cylinders are usually equipped with a backup electric element or gas booster, or (with low pressure only) a wood stove wetback for the sun-starved winter months.

An indoor temperature gauge helps users to plan best usage of solar-heated water and a tempering valve allows cold water to be added if the water overheats.

High-quality design and skilled instalment are essential. If installed correctly, little maintenance is needed, though panels can be damaged by winter freeze, so must have inbuilt protection in frost zones.

Wetbacks

Wetbacks can be attached to coal ranges and open, closed or free-standing fireplaces. A wetback is essentially a water jacket or pipe, usually made of copper, which circulates water between the fire and hot-water cylinder. Obviously, the hot-water cylinder and fireplace need to be in close proximity – preferably no more than 4 m apart.

Wetbacks may be fitted only to open vented systems to eliminate the risk of explosion. For this reason they are usually installed in low-pressure hot water systems with conventionally vented cylinders. (Wetbacks can be used in mains or high-pressure water systems, but such installations must have an additional, separately vented water circuit, which make them more complex and expensive.)

Wetbacks also create very high water temperatures, high enough to boil water, with attendant risks to users. As with all hot-water systems, a tempering valve must be included in the system to meet regulations governing water temperature at the point of supply (see above).

Unlimited water temperatures also pose a risk of damage to water pipes — especially non-copper pipes — and appliances that draw hot water.

Depending on the source of fuel, a wetback can be a stand-alone water heater or an energy-efficient backup to a mains- or solar-powered hot water supply. Wood-fired wetbacks can also heat water economically for use by a central-heating system, in which water is pumped to fixed radiators throughout the house, or through pipes buried in the floor.

Wetbacks are worth considering if you use a solid-fuel burner for space heating or cooking; if you have a reliable and cheap source of sustainable firewood; or if you live in a location where other energy sources are expensive, limited or intermittent.

Hot-water heat pumps

Heat-pump technology can be used to heat or cool both air and water. Heat-pump water heaters are uncommon in New Zealand but because they use much less energy than the amount of heat they move, they are an efficient form of water heating. Ideally, they are suited to buildings in mild or cool climates with large, steady hot-water requirements, such as families of four or more members.

They work by extracting 'free' heat from the surrounding air and transferring that heat to the water in the tank. The amount of electrical energy required to capture and transfer the heat is generally less than half the amount of heat that is finally transferred to the water. This means that for the same electrical input, a heat pump will heat more than twice the amount of water as that available from a standard resistance water heater, which makes it a very efficient system of water heating.

The electricity to run the heat pump can be supplied by solar photovoltaic panels, making it a cheaper and more self-reliant form of water heating. Other options involve the use of heat-recovery units to capture the warm exhaust of air conditioning systems, which would otherwise be wasted. Alternatively, the cool air expelled by the heat pump can be used to cool and dehumidify indoor air in summer.

Hot-water heat pumps can be fitted as an adjunct to an existing water cylinder (providing it is serviceable) or installed as a complete system with an inbuilt tank. The payback period of five to 10 years depends on the type of system purchased, its 'coefficient of performance' and the amount of hot water used.

LIGHTING

(Also see Chapter 11.)
Lighting accounts for about 10% of energy consumption in the home. This can be reduced with well-placed windows and skylights.

Fluorescent lamps use less energy than incandescent bulbs. Compact fluorescent lights (CFL) are four times more energy efficient than incandescent bulbs of the same intensity. Their higher initial cost is offset by their longer lamp life and lower running costs.

Appropriate lighting design and use also minimise wasted energy, by, for example, task lighting instead of flooding an entire room with light, or switching lights off when the room is vacated. If switching lights off is hard to enforce, occupancy sensors that turn off the light when the room is empty can be installed.

Outdoor solar lights store energy during the day for use at night.

APPLIANCES

New appliances sold in New Zealand must carry a mandatory 'Star' energy rating. The rating ranges from one to six stars, with one star being the least and six stars being the most energy efficient. Half-stars are also used. Each star can add up to 10% efficiency. Most appliances fall into the three- or four-star bracket.

Labels should also show an energy consumption estimate based on the appliance's expected annual consumption of kilowatts. The lower the estimate, the less energy used.

Energy consumption of appliances

The annual cost of running an appliance can be roughly calculated by multiplying the estimated power consumption by the cost of power per kilowatt. For example, if the estimated annual consumption is 540 kW and power in your region costs 13 cents/kW, the annual cost of running that appliance will be $70.20 (540 kW x $0.13 = $70.20).

This is just an estimate and will vary with household use. The actual amount of power drawn by a household appliance per day can be calculated using the formula:

$$\frac{\text{wattage} \times \text{hours used per day}}{1000}$$

For example: if a 2 kW electric heater is used for eight hours it will use

$$\frac{2000 \times 8}{1000} = 16 \text{ kW}$$

And if power costs 13 cents/kW the cost of running the heater for eight hours will be 16 kW x $0.13 = $2.08.

(Note: the cost of electricity per kilowatt is shown on monthly electricity accounts and is constantly changing — usually upwards. The cost per kilowatt does not include what is called a 'line charge', a fixed sum charged by your lines company to deliver the power to your home.)

Many appliances use 'standby' power to run electronic clocks, timers, remote controls and the like. It is estimated that electricity savings of close to 12% could be made by turning appliances off at the wall when not in use. However, even when plugged in but not switched on, they are still drawing power. The international 'Energy Star' guarantees that electronic appliances will automatically slip into a sleep mode, reducing the use of standby power, if the appliance is not used for a length of time.

WATTAGES FOR COMMON APPLIANCES

Appliance	Watts	Appliance	Watts
Clock radio	10	Dehumidifier	790
Computer (asleep)	30	Portable heater	750–2000
Electric blanket (double)	100	Vacuum cleaner	100–1400
Computer (awake)	120–150	Iron	100–1800
Heated towel rail	80–85	Toaster	800–1400
Ceiling fan	65–175	Hair dryer	1200–1900
Television	110–170	Dishwasher	1200–2400
Washing machine	350–500	Clothes dryer	1800–5000
Stereo	400	Hot-water cylinder	2000–3000

COOKING AND REFRIGERATION

Cooking and refrigeration account for 5% and 10% respectively of energy use in the average Kiwi home.

Microwave ovens

Microwaves draw a third of the energy of electric ovens. Little energy is wasted as most is absorbed by the food, unlike a conventional oven, which radiates heat into the kitchen. The shorter cooking time further reduces energy used in cooking.

Electric stoves

~ Radiant elements   Radiant elements are the most common but least energy-efficient method of cooking on the stove. Solid and ring elements work by sending energy into resistance elements where it is turned into heat. These types of element are slow to warm up and cool down, and lack precise temperature control.

~ Electric halogen elements   Electric halogen elements use halogen light to heat and radiate energy to a smooth-top cooking element. They are more energy efficient as they are faster to heat than radiant elements.

~ Electric induction elements   Electric induction elements are the most energy efficient. They use a magnetic field that is activated only when an iron or steel pan is placed on the smooth-top element. No energy is wasted in heating the element or stove top and they offer precise temperature control.

~ *Fan-forced ovens*   Fan-forced ovens use a combination of radiant heating (an element) and convection heating (the fan). The more efficient flow of heat tends to cook food faster than a radiation element on its own.

Gas stoves

Gas hobs offer instant heat and precise temperature control. A blue flame indicates efficient use of the gas, a yellow or orange flame indicates the gas is burning at less than full heat.

Solar ovens

Solar ovens will achieve heats of 180 to 200°C — enough to cook a roast — but are generally used only for camping.

Refrigerators

Refrigeration uses, on average, twice as much energy as cooking: 10% of household energy. An ideal running temperature is 2–5°C. Freezers are best set at around −18°C.

Energy is conserved if seals are kept in good repair. Failed seals are easily replaced. Opening the fridge often — gazing before grazing — wastes energy.

Freezers

Freezers use less energy when they are full. All that frozen food keeps the temperature down. Water-filled milk bottles can be used to fill up empty spaces in the freezer and save energy.

WASHERS

Dishwashers

Self-heating dishwashers are more energy efficient than those that draw hot water from the hot-water cylinder — unless the cylinder is solar heated. Many offer economy cycles with fewer rinses and reduced heating and drying times.

Washing machines

Clothes-washing and drying machines use relatively small amounts of household energy — about 3% on average — but overuse of a clothes dryer quickly drives this figure up. Cold washes are energy efficient and some machines make provision for water conservation by enabling water from a first rinse to be held over and recycled from a nearby tub.

Front-loading machines use as little as half the water required for the average top-load washer, so less energy is used in heating, pumping and disposing of the water. Because they also extract up to 10% more water during the spin cycle, they enable less energy to be used to dry the clothes. Whenever possible, dry your clothes using the sun and wind — these are healthy, free and entirely renewable.

MAKING YOUR OWN ELECTRICITY

Stand-alone power systems (SAPS) use renewable energy sources — solar, wind and water — to generate electricity. They are usually installed in areas where connection to the mains electricity network (the grid) is impossible or too expensive but also have the benefit of offering those who want it an independent and verifiable source of 'green' power.

SAPS need to be designed to suit specific locations and are sometimes designed to work one with another (such as solar and wind power) to cover the variability of supply. However, because SAPS typically generate low levels of power, the use of household appliances and energy-intensive activities such as heating and cooking need to be carefully and conservatively managed. Wood burners, wetbacks, passive solar design, and energy-efficient appliances and lighting fixtures will help reduce the load that would otherwise be placed on the SAPS.

Although hydro generation and wind generation are attractive propositions at a commercial level, at a household level their viability depends on the availability of suitable natural resources. (A resource consent is likely to be needed to harness both wind and water energy; check with the local council.) Micro-hydro generation is cheap and reliable but most residential sites don't have streams with the head or flow needed for year-round micro-hydro generation. And although many people think they live in a windy location most sites are not windy enough for wind power. Even if they are, a small wind turbine is expensive in relation to what it produces: a rotor diameter of 2 m might yield 500 kW/h of electricity annually, about 5–10% of that used by the average household. Furthermore, neighbours are unlikely to be enthusiastic about the lofty structures needed to support large turbines.

Photovoltaic energy

Solar energy is the best choice: it is plentiful, relatively easy to capture and installations do not require a resource consent. Solar energy is most commonly used to heat water via solar thermal panels but can also be used to provide electricity for household use. When used in this way it is referred to as photovoltaic energy (PV).

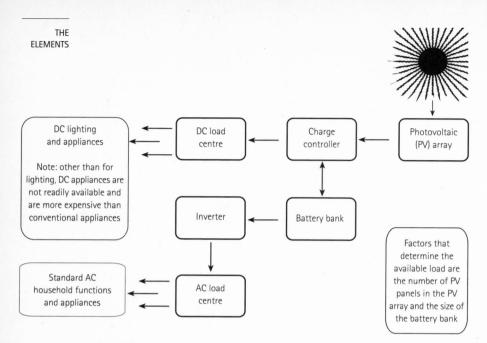

Stand-alone PV system with battery backup to power AC and DC loads

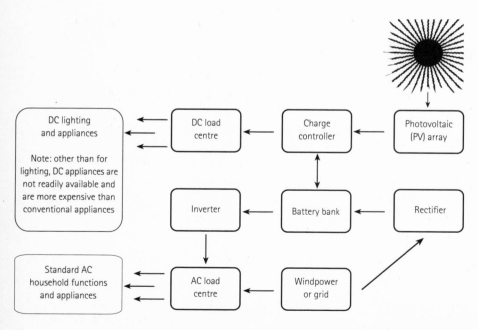

Hybrid PV system with grid backup to power AC and DC loads

PV systems are safe and reliable and have projected service lifetimes of 20–30 years. Energy independence and environmental compatibility make them attractive energy sources. They are modular, easily expandable and their only fuel — sunlight — is free. (One drawback, however, is that because of their small size, portability and suitability for use in isolated locations, PV panels can be easily targeted by thieves.)

PV systems can:

➤ be designed to provide direct current (DC) and alternating current (AC);

➤ operate interconnected with or independent of the national grid;

➤ be integrated with other types of alternative power systems, such as micro-hydro and wind power.

~ *PV cells, panels and arrays* PV cells containing the raw material silicon are the basis of PV systems. The current and power output of a typical silicon PV cell depends on its size (surface area) and is proportional to the intensity of the sunlight striking it; you get more power on clear, sunny days.

A typical PV cell the size of a 10-cent piece produces just a small amount of power (0–2 watts) but by linking a number of cells into a module, a module into a panel and a number of panels into a PV array, a system can be made large enough to deliver enough power to charge batteries and operate electric motors and small appliances.

To capture the power generated and make it usable a number of additional components are required. These typically include a DC-AC power inverter and a battery bank.

Batteries enable the power generated to be stored and supplied at a stable voltage when needed. An inverter changes DC into AC for use with conventional AC household appliances.

Solar PV panels are typically manufactured to deliver 12 volts DC, about the same amount as that of a car battery. At this low level it can be used for a number of functions (such as 12 V lighting). Most domestic installations are designed to deliver 12, 24 or 48 volts (one, two or four panels), depending on their application.

~ *Types of PV system* STAND-ALONE SYSTEMS are designed to operate independently of the grid with the DC output coupled directly to a DC load: a small circulation pump for a solar hot-water system, for example. As there is no storage it operates only during sunlight hours.

Adding a battery to the system allows the power to be stored and used at other times, and an inverter allows the DC current to be converted to AC current for use by AC loads, like standard household appliances.

HYBRID SYSTEMS are designed to accommodate other sources of power such as wind turbine, diesel generator or grid supply.

GRID-CONNECTED SYSTEMS are designed to operate in parallel with the national grid. Solar DC power is converted into AC power and fed through an electrical distribution panel to either directly supply household loads or to back-feed the grid when solar generation is greater than that required by the household, creating an effective power 'credit', which can be drawn from the grid when needed.

TOP TIPS FOR ENERGY

✓ A versatile approach, including energy-efficient design and varied energy sources, is preferable to heavy reliance on the national grid.

✓ Solar energy is free to run and easy on the environment.

✓ Check the 'star ratings' of new appliances.

Chapter 8

Radiation and electromagnetic fields and waves

RADIOACTIVITY

Radioactivity is the spontaneous emission of radiation at great speed from the nucleus of an unstable atom. We are all exposed to natural background radiation from cosmic rays, radon gas and radionuclides in our bodies.

Radon gas

Radon, which accounts for about half of natural background radiation, is an odourless, colourless radioactive gas, produced mainly by the decay of uranium and radium. It is found naturally in rocks, groundwater and soil. Radon decays into radioactive substances, which can affect respiration.

It may seep into a house through cracks, drains and concrete. If trapped in tightly sealed and insulated houses, concentrations can be hundreds of times stronger than outside. Building materials — especially granite and pumice — can release radon, as can bricks, plaster and concrete made from radon-rich sources.

New Zealand soils contain only traces of uranium and radium. A nationwide survey in 1986/87 measured natural radiation, including radon concentrations, in New Zealand houses. The occurrence seems to be moderate and even. Concentrations were similar to those found in most countries, with no evidence of the 'hot spots' found in some countries (parts of the United States have a significant radon problem).

You can check radon levels in your area through the local council. If radon is a concern, boosting ventilation under the house and sealing off the ground beneath floors with polythene sheeting and tape will reduce the risk.

Smoke detectors

Smoke detectors contain a minuscule amount of radioactive material, which is securely contained in a heatproof department. Even if the radioactive material escaped, the quantities are considered too small to be harmful.

ELECTROMAGNETIC RADIATION

Electromagnetic radiation (EMR) consists of a travelling wave motion comprising changing electric and magnetic fields. There is an EMR spectrum: gamma rays at the short wavelength end of the spectrum are followed by X-rays, ultraviolet light, visible light, infrared light, microwaves (including cell phone transmission) and radio waves. Household electrical appliances at the long wavelength end of the spectrum are experienced as an electromagnetic field rather than a wave.

Gamma rays and X-rays are used medically but are not a significant health hazard in the natural world, as few can penetrate the earth's atmosphere. However, ozone depletion has allowed greater penetration of ultraviolet light. Over-exposure can cause skin cancers — now a real danger in New Zealand. Infrared and visible lights pose little risk.

Electromagnetic fields are generated by power lines, household wiring, vehicles, computers, printers, fax and copy machines, fluorescent lights, scanners, portable phones, electrical instruments and household electrical appliances.

Effects of exposure

Some studies haven't found adverse effects from exposure to weak *electrical* fields in the home or workplace but there is conflicting evidence about the effect of *magnetic* fields. An electrical field operates if an appliance is plugged in; a magnetic field operates only if an appliance is in use.

Some studies link high magnetic fields in the home or proximity to high current power lines with a high incidence of cancers — particularly childhood leukaemia — but later studies have not always confirmed these findings. Virtually all research concludes that the health effects are from long-term, cumulative exposure only.

Understandably, people are wary of living close to electricity substations (which use transformers to break high voltage current into lower voltages for localised distribution), or of having an electricity transformer positioned outside their property. However, the iron core within a transformer is very good at confining its magnetic field — very little escapes.

Overhead high-voltage transmission lines generate strong electric and magnetic fields. Low-voltage distribution lines generate weaker electric fields, but can generate strong magnetic fields, depending on the number of houses they supply. Underground power lines produce a weak magnetic field.

Reducing exposure

The easiest way to reduce exposure to magnetic fields is to increase the distance from the source. Locating bedrooms towards the rear of the house reduces dramatically the exposure to distribution lines in the front of the house. Moving beds away from an outside wall that has an inbuilt electric meter board or hot water service also reduces exposure. Other precautionary measures are turning the electric blanket off before hopping into bed (and other appliances when not in use); keeping at least more than 50 cm away from televisions and microwave ovens when in use, and minimising cell phone use.

~ *Microwave ovens* The water in food absorbs microwaves in a microwave oven. It is the heating of the water molecules that cooks the food. When the microwave oven is turned off, there are no longer microwaves present in the oven — their absorption by the food is instantaneous.

A damaged oven door may release microwaves. You can buy a microwave detector but provided the oven door is secure, there is little need to have it checked for leaks. However, when in use, the microwave oven does generate a strong magnetic field.

~ *Cell phones* Cell phones also use microwave energy but you can't close the door on them as you can with an oven. The scientific jury is still out on whether cell phones pose health risks. Limiting call length and, if possible, avoiding direct contact with the head are precautionary measures.

Microwave ovens

The National Radiation Laboratory has tested leakage from many new and used microwave ovens. Any leakage has been less than the maximum allowed by the Microwave Ovens Regulations 1982. Most ovens were 10 to 100 times better than are required by law. There was no evidence that old ovens leak more than new ones, or that leakage increases as the oven gets older.

RADIO WAVES

Radio waves are emitted naturally in minuscule amounts by stars and in brief bursts by lightning (which is why you hear interference on your radio in a thunderstorm). Artificial sources of radio waves are broadcasting, radar use and mobile phone transmitters. The World Health Organization (WHO) has set safe limits for exposure.

The radio waves from antennae placed on buildings for mobile phone transmission are within these safety limits apart from the space a few centimetres directly in front of the antennae. The people in the building on which the antennae are mounted are not affected as radio waves move out from their source, a little like car beams which light the road ahead but not the car itself.

TOP TIP FOR RADIATION

✓ The key to living safely with radiation and electromagnetism is to understand the science behind it.

Chapter 9

Water

Water is blue gold — one of our most precious resources. Yet the United Nations estimates a sixth of the world's population (around a billion people) lack access to clean water. By 2025, it is estimated this proportion will rise to two-thirds.

In the more arid parts of the world, an air of conflict between neighbouring states over who owns particular water resources is already apparent, and future wars are likely to be fought over scarce water resources. This is a foreseeable consequence of a failure to treat sustainable fresh water supplies with the respect they deserve. It is not that we have any less water — there is the same amount as when the earth began billions of years ago — but contamination is outstripping its rate of purification. We have plenty of grey water, black water and salt water but rapidly dwindling supplies of clean, fresh blue water.

Water is very resilient and responds well to recycling. In its journey, water absorbs chemicals from the air, loose matter from the earth and minerals from the rocks. However, at the same time a cleansing process occurs. Vegetation provides a natural filter for surface water and earth, sand and rocks for water absorbed into the ground. As water gathers in surface and underground streams and rivers, heavy matter sinks to the bottom, while the moving water is oxygenated and vitalised. For water that finds its way to the sea, salt acts as a strong antiseptic. Evaporation from the earth and sea completes the purification and water vapour gathers in clouds, ready for its return to earth.

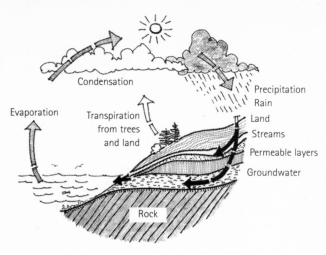

The water cycle

WATER CONTAMINANTS

Pure water is tasteless and insipid. Even the most pristine water contains low concentrations of salts and minerals, which are harmless or beneficial. However, with changes to the natural environment, high concentrations of these elements and additional toxins can enter the water cycle at every stage. Widespread clearing of land removes the natural green filter provided by vegetation and accelerates erosion. Roading and stormwater drainage allow

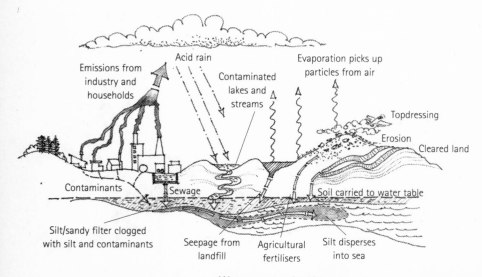

Water contamination

COMMON WATER CONTAMINANTS, THEIR SOURCES AND EFFECTS

Contaminant	Source	Effect
Synthetic organic chemicals (VOCs)	Household cleansers, seepage from landfill	VOCs can be inhaled or absorbed. Wide-ranging health effects; suspected to be carcinogenic
Phosphates	Cleansers, fertilisers	Over-fertilise algae, exhausting oxygen supplies in the water
Mineral acids, e.g. sulphuric, sulphurous and nitrate acids	Form in the atmosphere as smog, fall as acid rain	Corrosive — release more metals from pipes Destroy plant life Attack masonry buildings
Nitrates	Chemical fertilisers that leach into rivers	A danger for babies; at high enough levels they interfere with the ability of the blood to carry oxygen
Copper	Copper pipe corrosion	Linked with anaemia, digestive disturbance
Lead	Old pipes, paint, solder on pipes and roofing components	Nerve and brain damage Damage to foetuses and young children
Aluminium	Water treatment	Nervous system damage Possibly linked with Alzheimer's disease (though this is widely disputed)
Iron and magnesium	Groundwater supplies	Corrode steel and iron pipes Turn water brown and cloudy
Chlorine	Water treatment	Absorbed through skin, inhaled. At high levels may form suspected carcinogens by reaction with organics in water
Giardia	Faeces	Severe enteritis
Campylobacter	Faeces	Severe enteritis

Note: There are also many other waterborne micro-organisms that may cause diseases.

rapid transport of excess water to the sea, taking with it toxins from households, industry, transport and agriculture. Pollutants in the air attach themselves to water vapour as it evaporates to form clouds and as it falls again as rain. Seepage from landfill can enter groundwater supplies. As deep underground aquifers fall, concentrations of minerals and metals are intensified.

By the time chemical sterilisers such as chlorine, flocculants such as alum, and dental decay preventives such as fluoride are added at water filter stations, we wind up with water that is far from pure.

WATER SOURCES

In New Zealand about 60% of water for households, industry and agriculture is surface water drawn from dams and rivers. The remainder comes from groundwater. Groundwater can rise to the surface naturally through springs or constructed wells. It also acts as a natural equaliser, by discharging water into wetlands, streams and lakes during dry seasons and soaking up water and preventing flooding during wet seasons. Drawing excessive water from groundwater upsets this natural balance.

Town supply

City water supplies are required by law to be of a minimum standard for health. Supplies are monitored and rated. All are subject to contamination and many require sophisticated filtration and treatment to ensure public safety. The water supply authority does this as a matter of course.

Home supply

Catching rainwater from roofs and storing it in galvanised iron, concrete or plastic tanks is the most common means of private water collection (see page 108). Less common sources are streams, springs, and wells. Streams, lakes and shallow wells are more likely to contain disease-causing organisms than deep wells and springs but groundwater is likely to contain concentrations of minerals and salts, which may taint the water. Landfills, septic tanks, leaky underground petrol or oil tanks and overuse of fertilisers and pesticides can also pollute groundwater.

Surface water — both roof runoff and that found in streams — is likely to contain particles of dirt, vegetable matter, animal droppings and other potentially unhealthy substances. Research shows over half the collections of drinking water from roofs contains contaminants such as *Salmonella*, *Campylobacter* and *Giardia*. Dust, paint by-products and heavy metals such as lead, iron and zinc are also known to contaminate house water supplies in

WATER QUALITY TROUBLESHOOTING

Tinged water	Trouble spot
Blue/green	Copper
Dark brown/black	Manganese
Reddish/orange	Iron

Smelly water	Possible cause
Bleach	Chlorine
Fish	Barium, cadmium
Rotten eggs	Sulphur
Sewage	Selenium
Sweet solvent	Methyl tertiary-butyl ether (MTBE)

Tainted water	Trouble spot
Salty	Chloride-sulphate
Metal	Iron, zinc

Scummy water	Trouble spot
Soap scum on bath	Hard water, i.e. high calcium carbonate, magnesium carbonate or calcium/magnesium sulphates
Whitish scale	Hard water, e.g. high calcium carbonate

Spotty water	Trouble spot
On glassware	Hard water: high total dissolved solids (TDS)
On clothes	Hard water: high TDS
White spots on teeth	fluoride

concentrations strong enough to affect health. In city areas, acids in the air can contaminate the rainwater.

If roof water is destined for drinking or for the garden, a diversion system for the initial runoff that contains the bulk of contaminants, and a filter or debris trap, are essential. It is imperative to avoid runoff from roofs with treated timber shingles, lead flashings or lead paint.

DIAGNOSING WATER QUALITY

Whether from home or city supply, above ground or below, if your water is discoloured, smells or leaves strange deposits on utensils and clothes, try the troubleshooting list above.

WATER PIPES

Domestic water supply pipes are typically either copper, or plastic (poly-butylene and polyethylene) piping. Accessible reserves of mineral copper are limited and copper mining is very destructive of the environment. More than half the copper used in industry is recycled.

Copper

Copper piping and fittings are widely used in household supplies. Although copper is an essential micronutrient, it is required by the body in very small amounts. Copper does not occur naturally in water supplies but can occur through corrosion of copper piping and fittings. Low levels do not pose health problems but too much will cause stomach and intestinal distress. Soft water with a low pH level and low mineral content is generally more corrosive than hard water. In the case of hard water, a layer of minerals is slowly deposited inside the piping, forming a chalky lining, which protects against corrosion and copper contamination. Grounding electrical equipment through copper water pipes increases corrosion. (This practice is no longer favoured in new construction.)

As a simple health measure, if a copper supply system has not been used for some hours, flush the system before using the water for drinking or cooking, particularly if it comes from a copper hot water cylinder. Let the tap run for 10–15 seconds. If possible, use the water runoff for non-consumption purposes.

Plastic

Plastic polyethylene and polybutylene water piping are manufactured without using chlorine and are regarded as being more environmentally friendly than PVC plastics. They are used in many situations as an alternative to copper.

Lead and clay

Lead waste pipes, once common beneath kitchen, bathroom and laundry fittings, have largely been replaced by PVC waste pipes and fittings.

Ceramic (clay) pipes remain the most eco-friendly material for exterior drains, although significant energy is used in their manufacture.

WATER PURIFICATION

Home purification systems range from basic to very sophisticated technologies. Choice of a system will depend partly on the source of water supply.

Cool, running water

Whether from the tap or the stream, it is best to use moving water. Water that has been sitting in pipes, or is from the hot water supply, is more likely to have absorbed contaminants and to have a discernible metallic or plastic taste. For drinking and cooking, use the cold supply — let it run for a few seconds to clear the pipes.

Bottled water

Analyses of bottled water have found it to be of variable quality, often no better than that available through town supplies (and often worse). Studies have found that microbes can increase with shelf life.

Standing water

Leaving tap water standing in a jug for around 48 hours allows chlorine to fully evaporate (although not necessarily the chlorinated organic compounds), noticeably improving the taste.

Boiling water

Boiling water will destroy disease organisms (including *Giardia*, which is a protozoan) — one minute for water from streams at sea level and three minutes for higher elevations.

Filtration

~ *Jug filters*   Jug filters remove some contaminants and improve the taste of water. They use a granular activated carbon filter with a life of about 100–150 litres. Some jug filters incorporate de-ionising crystals but this effect will only last a few jug fills. They are a cheap, easy option. Refill filters are available.

~ *Fixed filters*   Filters can be installed on the bench top, under the bench or at point of entry. Filters used include: sediment, carbon, metal and resin filters. If you want the filter to remove chemical contaminants check that it complies with an accepted performance standard: AS/NZS 4348 (local) or NSF 53 (United States).

~ *Filter cartridge replacement*   Depending on the type of filter and the use it is put to, cartridges need replacement at regular intervals. Some filters are designed to let you know when this should occur, such as by reducing the flow. It is a good idea to write the date it was installed, or when you expect it to expire, on the cartridge. Otherwise, look for signs that filter activity is impaired, such as poor taste and slow water flow.

~ *Sediment filters* Sediment filters are used to screen out particles in water supplies that are visibly dirty or have a risk of *Giardia*. *Giardia* has a micron rating of five, so a *Giardia*-safe filter will need to have a rating of one micron. The sediment filter is often used as a pre-filter for other types of filter. Sediment filters of over five microns are washable.

~ *Carbon filters* Granular activated carbon (GAC) and carbon block filters contain a disposable cartridge of activated carbon. As carbon is extremely porous, it provides a vast surface area to attract and hold impurities. It bonds with chlorine by-products, pesticides, lead and sediment but not with trace elements such as dissolved calcium and magnesium, so the health-giving properties of water are retained. It will not remove nitrates or sulphides (possible by-products of chemical fertilisers), or disease-causing pathogens.

There are varying grades of carbon. Some improve the smell and taste but remove few impurities; finer grades remove a greater number of impurities. The critical factors are water flow — a poorly designed cartridge lets water through too quickly to capture much matter — and carbon particle size: the smaller the particle, the more surface area is available to attract impurities.

Loose GAC is found in most domestic water filters but the small amount in most filters leads to very quick saturation and the need for frequent replacement. It can also act as a warm, moist medium in which bacteria can breed, meaning more bacteria can exit the filter than entered with the water supply. Because there is no chlorine left to limit their numbers, they multiply quickly, feeding off the trapped organic matter in the filter. Some filters contain a chemical, usually silver nitrate, to limit the growth of bacteria. GAC has a typical micron rating of 25. Carbon block cartridges use a dense brick of activated carbon. The increased density slows the water down and increases the carbon contact time, allowing more bonding with impurities. Block cartridges have micron ratings as low as one.

~ *Resin filters* KDF resin filters are used mainly for chlorine removal but a large amount of KDF resin, and lengthy contact with the water, are required to do so, which makes it better suited to large commercial rather than domestic situations. Combined with carbon filters, KDF filters typically use copper and zinc to create electrolysis, thus keeping bacterial growth to a minimum in the carbon filter. KDF filters remove organics and some heavy metals but tend to clog relatively quickly (six to nine months).

~ *Mixed-bed resin and de-ionising crystals* Ion exchange uses resin to attract either positively or negatively charged chemicals such as fluoride, or nitrates. They are usually combined with carbon and sediment filters to

eliminate solid particles, pesticides and chlorine. This system requires frequent
resin replacements to maintain efficiency.

Distillers

Distillers work by evaporating water, recondensing it and collecting it in a
container. Distillers remove approximately 99.99% of total dissolved salts
from the water, including fluoride. They also remove free oxygen from the
water, resulting in flat oxygen-less water. VOCs, however, may recondense
and drop back into the water so the distiller is usually combined with a
carbon filter. The mineral-free water may be specified for certain health
conditions but can be detrimental to the health of bones, teeth and tissue, if
drunk exclusively for a long period of time. Distiller boiling trays need to be
cleaned regularly.

Reverse osmosis

Reverse osmosis was originally designed to desalinate sea water. It uses water
pressure to force water through a very fine membrane. Most gases pass
through this membrane but most water contaminants will not. It won't
remove chlorine by-products, so usually incorporates a GAC filter as well.

The purified water is mineral free — so should not be drunk exclusively
over a long period of time — but is well oxygenated and does not have the
flat, lifeless taste of distilled water. Combined with the sediment and
activated carbon filters, reverse osmosis will remove fluoride, bacteria,
protozoa and viruses, and significantly reduce organics, salts, metals, nitrates
and pesticides. It is often used in situations where there is extreme
mineralisation of the water or high nitrate levels from agriculture. The
method is wasteful: it disposes of four times as much water as it purifies. The
membrane is fragile and needs regular replacement.

Ultraviolet light

Ultraviolet light kills waterborne disease-causing micro-organisms, such as
bacteria, viruses, some algae, and fungi by delivering concentrated amounts
of UV light energy to the reproductive mechanism of the microbe. However,
it does not eliminate protozoa such as *Cryptosporidia* and *Giardia*. Virtually
all chlorine is also removed (but maybe not the chlorinated organics that
might have formed). It won't remove lead, asbestos or particles such as dirt
or leaves and so needs to be combined with a sediment and/or carbon filter.

Filtration can be at point of entry, so that all water in the house is
sterilised, or at point of use with a single faucet for a drinking tap. The only
homeowner maintenance is to replace the UV bulb once a year.

Ozone

Ozone, produced by an ozone generator, 'super oxygenates' water, which, after sufficient contact, kills bacteria. It also breaks up organic contaminants and converts iron to an insoluble form, allowing them to be removed by a supplementary filter. Ozone generators require no maintenance and draw very little power — less than 100 watts, the same as a light bulb. However, some of the created by-products may increase the chance of bacterial growth in the pipes down the line.

WATER PURIFICATION

Pollutant	Carbon Filter	Reverse Osmosis	Steam Distillation
Aluminium			
Arsenic			
Bacteria			
Cadmium			
Calcium			
Chlorides			
Chlorine			
Copper			
Cryptosporidium			
Detergents			
Fluorides			
Pesticides/herbicides			
Iron			
Lead			
Magnesium			
MTBE			
Nitrates			
Organic matter			
Phosphates			
Sediment			
Selenium			
Sodium			
Sulphates/sulphides			
Viruses			
Zinc			

Key: ▨ no reduction; ▦ significant reduction; ▬ effective removal; ▬ effective removal with the addition of carbon filtration.

MTBE

Methyl tertiary-butyl ether (MTBE) is a petrol additive that boosts octane rating and improves combustion. It has been widely used worldwide to reduce smog and ozone depletion. Unfortunately, MTBE and most other oxygenates have an affinity for water. If water is present in a fuel (or the storage vessel), oxygenates will preferentially blend into the water and out of the petrol. The chemical is released into the environment via leaking storage tanks and petrol spills, including small spills such as those that occur when filling up at the service station or refilling lawnmowers, chainsaws, brush cutters and the like at home. Uncertainty surrounds the extent of the health risk posed by chronic, low-level exposure to MTBE via drinking water but MTBE is persistent and imparts an unpleasant taste and odour, even at very low concentrations. Significant MTBE pollution of drinking water in many areas of the United States has led to a call for use of the additive to be banned. New Zealand banned the use of MTBE in petroleum as of March 2003.

WATER CONSERVATION

With New Zealand's abundant rainfall it is tempting to use water freely and carelessly. However, we don't have a limitless supply of *clean* water. Purifying and processing water is economically and environmentally costly. Only 5–10% of the water we process is used for drinking and cooking. Toilet cisterns are greedy, accounting for 20–50% of household domestic water use. Showering and bathing account for about 30%. There are many simple ways of saving water.

Check for leaks

Check for leaky taps and corroded water distribution pipes. Older galvanised piping is particularly susceptible — once corroded it loses water at a steady rate. An unusually hefty annual water account is often a sign of an undetected leak. It is easy to check for water loss. Simply check the outside water meter over a period of non-use, perhaps one evening before going to bed and again in the morning when you first get up. If you are losing water, check the supply pipes, all valves and taps, and the toilet cistern for leaks.

Around 20% of toilet cisterns leak. A simple test is to add a few drops of food colouring to the cistern. If it is leaking the colouring will appear in the bowl within seconds.

Toilet cisterns

Toilet cisterns range from 4 to 11 litres in size. Dual-flush cisterns offer a full and a half-size flush. Before the days of dual-flush toilets it was common in areas where water was in short supply to put a brick in the cistern. If the flush is excessive or water is dripping from the cistern overflow pipe (it sometimes drains outside), bend the arm of the cistern float downwards to lower the water level in the cistern. Fastening a small weight to the float will also reduce the size of the flush.

Using tank water from the roof for the toilet cistern can halve your use of tapped water. Composting toilets (see page 105) can be used in some areas, eliminating water from the process completely.

Showers

A standard bath uses about 100 litres of water. A standard shower delivers about 12–20 litres of water a minute. So a three-minute shower uses around half the water of a bath but a 10-minute shower uses twice the amount.

A water-saving head can halve the shower flow. An aerator showerhead gives the impression of a luxurious shower — never mind that it is more hot air than water. Turning the shower off while lathering and shampooing, keeping the shower short and sharing a shower will save more water still.

Tinkering with the taps

Standard taps deliver 10–20 litres of water a minute. For most purposes a flow of 3 litres is adequate. Flow control regulators can be fitted to most taps.

Washing hands or face with a running tap uses about 5 litres of water, brushing the teeth about 1 litre. A fraction of this amount is needed, if a basin or cup of water is used instead of running water.

Washing clothes

Washing machines use 110–220 litres per load. Front loaders use about half the water of a top loader. Some machines will recycle the rinse water; some have an economy cycle. Take the time to adjust the water level or rinse programme to match the size of the load. When investing in a new washing

---

TOP TIPS FOR LESS GARDEN WATERING

✓ A lawn height of 70–100 mm helps protect the roots from heat and reduce evaporation.

✓ Plant shrubs and trees rather than grass in areas that are difficult to irrigate such as steep slopes.

✓ Water infrequently but thoroughly to promote deep root growth.

✓ Mulch around plants to retain moisture.

✓ Use porous materials for walkways and patios to prevent runoff.

---

machine make low water usage a priority. Look for appliances with the 'AAA'
Water Conservation Label — the more As, the more water-efficient it is.

Washing dishes

Hand washing for a small family uses 15 litres a load, if a double sink is used
for rinsing dishes rather than a running tap. An automatic dishwasher uses
approximately 60 litres a cycle. Some will run half loads and economy cycles.

A waste disposal unit installed beneath the sink typically uses 28 litres per
session. Composting and a worm farm use none.

Watering the garden

Hoses and sprinklers use about 15 litres a minute. Using watering cans for the
garden and a bucket to clean the car is less wasteful than using a hose.
Collected rainwater can be used for the garden, washing the car, filling spa
pools and the like.

WASTEWATER

Three types of wastewater flow through or around the typical home: blackwater, greywater, and stormwater.

Blackwater contains human waste and poses a significant health risk.
Greywater is mainly effluent from washing machines, dishwashers, kitchen
sinks and the like, and poses a much lesser health risk.

Stormwater falls as rain. It is clean at the outset but open to contamination as it travels through gutters, drains and natural waterways on its way
back to the ocean.

Black and grey wastewater

Thanks to the wonders of reticulated sewerage, and modern plumbing and
drainage systems, few householders need concern themselves with either
black or grey wastewater beyond pushing a button or pulling a plug to get
rid of it. City residents enjoy the most convenient solution — underground
sewers, a centralised waste treatment plant and a discharge pipe into a river
or the ocean.

Though these all-encompassing waterborne sewage systems are the norm,
they do not make good ecological sense. They are wasteful of fresh water,
cause heavy metal and organic pollution of the oceans and make little
attempt to save and recycle the energy and nutrient value of the organic
waste component. Yet in sewered areas it is invariably a public health
requirement that households be connected to it.

There is some flexibility in the disposal of greywater: water from the washing machine, bath and shower can in theory be used to water non-food crops but there is a risk of contamination if the water is not treated to destroy bacteria, and of damage to plants if the wastewater contains synthetic soaps or detergents. Pre-treatment of greywater is therefore advisable.

ALTERNATIVE TREATMENT SYSTEMS

In areas without reticulated sewerage, septic tanks have traditionally been considered the most reliable onsite alternative. They work well in pre-treating sewage but problems are often encountered when effluent is discharged into poorly drained soils. This has led to a number of systems other than septic wastewater treatment systems being approved for use in non-reticulated areas. Whatever the type, wastewater installations must be designed by geotechnical engineers with experience in effluent disposal.

Correct design, proper installation, good management and regular maintenance are needed for onsite disposal systems to work effectively. Factors that influence selection include soil types, the height of the water table, soil percolation rates and the overall ecological sensitivity of the area.

Here are short descriptions of the various types:

Septic tanks

A septic tank uses a relatively slow anaerobic (without air) bacterial process to break down organic waste matter. The waste matter flows into a single- or double-stage tank where it settles and is acted on by the bacteria. As additional waste enters the system, partially treated liquid effluent flows out the other end, through a series of slotted pipes and into a soakage field. The tank, which should be specifically designed to cope with a type and volume of effluent, needs to be kept free of detergents and chemicals toxic to bacteria, and emptied of sludge every few years.

Aerobic treatment systems

Aerobic (or aerated) treatment systems put wastewater through a four-stage programme. First, it enters a slow-acting digestion chamber where solids settle and are broken down by anaerobic bacteria, in much the same way as a conventional septic system. Effluent then passes to a secondary chamber where air is blown into it, creating an environment for fast-acting aerobic bacteria. (A suitable culture medium in the secondary chamber assists fast bacterial growth.) A third settlement or clarification chamber allows residual sludge to settle and be recycled to a previous chamber for reprocessing. Liquid is pumped from the fourth chamber through small-diameter irrigation hosing to a landscaped (mulched) garden.

Aerated systems require less space in which to operate than a conventional septic system. They also require a small amount of maintenance (filters need cleaning approximately once every six months) but in return deliver a cleaner effluent low in organic matter and high in dissolved oxygen. Power consumption is similar to that of a refrigerator.

By adding an aerobic sand filter between the outlet of a septic tank or aerated treatment system and the soakage field, effluent can be treated to a much higher level (suitable for reuse in garden irrigation or toilet flushing) before it is released.

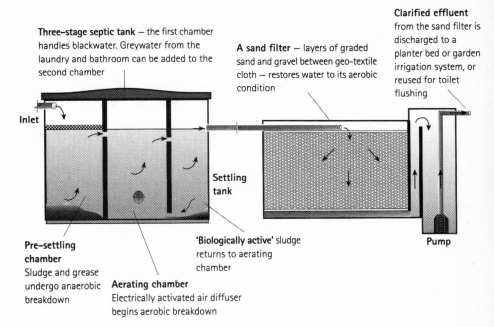

Three-stage septic tank – the first chamber handles blackwater. Greywater from the laundry and bathroom can be added to the second chamber

A sand filter – layers of graded sand and gravel between geo-textile cloth – restores water to its aerobic condition

Clarified effluent from the sand filter is discharged to a planter bed or garden irrigation system, or reused for toilet flushing

Inlet

Settling tank

Pre-settling chamber
Sludge and grease undergo anaerobic breakdown

'Biologically active' sludge returns to aerating chamber

Aerating chamber
Electrically activated air diffuser begins aerobic breakdown

Pump

Alternative treatment system: Septic tank and sand filter

Composting toilets

Composting toilets are a sensible and eco-friendly solution to waste disposal. They are suitable for sites that can't support septic tanks, and can even be installed in sewerage-reticulated areas with the approval of the local council. There are a variety of manufactured and owner-built designs available, including one which utilises a conventional flush.

~ *Types and process*   Compost toilets are essentially of two types. A batch system uses a replaceable container. When it is filled, it is replaced and left to fully compost. A continual-process system is a gravity-fed system in which

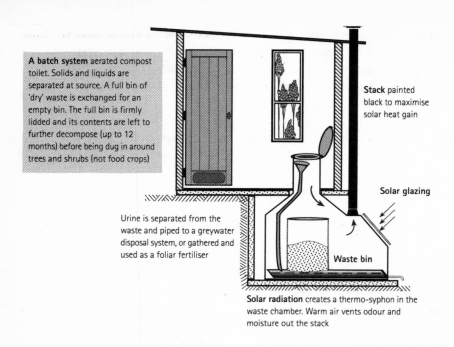

A batch system aerated compost toilet. Solids and liquids are separated at source. A full bin of 'dry' waste is exchanged for an empty bin. The full bin is firmly lidded and its contents are left to further decompose (up to 12 months) before being dug in around trees and shrubs (not food crops)

Stack painted black to maximise solar heat gain

Solar glazing

Urine is separated from the waste and piped to a greywater disposal system, or gathered and used as a foliar fertiliser

Waste bin

Solar radiation creates a thermo-syphon in the waste chamber. Warm air vents odour and moisture out the stack

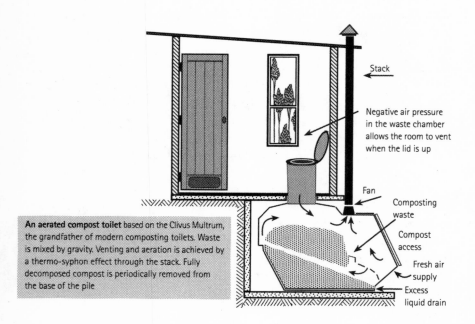

Stack

Negative air pressure in the waste chamber allows the room to vent when the lid is up

Fan

Composting waste

Compost access

Fresh air supply

Excess liquid drain

An aerated compost toilet based on the Clivus Multrum, the grandfather of modern composting toilets. Waste is mixed by gravity. Venting and aeration is achieved by a thermo-syphon effect through the stack. Fully decomposed compost is periodically removed from the base of the pile

Composting toilets: A batch system (above) and an aerated compost system (below)

solid and liquid wastes are separated and aerated. Solids are broken down by
aerobic action, and liquids by evaporation. (Aerobic composting minimises the
rotten egg odour typical of the traditional one-holer, or long drop.) A handful
of dry flush material — sawdust, cardboard or peat — with every use assists
bacterial decomposition. Small quantities of food scraps and organic garden
matter can also be added. Decomposing material falls away from the
operational end of the toilet, moving slowly under its own weight towards
the lower end of the chamber. Fully composted material is removed once
every one or two years and used as fertiliser for flower gardens or trees. A
reasonable amount of space, preferably external, below the level of the
throne is needed to hold the composting container, and it must be possible to
easily access the container for servicing and waste disposal.

Compost toilets are not pit latrines. If they're not well designed and well
managed your nose will soon tell you! To work properly they need the right
balance of oxygen, nitrogen, carbon and moisture. The most common
problem is urine build-up. A blend of urine/faeces contains too much
nitrogen to allow effective composting. The urine needs to be balanced by the
addition of sufficient carbon-based bulking material to absorb the urine and
set the stage for composting.

Alternative systems avoid the build-up of urine by diverting it into a
separate container, and by providing additional fan-assisted or solar-heated
ventilation through the composting chamber to evaporate the liquids. Human
urine is sterile as long as it has not been contaminated with faecal matter.
Diverted urine can be plumbed directly into a greywater treatment system
such as a septic tank and sand trap, or UV treated before being dispersed
through surface irrigation, or applied directly to a compost heap as a source
of nitrogen.

A joint New Zealand and Australia standard (AS/NZS 1546.2:2001 On-site
domestic-wastewater treatment units) covers the construction of waterless
composting toilets.

Chemical toilets of the porta-variety offer only a temporary measure of
chemically sanitised containment. The removal and disposal of waste matter
in some other sewerage system is still needed.

Keeping stormwater separate

Conventional waste disposal systems treat blackwater and greywater as one
and the same thing, piping it through a reticulated sewer to a central waste
plant where it is treated then released, usually into the sea.

Stormwater — all that which falls onto a property as rain — is channelled
across roofs, down gutter pipes and back into the environment via a network
of stormwater pipes.

The two systems are separate and should at no stage be mixed. Because stormwater is fed directly back into the environment without further treatment it is important it be kept pollutant free. Typical sources of household pollution include the disposal of paints and hazardous chemicals directly into sewerage and stormwater systems. Municipal sewage systems in turn are susceptible to overflow if stormwater finds its way into the sewerage system during a storm, resulting in discharges of raw sewage into streams and onto beaches.

RAIN HARVESTING – USING RAINWATER AROUND THE HOME

In New Zealand, rainwater is a primary water supply for many rural and small-town residents. Our larger communities have become accustomed to a centralised water supply but there is a good argument that all households should catch and use rainwater for part of their water needs.

Household water services are charged on a user-pays basis to cover the cost of supply and disposal. If you are connected to a reticulated system the installation of a tank may do little to reduce your water rates – part of the council charge for a reticulated supply is a fixed charge regardless of whether you use it. Costs are also worked out on a discharge basis, because waste pipes are needed to remove used water regardless of its source of supply.

Rain harvesting has advantages for all, however, and some city councils (e.g. North Shore City) actively encourage its adoption by offering rebates on tank installations. Capturing and using rainwater lowers the volume of stormwater flowing through an urban environment, reduces the likelihood of local surface flooding and reduces the overloading of underground sewerage systems in sudden downpours.

Not only does tank collection conserve a valuable resource, it reduces the overall need for a centralised water supply with its treatment and pumping stations, thereby lowering greenhouse gas emissions.

Health issues

Health authorities are keen to stress that tank water should be 'appropriately treated' if it is to be used for drinking. Tanked water supplies can be easily contaminated by agricultural spray drift, bird and animal droppings, nasties (dead birds, rodents and the like), lead contaminants in dust and lead roof paints, lead, copper and zinc contaminants from roofing materials and flashings, and the general debris that finds its way into roof gutters. But if sensible precautions are taken and the system is maintained in good repair, it can deliver excellent potable water that is free of the chlorine and fluoride often found in reticulated town supplies.

If you intend drinking water collected off a roof, check that the roofing and guttering material is sound, that there are no lead flashings, lead paints, or treated timber shingles. Gutters should be regularly cleaned and the tank occasionally de-sludged.

Asbestos roofs should never be waterblasted to make them cleaner for water collection (or to prepare them for a coat of paint). Waterblasting dislodges millions of microscopic asbestos fibres which, when dry, become a serious airborne health hazard. There are many asbestos-cement water pipes in use throughout New Zealand and a significant percentage of tap water contains large numbers of asbestos fibres. There is no clear evidence, however, to suggest asbestos fibres are harmful in drinking water.

Potable water should at all times look, smell and taste healthy. Tank water can be filtered or purified (chemical or ultraviolet light disinfection) before use but if there is any question over its quality, a sample should be laboratory tested (ask your council or local public health service for an approved laboratory).

Rain-harvesting options

There are several straightforward rain-harvesting options but if you plan to do anything more than water your garden, a building consent is generally required. This is because the tanked water supply connects into the existing household plumbing system. (The use of a registered plumber to carry out the plumbing work is a requirement of the building consent.)

Tanks larger than 6000 litres may also require resource consent, depending on their proximity to boundaries.

➤ Option 1: Water for the garden — no building consent required.

➤ Option 2: Water for the garden, laundry and toilet cistern, without mains backup — building consent required.

➤ Option 3: Water for the garden, laundry and toilet cistern, with mains backup supply — building consent and an approved (i.e. not just a non-return valve) backflow-prevention device required on the mains inlet. (This is to stop water being siphoned out of a self-contained system and back into the mains supply, where it could possibly contaminate supplies to other households.)

Tanks

Storage tanks should be opaque, with smooth internal walls and a tight-fitting cover to keep insect, bird and animal pests out. They should be situated in a cool or shady spot to discourage algal growth.

Precast concrete, corrugated galvanised steel and plastic tanks are common. The ecological implications of tanks manufactured from all three materials are arguably equal.

Concrete is durable and keeps water cool but is a heavyweight material, which makes it difficult to install in some locations. Tanks can be precast or built on site to almost any size or shape.

Steel is lightweight and cheap but comparatively short-lived; it rusts in time.

Newer, plastic tanks are made from polyethylene — a non-sustainable material which is, nevertheless, often marketed as 'environmentally friendly' because it can be 'recycled'. It doesn't rot or corrode and is lightweight, making it very easy to install in tricky locations. It can be repaired by heat

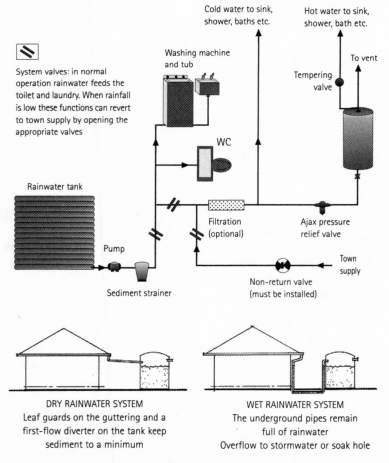

Cold water to sink, shower, baths etc.

Hot water to sink, shower, bath etc.

System valves: in normal operation rainwater feeds the toilet and laundry. When rainfall is low these functions can revert to town supply by opening the appropriate valves

Washing machine and tub

To vent

Tempering valve

WC

Rainwater tank

Filtration (optional)

Ajax pressure relief valve

Pump

Town supply

Sediment strainer

Non-return valve (must be installed)

DRY RAINWATER SYSTEM
Leaf guards on the guttering and a first-flow diverter on the tank keep sediment to a minimum

WET RAINWATER SYSTEM
The underground pipes remain full of rainwater
Overflow to stormwater or soak hole

Integrated water management

welding if damaged. Its formulation also resists algal growth, through some
means other than the addition of fungicides.

~ *Tank size*   Tank size is best determined by the frequency of rainfall, the
intended water use and the size of the roof collection area. Whether or not
you have mains backup is also critical.

An average-sized roof (150 sq m) in a location with an average annual
rainfall of around 1000 mm will catch enough water to provide 150,000 litres
per year (150 sq m x 1000 mm = 150,000 litres). A 10% allowance for spillage
and evaporation still leaves enough water to meet the reasonable needs of
most households.

A tank as small as 200 litres will support much of the average home's toilet
water use if rain occurs every few days (200 litres ÷ 5 litres = 40 flushes).

A tank of 4500–9000 litres will provide storage for 50–75% of the water
needed to supply the combined average needs of a garden, toilet and laundry.

~ *Tank placement*   Tanks can be sited on the ground, under the ground or
on a raised platform. Tanks can sometimes be sited in such a way that they
deliver sufficient pressure on a gravity-feed basis. Often, a pump is needed to
either pressurise the system or to feed a small header tank. (The pump can be
run by a solar panel.)

Rainwater-collection systems are either wet or dry. A wet system does not
allow the delivery pipes to drain out and should therefore be fitted with
screens at each end to ensure mosquitoes can't enter and breed. A dry system
allows the delivery pipes to completely empty of water after rain.

Screens and leaf guards are a good idea in that they prevent unwanted
material finding its way into the tank. So too is a first-flow diverter that
diverts the first flush off a roof, the water most likely to contain contaminants, into a separate chamber that drains
before the next rain. Tanks should be drained
and cleaned out once every couple of years.

~ *Gutters and downpipes*   Gutters and
downpipes should be installed with sufficient
slope to deliver the water and then drain dry —
mosquitoes will breed in the small residues of
water left in the open system.

Gutters, even when kept free of over-
hanging vegetation, need to be inspected and
cleaned regularly (don't forget to divert the
dirty water away from the tank!).

TOP TIPS FOR WATER

✓ Install your own rainwater tank.

✓ Use a dual-flush cistern; adjust
the float.

✓ Put a brick in older toilet
cisterns.

✓ Add an aerator to the shower.

✓ Choose water-efficient
appliances.

✓ Purify drinking water.

Chapter 10

Air

Air, like sound, light and water, is common property. We share the air we breathe with our neighbours and as nation states we share the effects of global warming, extreme weather patterns and ozone depletion.

Yet regardless of general air quality, each home encapsulates an atmosphere of its own. Research by the US Environmental Protection Agency indicates that indoor air can be six to 10 times as polluted as outside city air — though, sensibly, this would depend on where you lived. Contributors to pollution are building materials, interior finishes, furnishings and the activities of occupants. Each house has its own mini climate, its own rate of air exchange and its own distinctive smell. The air inside a dwelling can be healthy or unhealthy, pleasant or unpleasant. It can be fresh and fragrant or stale and musty. It can smell of natural oils and essences or of plastics, vinyls and polyurethanes.

Although smell is the first, it is not the complete test of air quality. There can be pollutants in the air that are imperceptible yet harmful. Possible symptoms of air pollution are headaches, vertigo, nausea, nose or throat irritation, asthma, bronchitis and allergies. If these occur in one environment but not others, air pollution is a possibility.

AIR CIRCULATION

A complete air change within the home every hour is ideal. This was easily achieved in older, draughty homes, even when windows and doors were shut. But with new homes more tightly sealed to conserve energy, air replacement occurs only every five or six hours.

Natural diffusion of air through porous building materials such as earth, wood, brick, stone and plaster allows a building to 'breathe'. An airtight home with non-porous materials, sealed with paints, varnishes and plastics, is like a body wrapped in plastic — it sweats and smells.

Air moves naturally through a house due to pressure and temperature differences. As well as creating a through-breeze, you can maximise air circulation with the 'stack effect', where warm air rises and is vented through upper floor windows, skylights or clerestory windows.

OUTDOOR AIR QUALITY

Ozone, better known as the protective atmospheric layer that shields the earth from the sun, consists of molecules of three bound oxygen atoms (O_3) rather than the two found in oxygen (O_2). The extra atom makes it an unstable, poisonous gas with a distinctive smell.

Ozone is present in small amounts in air. It is generated when ultraviolet rays in sunlight act on hydrocarbons and nitric oxides in polluted air, recreating smog conditions. Smog is a problem in some places, especially where there is heavy industry, traffic congestion or still, cold conditions coupled with many wood or coal burners. Electrical discharges from appliances with brush-type motors and photocopiers can also produce small amounts of ozone smog.

Ozone can affect respiration. In plants it inhibits foliage growth and reproduction, often leaving plant life weakened and susceptible to insect infestation and cold-weather damage.

There's little point in opening a house up to outside ventilation if the air outside is heavily polluted. Sources of general air pollution include natural sources such as volcanic activity, sea spray and pollens and created sources such as industry, agriculture, transport, waste incineration and home fire-places. In heavily polluted environments, filtered air conditioning (see Chapter 7), though expensive to install and run, is perhaps a healthier option.

Industrial and agricultural pollution

Industry is estimated to produce 60% of New Zealand's total emissions. Pollutants include industrial chemicals which may be toxic in their own right but also contain dioxin, polychlorinated biphenyls and pentachlorophenol. Medical and industrial incineration is a source of dioxins.

However, on a world scale, New Zealand has relatively little industrial air pollution. Most pollution can be controlled at its source with good management.

Regional councils regulate for emissions and will act on complaints of visible, smelly, or noxious emissions.

The use of agrichemicals is subject to a hazardous-chemical control regime but agricultural odours and chemical emissions are often difficult to contain. Many district councils require offensive odours to be contained within the property and suggest farmers make regular olfactory boundary checks. Spray drift in horticultural areas is a major hazard but is difficult to prove and hard to stop. Incidents can be reported to local councils. Intensity, duration and health concerns are all considered.

On a wider scale, New Zealand's agriculture produces about 40% of our greenhouse gases, which in turn contribute to global warming. These include methane from digestion (cows burping) and nitrous oxide formed when urine reacts with soil.

Transport

According to the Ministry of Transport (January 2002), vehicle emissions are credited with about 400 premature deaths in New Zealand each year, mostly from cardiac and respiratory disease. Altogether, close to 1000 people per year are estimated to die prematurely from causes exacerbated by general air pollution.

In Auckland on still days, roadside air pollution often exceeds World Health Organization guidelines. Dwellings in areas where traffic density is high inevitably suffer constant exposure to airborne pollution from fuels and road wear and tear.

Petrol pollutants include the oxides of nitrogen and sulphur, benzene and carbon monoxide. Lead emissions are negligible, following the mandatory removal of lead from vehicle fuel in 1996.

Diesel exhaust is a mixture of a number of dangerous chemicals, including benzene, formaldehyde and polycyclic aromatic hydrocarbons.

Walking, cycling, using public transport or travelling at off-peak times all help reduce air pollution. Regular vehicle tune-ups lessen noxious emissions significantly and are at least as effective as fitting a catalytic converter to a vehicle. There are national regulations to keep smoky vehicles off the road, although they are not yet part of vehicle warrant of fitness checks.

Garages should not be connected to the home. If they are they should be well vented.

Outdoor fires

It may seem a great way to get rid of garbage, but airborne pollution from backyard fires typically travels about 100 m downwind from the fire before settling again. Plastics, rubber, green waste and painted and treated wood give off noxious and toxic chemicals when burnt, and contaminated fire ash pollutes groundwater.

Fires are often restricted in the summer months by local councils. Otherwise, only social restrictions apply: you smoke out your neighbours at your own risk.

Recycling paper and plastic and mulching or composting garden waste are better solutions. Hazardous materials, such as treated wood and tyres, are best disposed of according to council guidelines.

Indoor wood fireplaces and burners are still very popular in heating homes but contribute significantly to smog.

~ *Christchurch smog*   Coal fires are banned in Christchurch. The ban is the first of a number of measures to be taken by Environment Canterbury to minimise winter smog problems. Other measures to be taken in the Christchurch urban area are:

➤ Homes with open fires will not be allowed to use them from 1 January 2006.

➤ Homes with high-emission solid-fuel burners (emitting more than one gram of particulate per kilogram of fuel burnt, and/or not meeting 65% heating efficiency) will need to be replaced 15 years after installation, but not before 1 January 2008.

➤ Homes currently not using wood or coal for home heating, and new homes, will not be allowed to install solid-fuel burners from 1 January 2003.

➤ For all homes using open fires and burners for heating: from 1 January 2004 only low-emission burners will be installable.

Manufacturers are producing special models to meet the low-emission standards required by the Christchurch Council. These new models should benefit air pollution nationwide.

INDOOR AIR POLLUTION

Common sources of indoor air contamination, mainly through the release of VOCs, are building materials, home furnishings, cleansers, heating appliances, aerosol sprays and beauty products.

The following table indicates types, sources and effects of typical indoor air pollutants.

INDOOR POLLUTANTS

Pollutant	Source	Effect
VOCs	LOSP-treated framing timber, plywood panels, mouldings Solvents in paints, varnishes, lacquers, glues, resins, waxes and oils, cleansers, polishes, air fresheners and personal beauty products	Damage to the nervous system Behavioural and emotional problems
Formaldehyde	Glues in particleboard, plywood, medium-density fibreboard and other manufactured wood products Plastic furnishings, printer inks	Probable carcinogen. May cause headaches, eye, nose and respiratory irritation. Also linked with menstrual and pregnancy disorders in female workers
Dioxin	PVC products	Known human carcinogen
Carbon monoxide	Coal and wood fires: inefficient fireplace design, wet, green or chemically treated wood, blocked chimneys or damped-down fires resulting in poor combustion, and causing release of gases into the room	Early symptoms of carbon monoxide poisoning are irritated eyes, headache, nausea, weakness, and dizziness. Prolonged exposure to low concentrations or very short exposure to high concentrations can be fatal

DEALING WITH AIRBORNE MOISTURE

Just by breathing, eating and washing, a family of four generates about 12–20 litres of moisture a day. Unless expelled, the moisture circulates throughout the house as humidity. When it hits a cold surface — be it a wall or a window — it condenses again. Rivulets of moisture on walls and windows, and pools of condensation on window sills, are signs of excessive indoor humidity.

In summer, high humidity is experienced as a sweaty stickiness; in winter a damp clamminess. The first step is to locate the source of humidity. It may be generated by everyday household activities but leaks in roofs, wall claddings, around windows and doors, and in plumbing systems can also create sources of moisture. If left untreated, these will contribute to damp or

Pollutant	Source	Effect
Sulphur dioxide	Coal and wood fires (as above)	Sulphur dioxide is associated with respiratory and cardiac problems In the atmosphere, sulphur dioxide mixes with water vapour, producing sulphuric acid. This acidic pollution can be transported by wind over many hundreds of miles, and deposited as acid rain
Carbon monoxide, nitric oxide and nitrogen dioxide	Flueless heating appliances: kerosene, gas and oil heaters	(As above) Nitrogen dioxide can cause eye, nose, throat and breathing problems
High humidity and condensation		High humidity and condensation levels can cause respiratory ailments
Asbestos fibres	Asbestos in vinyl flooring, exterior cladding, textured ceilings (mainly pre-1980s houses)	Asbestosis, mesothelioma, both of which are lethal
Lead particles	Lead paint (mainly pre-1970s houses)	Brain damage

SOURCES OF AIRBORNE MOISTURE

Activity	Water vapour produced
Unvented clothes dryer	3 litres per load
Bath or shower	1–2 litres per person
Dishwasher	1 litre per load
Cooking	3 litres per day
Unflued gas heater	1 litre per day
Pets and people	1 litre per day

humid conditions, the growth of unwanted moulds and fungi and, possibly, a
rotting building.

If the weather is warm and dry, or even cool and dry, natural ventilation
may be all that is needed to lower indoor humidity and reduce condensation
– open the windows and doors. North-facing orientation and energy-
efficient design also help. If it is cold and wet outdoors, however, natural
ventilation is likely to be less successful. It then becomes a matter of using
mechanical ventilation to minimise the problem.

Dehumidifiers

Dehumidifiers are designed to extract moisture from the air. They are seen as
a convenient solution to health and decor problems caused by cool, wet,
wintry conditions. They work best when the house is warm, so should be used
alongside a heating system. In winter, keeping the house at least 7°C warmer
than the outside temperature discourages dampness and condensation. The
wrong type of heating, however, exacerbates the problem. Unflued gas
heaters – those that run off bottled gas – displace moisture into the air. It
doesn't make sense to create moisture with one appliance (the gas heater)
and extract it with another (the dehumidifier).

If allergies are a problem, dehumidifiers with specific and accurate
humidity settings are preferable but even these, under optimum conditions,
do not remove enough moisture to control dust mites – a common asthma
allergen. To control dust mites, humidity needs to be less than 50%. Even the
best dehumidifiers are unlikely to reduce humidity to less than 70% at
temperatures around 15°C. Some asthma, like that which is exercise-induced,
benefits from higher humidity levels. In these cases wrapping mattresses in
closely woven material and thorough, regular use of an efficient vacuum
cleaner helps with dust mite control.

Domestic ventilation system

A domestic ventilation system (DVS) is a more effective means of removing
moist air than a dehumidifier. It displaces the damp air in living spaces with
warm, dry air from the roof space (as long as there is a roof space),
channelling it via a network of ceiling ducts to wherever it is needed. The air
is filtered in the process and the fan is quiet and unobtrusive. Though more
expensive to install, a DVS can be run at less than half the cost of a
dehumidifier, does not need emptying (it does not gather water) and can be
retro-fitted to existing homes. Unlike a dehumidifier, it treats more than one
room at a time.

Even less expensive than a DVS, a ventilation grille between a wardrobe
and the warm roof space can help keep stored clothes warm and dry in winter.

Mechanical extraction

The Building Code stipulates that bathroom extractors have a 25 litres (of air) per second rating, kitchen rangehood extractors a 50 litres/second rating and laundry extractors 20 litres/second.

Rangehoods in the kitchen, extractor fans in the bathroom and laundry, and clothes dryers must be vented to the outside and not into ceiling or wall cavities. Where ducting is difficult to install, manufacturers offer recirculating rangehoods which filter air through a carbon filter and recirculate it back within the room. Carbon filters must be replaced periodically.

Rangehoods should have washable filters (aluminium or stainless steel) to trap the oil and grease that condenses within the baffles.

Gas cook tops and ovens should always be used with some form of exhaust ventilation to remove the products of combustion, water and carbon monoxide.

Mould and rising damp

A timber dwelling built low to the ground sometimes suffers rising damp — the penetration of cold, wet air through the floor of the house. Sealing the ground with heavy-grade polythene taped against the foundation walls is an effective way of stopping the moisture rising into the house.

Water needs to be able to drain freely away from exterior walls and paving, and outdoor flower gardens should not be built up against wall claddings.

Moulds are a natural part of outdoor environments and mould spores can be detected in the air year round. Given the right conditions, they will readily establish themselves indoors as well. Moulds need moisture to breed and survive. Stale food can be a prime source of mould growth but in terms of indoor air pollution, lax internal moisture management (insufficient heating, poor ventilation and a lack of insulation) and a failure to keep the building envelope dry (leaks in cladding systems and plumbing and drainage) are the prime contributors.

Moulds are no more attracted to timber than any other building material — they will grow on almost any surface. In any place where there is high humidity, such as bathrooms, laundries, kitchens and poorly vented ceiling and basement spaces, mould will thrive.

Two health risks are associated with moulds: asthma-type symptoms (especially in those predisposed to asthma) caused by the inhalation of mould spores and, more seriously, poisoning caused by the inhalation or ingestion of mycotoxins produced by toxigenic fungi. Both are serious if not attended to.

How to decrease mould exposure

Humidity levels lower than 40% will not readily support mould growth. Good, natural or mechanical ventilation and the use of 'breathable' building materials will lower indoor humidity levels sufficiently. Carpets should be avoided in bathrooms and basements — anywhere they can support damp conditions.

How to get rid of mould

If you can see or smell mould, you have a problem. (Moulds usually have a woolly or powdery appearance and come in a range of colours — green, pink, orange, black and blue. The smell is earthy and musty.) Until the source of moisture is removed and the area is cleaned and decontaminated, mould growth, though removed, is likely to recur. Standard white vinegar is an adequate cleanser and decontaminant. A less eco-friendly decontaminant is a 10% solution of household bleach (using a chlorine bleach straight from the bottle is no more effective) but it should never be mixed with ammonia-based cleansers — the fumes are toxic.

'Toxic mould'

Stachybotrys chartarum is one of several toxic fungi that grow readily on building materials containing wood fibres. This includes the paper backing on plasterboards, fibreboards and wallpapers and on carpets made of natural fibres or the like. The fungus does not grow directly on timber and does not cause significant decay, though it does need a period of wetting to take root and thrive — hence its association with weather-tightness failure.

It can be hidden from view in the ceiling or walls yet, aided by negative air pressure, contaminate living spaces with live spores.

In North America and Europe considerable attention has been given to the health risk associated with 'toxic moulds', that is, *Stachybotrys*, following incidents of pulmonary haemorrhage and haemosiderosis thought to have been caused by mould contamination in homes which, some time earlier, had sustained water damage.

Stachybotrys is greenish-black in colour and its presence is often discovered only when building repairs or alterations are done. Infected material must be removed and replaced. People with allergies, immune suppression or lung problems should avoid contact with the mould and the airborne spores likely to be present in an affected area.

HOUSEHOLD DUST

A moderate quantity of what we call dust is always present in the air inside the average home and it is a known asthma trigger. Dust is a handy name for a wide range of microscopic organic matter, mould and mildew spores, dust mite corpses and faeces, animal detritus, and particles created by everyday life within the home. You can keep much of it out: about two-thirds is

tracked into the home on feet. A good doormat or a policy of 'shoes off' will
keep most of it outdoors. The age-old solution of dusting and sweeping is
ineffective – it often just moves dust around. Wet wiping and vacuuming are
better remedies.

Vacuum cleaners

Most vacuum cleaners have a four- or five-stage filter, a dust bag of two or
three layers, a filter before the motor and an exhaust filter. To trap the fine
particles such as cat allergens and dust mite faeces and body parts (what a
charming thought), a 'HEPA' or 'S Class' exhaust filter is required. Dust mites
are able to cling to soft surfaces so are difficult to expel. However, their
faeces (the main allergen) are captured quite readily by the HEPA filter.

Air filters

Air filters are an integral part of extractor fans, rangehoods, most modern
vacuum cleaners and some dehumidifiers and heat pumps.

Filter systems vary in efficacy. Systems include an initial filter that
removes dust, lint, carpet fibres and pet detritus. A HEPA filter that removes
microscopic particles, larger than 0.3 microns, is more effective. This will
catch fine dust, smoke, pollen, bacteria, mould spores and viruses. An
activated carbon filter may also be used to remove odours and volatile
organic compounds (VOCs) arising from furnishings, aerosols, carpets and
smoke.

BENEFICIAL PLANTS AND FLOWERS

Smells and substances carried on the air are not all
bad. Sometimes you may wish to add fragrance with
pots of herbs, potpourri, cut flowers, stringed herbs,
naturally scented woods such as sandalwood and oils
such as linseed.

Not only do some plants and flowers add
fragrance, a joint study by NASA and the American
Landscape Contractors Association indicates that some
indoor plants absorb pollutants such as formaldehyde,
benzene and carbon monoxide from the air. In the
study, each plant type was placed in a sealed chamber
into which chemicals were injected. Philodendron, spider plant and the
golden pothos were found to be the most effective in removing formaldehyde
molecules. Flowering plants such as gerbera daisy and chrysanthemums were
more effective in removing benzene from the air.

> *TOP TIPS FOR A FRESH,*
> *FRAGRANT HOME*
>
> ✓ Good ventilation
> ✓ Natural, energy-efficient
>   building materials
> ✓ Efficient appliances and
>   vehicles
> ✓ Natural furnishings
> ✓ Natural cleansers

The top pollutant busters were:

- Bamboo palm/reed palm (*Chamaedorea seifrizii*)
- Chinese evergreen (*Aglaonema modestum*)
- English ivy (*Hedera helix*)
- Gerbera daisy (*Gerbera jamesonii*)
- Janet Craig (*Dracaena* 'Janet Craig')
- Marginata (*Dracaena marginata*)
- Mass cane/corn plant (*Dracaena massangeana*)
- Mother-in law's tongue (*Sansevieria trifasciata* 'Laurentii')
- Pot mum (*Chrysanthemum morifolium*)
- Peace lily (*Spathiphyllum* 'Mauna Loa')
- Warneckii (*Dracaena warneckii*).

Pomander

- Press cloves into a lemon, orange or lime until the surface is covered.
- Roll in cinnamon, nutmeg or ginger, and orris (orris is a fixer) for a stronger scent.
- Leave somewhere dark and dry until hard. The fruit will shrink a little.
- Hang or place wherever you like.

Potpourri

- Dry leaves and petals separately.
- Place in layers (about 2.5 cm deep) in a glass jar.
- After each layer, sprinkle half a teaspoon of coarse salt and the same of orris root.
- Close the jar tightly and store in the dark for three weeks.
- Mix in an open bowl or jar with spices and a few essential oils.

Herb sachets

- Fill small cotton bags with potpourri and dried herbs.
- Add a few drops of lavender, rose or rosemary oil; tie at the top.
- Place in cupboards and drawers.

Chapter 11

Light

The circadian cycle has a profound effect on our body functions. Body temperature, heart beat, blood pressure, hormone levels and urine flow rise and fall in a predictable, rhythmic pattern — a pattern initiated and governed by exposure to sunlight and darkness. Light is the time keeper that synchronises these body rhythms, by triggering a tiny cluster of cells behind the retina, setting in motion a complex chain of reactions.

We can function without natural light but risk gradually falling out of rhythm, resulting possibly in sleep disturbance and emotional and mental imbalance: effects similar to jet lag. Research shows that there is a marked seasonal variation in depression — Seasonal Affective Disorder (SAD) — with an increase of symptoms in winter months, especially in countries in the high latitudes with low daylight hours.

In the industrialised world, few people can live in harmony with the sun's cycles. Even in earlier times, twilight was extended with firelight or candlelight. However, the pace of life today requires that bright, artificial lighting extends full daylight until late at night and true darkness has been banished from the cities and suburbs. Even during the day, many people work in buildings illuminated by artificial lighting. However, it is still possible to maximise the use of natural light and mimic its qualities with artificial lighting.

USING NATURAL LIGHT

Light quality
Natural light is moving, variable and dynamic. Its quality and colour change with the seasons, time of the day, weather and terrain.

Direct sunlight throws light and shadow into sharp relief. It is the most intense light but may cause glare.

Direct light is best in workspaces such as kitchens, offices and playrooms. Large windows to the east and north will bring in strong, direct light without producing the glare often experienced from the west.

Direct shafts of light through small, high windows or skylights are also good for highlighting focal points such as a painting, sculpture or water feature or for lighting hallways and stairs.

Reflected light is gentler and more varied as it takes on some of the hue, intensity and texture of the reflective surface.

Diffused light, which has passed through a filter such as net curtain, frosted or stained glass, blind or screen is a soft, almost shadowless light.

Reflected and diffused light produces a gentler, more relaxed atmosphere than direct light and is favoured in bedrooms, sitting rooms and entranceways.

Orientation

A dwelling's orientation is a critical factor in using natural light. A north-facing aspect is ideal. The penetration of sunlight into a home varies dramatically with the height and angle of the sun. In winter, the low angle of the sun brings it deep into the home but because it rises and sets later, less of the house is encompassed. In summer, the higher angle of the sun means penetration is less during the height of the day but the wider sweep across the sky means more of the house is enveloped.

The layout of the house should ideally follow the path of the sun, with 'morning rooms' (bedrooms, kitchen, study) facing east; day rooms and living rooms to the north; evening spaces (sitting rooms and lounges) to the west and utility areas (laundry, bathrooms and storage spaces) to the south.

Surrounding features

As well as orientation, it is important to consider surrounding features that might interfere with the spread of natural light — hills, trees or neighbouring properties. (There are bylaws governing the proximity and height of neighbouring buildings to allow fair distribution of light.) Similarly, street lighting, brightly lit stadiums and city lights will influence the depth of darkness that falls at night.

Windows

Windows are our main means of bringing light into the home. Light coming from different directions creates the most natural effect.

North-facing windows maximise the reach of sun into the home in winter but minimise it in summer, affording valuable warmth in winter but not admitting direct sun during the hottest hours in summer.

To the north, the higher or taller the window the more sky area is revealed and the greater the penetration of light and sun. To the east and west, wide, low windows admit the most sun.

Clerestory windows high in the walls and skylights allow light to reach the backs of rooms and bring sunlight into previously sunless spaces.

Skylights can be placed on a flat or angled roof. Unlike north-facing windows, north-angled skylights catch maximum light and sun all year round. South-facing skylights bring in constant, soft, diffused light. (Be aware that skylights are not good from the perspective of heat control: unless shaded, or fitted with tinted or UV-resistant glazing, they allow heat to escape in winter and penetrate in summer.)

Light shafts can provide a more indirect source of light and 'warmth' deep into the home from glazed dome inlets on the roof. A flared light shaft brings in more light than a straight shaft and a reflective surface within the shaft boosts light levels further.

~ *Window design* Window surrounds that are splayed, and bay windows, bring in more light than conventional windows. Picture windows or ranch sliders allow in more light than windows divided into small sections or sashes. Curtain tracks that allow the curtains to completely clear the window also allow in substantially more light.

Glass expels most ultraviolet light but lets in the visible spectrum. Plastic or acrylic, which is sometimes used in mobile homes or skylights, filters visible light slightly, lending a diffused, gentle light, but also lets in UV rays.

Frosted windows and stained glass also change light quality in a room.

Decor

Garden design and indoor decor can be used to reflect and maximise light. Lightly coloured paving can reflect light into the home and internal glass doors or shoji screens allow light to pass from one room to another. Light-coloured furnishings and reflective surfaces and ornaments reflect light within a room.

Glare, especially from the low western sun, can be a problem. Gauze curtains will diffuse glare without expelling light; Venetian blinds, which can be angled to bring in as much light as wanted, diffuse the glare and bring soft, dappled light into the room.

Wooden blinds have a cool, shaded effect. Light-coloured aluminium or synthetic blinds produce a more dynamic effect by bouncing light deep into the room, creating sharp contrasts between shadow and light.

Rediscovering darkness

Like the day, the night contains shifting patterns of light and dark. In the city we are unlikely to experience true darkness or the full effect of starlight and moonlight. It is very difficult to reproduce these conditions artificially as heavy curtains blanket out all light but lightweight curtains admit illumination from streetlights and city lights.

Turning off lights on your own property and electrical appliances that glow in the dark at night helps create more natural conditions. Positioning bedrooms away from the road is also helpful.

ARTIFICIAL LIGHTING

Light types

Nothing compares with natural light but we can try to mimic its qualities with artificial lighting. Lighting can be incandescent or fluorescent. Incandescence is the glow produced by heat. Fluorescence is the glow created when electrons strike a surface.

~ *Incandescent tungsten lights*   Though it gives off a warm, yellow glow, the standard incandescent light is so inefficient that 90% of the energy it consumes is given off as heat rather than light. It is really just a miniature space heater, which gives off a little light. As well, the heat may damage the plastic fittings, causing it to off-gas VOCs. Where possible, look to replace the standard 'bayonet'-type incandescent fitting with a screw-type fitting to accommodate much more efficient compact fluorescent lights.

Incandescent lights consume power according to their wattage. Choose lights of different wattage to suit the amount of light needed, and a shade or globe that doesn't obscure the light — some emit as little as 30% of available light. Incandescent light bulbs are short lived, generally lasting about 1000 hours. Dimmers save energy and extend the life of incandescent bulbs.

~ *Tungsten-halogen lights*   A halogen light encases a tungsten filament in a much smaller quartz envelope filled with halogen gas. The halogen combines with the tungsten vapour and redeposits it on the filament, increasing the lifespan of the filament. This allows it to burn hotter and produce a bright, white light, close to daylight quality.

There are two types of tungsten-halogen light: powerful, high-voltage lights are best for general illumination, especially up lighting; low-voltage lights are ideal for accent or task lighting.

Initial costs are high but tungsten-halogen lights are long-lasting and energy efficient, typically giving 4000 hours of use.

~ *Metal-halide lights* Metal-halide lights produce the same powerful white illumination as tungsten-halogen lights but are as energy efficient as fluorescents. Initial costs are high but they are long-lasting, giving up to 6000 hours of service.

~ *Fluorescent lights* In fluorescent lights, electricity passes through electrodes at each end of a sealed fluorescent tube which contains mercury vapour in an argon gas. The generated electrons form an arc, which knock electrons in the mercury atoms out of their normal position. In returning, they produce an ultraviolet light that strikes phosphorus particles coating the wall of the tube, creating a fluorescent glow.

Fluorescent lights generate a flicker that occurs at 50–60 cycles per second, meaning the tube is effectively switched off or on 100 or 120 times per second.

Pre-1978 fluorescent lights have starting devices containing highly toxic polychlorinated biphenyls (PCBs). These PCBs can leak and produce high concentrations in the room in which they operate. The disposal of PCB-containing materials in landfills is also a problem. Early-model fluorescents emit higher electromagnetic fields, and headaches and visual stress have been linked to their perceptible 'flicker'. There is no perceptible flicker in newer fluorescent tubes, which are typically five times as efficient as incandescent bulbs and use only 20% of the electricity.

~ *Compact fluorescents* Compact fluorescent lights (CFLs) have at least 10 times the lifespan of incandescent lights and use a quarter of the electricity. The higher initial cost of CFLs is offset by their longer life and lower running costs, and their production places much less demand on global resources. They are best used in locations where lights are left on for an extended length of time (two to three hours or more), such as kitchens, lounges, and bedrooms. Some CFLs have an electronic ballast unit built into the base of the light. (A ballast is a device that starts and regulates fluorescent lights.) An alternative option is to replace standard light fittings with ballasted fittings which allow the use of cheaper non-ballasted CFLs.

While standard fluorescents give off a hard, white light, newer CFLs are designed to give the same warm, yellow glow as incandescent lights. They are not yet suitable for use with dimmers.

CFLs are available with screw-in and bayonet fittings. However, when replacing standard incandescent lamps with compact fluorescent lamps be aware that those CFLs with a ballast mechanism in the base of the lamp are bigger than standard incandescent lamps, and the fitting may require a change of lampshade.

Light positioning

~ *General lighting*   Ceiling lights cast the most light but generally it works best to use several different light sources — some up lighting and some down lighting. Naked bulbs will need shading as they can become unwanted focal points.

~ *Task lighting*   Spot lighters, lights or shaded fluorescent lights can be used for specific purposes such as illuminating a desk or reading chair. Lights that can be redirected as required are useful.

~ *Atmospheric lighting*   Atmosphere can be created using low-level lighting with lamps or concealed lights using soft-toned incandescent bulbs. Dimmer controls can give extra flexibility. Traditionally, incandescent or tungsten filament lights are weak in blue wavelengths but rich in red and yellow wavelengths. This intensifies warm colours in the room so these lights are often chosen for sitting rooms or bedrooms.

Fluorescent lighting casts cooler green/blue light and is often preferred for workspaces.

Full-spectrum fluorescent tubes and incandescent lights can be obtained but emit slightly higher levels of ultraviolet light than traditional lights.

TOP TIPS FOR LIGHTING

✓ Orientate the dwelling to the north.

✓ Maximise the use of natural light.

✓ Minimise the use of artificial light.

✓ Vary light sources.

✓ Tailor lighting to specific needs.

Chapter 12

Sound

Sound affects our bodies and emotions. We tend to switch off to background noise but our bodies react even as we sleep. Soothing, rhythmic sound that matches our heart beat increases learning capacity; a fast tempo is invigorating and arousing. The industrial age arrived with a clang; we now live with unprecedented noise levels that influence our well-being more than we realise. Loud or unceasing sound causes stress and tension, increased heart beat, heightened blood pressure, sleeplessness and even violence; very loud noise permanently damages our hearing.

Sound is something we share; it is common property for better or worse but we can minimise its impact in planning our homes and lifestyles.

LOCATION AND ORIENTATION

Before you buy a home or move into a property, consider possible noise sources and how they might affect you. Sound travels great distances, particularly across water and in the stillness of the night. It also tends to rise. Hills and trees act as sound barriers, so do buildings. Use a map to identify industrial areas, airports and flight paths, traffic routes, railways, race tracks, schools, sports and music stadiums. Most importantly, talk to neighbours about local noise.

Assess the house itself: how close is it to roads and neighbours? What is the frequency, timing and type of passing traffic? How is the house orientated? Are the sleeping spaces protected from noise? Do the living spaces open onto quiet spaces? Is there landscaping or fencing of a type which will help buffer unwanted noise from roads and neighbours? If personal security is of concern, balance the need for sound screens against visibility.

FACTORS IN NOISE

Types of noise

There are two types of building noise.

➤ Airborne noise travels through the air, such as traffic, stereo, speech.

➤ Impact noise travels through the structure, such as footsteps, or the scraping of furniture on a concrete floor.

Ratings

The Building Code uses a STC (Sound Transmission Class) rating to measure how effective walls and ceilings are at screening noise. The noise insulation of floors is rated according to their Impact Insulation Class (IIC). In both cases, the higher the rating, the better the soundproofing. Different types of construction typically carry different ratings.

Situations

In any building the situations that need consideration are: outside-to-inside noise; room-to-room noise; and flanking noise. If dwellings are physically connected, sounds not only pass directly through walls and floors but travel along them from one space to another. This is called flanking noise and is partly why, despite an architect's best intentions, noise transmission between neighbours in adjoining dwellings is difficult to anticipate and prevent.

REDUCING NOISE

Nobody wants to live with deathly silence — without the constant stream of information about our surroundings provided by sound, we can feel isolated and uneasy. We want to repel some sounds but allow free access for others.

The science of sound insulation in buildings is complex, and the design and construction costs associated with installing it effectively are a disincentive to many developers and builders. To be effective, sound insulation must be installed correctly — it requires good design and careful attention to detail. It can be difficult to do anything comprehensive about a noise nuisance in an existing building but some reduction is usually possible.

Apartments

Residents in apartments and semi-attached dwellings are far more likely to be bothered by noise than residents in detached houses, which is why territorial authorities require minimum sound insulation ratings in medium- and high-density accommodation. The Building Code requires shared walls and floors to have a minimum rating of STC 55, an insulation level at which loud speech cannot be heard.

Speech is an airborne noise and is relatively easy to contain. Footsteps are an impact noise and are difficult to contain, especially when transmitted from a room situated one level above another. Such floors may meet the Building Code requirement but not meet the expectations of the residents.

When buying a recently built apartment or terraced house, ask to see design specifications, take note of the construction type (timber or concrete) and link noise performance to the purchase contract. If in doubt, employ a noise consultant to carry out an onsite check.

Outside-to-inside soundproofing

Exterior walls are typically made of either high-mass materials such as concrete and brick, or low-mass materials such as timber framing and cladding. In general, heavy, dense building systems provide better insulation against airborne noise than lightweight systems, but have the disadvantage of readily transmitting impact noise. A combination of low- and high-mass materials provides the best noise insulation.

The first step in noise proofing an existing house is to improve doors and windows. Solid doors are more effective sound insulators than hollow doors. Standard double glazing is not a good sound insulator. A more effective option is laminated glass with a special noise-control resin separating the two faces. Compared with plain glass, one layer of 7 mm laminated glass achieves a 40% reduction of perceived sound. Unfortunately, it doesn't have much better thermal performance than plain glass but does eliminate most ultraviolet light (which causes fading). To gain the best of both worlds install double glazing with one layer being laminated glass.

Room-to-room party walls

Under the Building Code, party walls between self-contained units must meet minimum fire and STC ratings. A concrete wall lined with plasterboard meets both requirements, but to cut down the high-frequency noise of human voices this type of wall requires a lined cavity, at least 50 mm deep and filled with insulation, to be added to either side of the concrete wall. Alternatively, a lightweight, insulated, timber-framed wall lined with multiple layers of acoustically rated plasterboard achieves the same effect.

~ *Partitioning* Uninsulated timber-framed cavity walls provide very little sound insulation but instead act like sound boxes to amplify certain sound frequencies. To gain good sound insulation internal timber-framed partitions are best constructed using resilient rails between the plasterboard and timber

  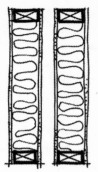 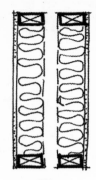

STC 33	STC 36	STC 40	STC 57
No acoustic insulation, 9.5 mm plasterboard each side of a 95 x 45 mm stud wall	Acoustic insulation added	Double insulated stud wall (Note: this is not 2 x 36 STC of a single insulated stud wall)	Isolated double stud wall, internal layers of plasterboard removed

Acoustic insulation: typical STC ratings of standard plasterboard-lined timber-framed partitions

frame, and filled with an absorbent insulation material. Or, better still, a double wall with both walls physically isolated from one another and the gap filled with insulation.

Areas of low sound insulation include gaps or holes in walls (especially windows and doors), and back-to-back electrical sockets.

Floors

Concrete slabs provide good low-frequency *airborne* noise insulation but readily transmit *impact* noises such as footsteps. A floating timber floor, fixed to resilient mounts, reduces the problem. Otherwise, the hard upper surface of the slab needs to be insulated as does the ceiling structure suspended beneath the slab. A thin layer of cork placed beneath the main floor covering acts as a good impact insulator. Cork is available in sheet form for this application and can be laid over any type of sub-floor as well as under ceramics, vinyl, timber, marble, natural stone or carpet. Carpet does little to reduce airborne sound but does raise the impact insulation level (IIC). Noise-reduction underlay is also available.

Mid-level lightweight floors built of timber present a more difficult problem. While resilient ceilings, floating floors and soft coverings reduce low-frequency impact noise on concrete floors, they do little to improve the same problem, particularly that of footfall impacts, on timber floors.

The most satisfactory solutions yet designed (which have layers of flooring board, insulation, plasterboard, and more flooring board on top of the floor joists, and resilient channels and fire-rated plasterboard below the joists) deliver an IIC of 60–70 decibels but are complex and difficult to construct.

Simpler but less effective solutions include placing a layer of sound-absorbing insulation between the flooring material and the floor joists, and sheets of acoustically rated plasterboard on furring channels and resilient mounts below.

APPLIANCES

To minimise noise at its source, check the decibel (dB) ratings when buying appliances. It is not compulsory for New Zealand manufacturers to indicate

AVERAGE DECIBEL (DB) LEVELS OF APPLIANCES			
Refrigerator	50 dB	Hair dryer	75 dB
Microwave	57 dB	Coffee grinder	80 dB
Clothes dryer	57 dB	Wastemaster	80 dB
Dishwasher	65 dB	Vacuum cleaner	81 dB
Washing machine	68 dB	Lawnmower	86 dB
Electric mixer	75 dB	Food processor	95 dB

decibel ratings on their appliances but they can generally give them on request. Manufacturers of quiet machines aim at 45–50 dBs, about the loudness of a trickling stream.

Average ratings for common appliances are listed on page 133; anything less is a bonus.

Placing appliances slightly away from walls will cut down on noise transmission. Vibration mounts, acoustic floor mats or simply rubber mats or concrete floors can absorb the vibrations of noisy appliances such as washing machines and refrigerators.

DOGS, LAWNMOWERS AND LATE-NIGHT PARTIES

Ask any city council and they'll tell you that the neighbourhood noises that cause the most distress are barking dogs, late-night parties and lawnmowers — just about in that order. The party problem is the easiest to solve: just put on your best hat and join in.

Neighbourly consideration and communication should take care of the other noise problems but where tact and persuasion fail, local councils have noise control officers who will investigate excessive noise and, if they find it, do something about it. You have a right to ask their assistance if noises:

➤ prevent sleep at night
➤ seriously intrude on work and concentration during the day
➤ prevent normal conversation in a neighbouring property
➤ require radio or television to be turned up significantly in order to be heard.

As well as noise control, local building regulations sometimes control outdoor-to-indoor noise transmission in new homes. For example, homes close to a noisy highway may be required to install laminated soundproof glazing to cut down decibel levels inside.

CREATING HARMONY

If intrusive noise is minimised, you are free to create a harmonious acoustic environment, not forgetting that the primary purpose of sound is information. In the garden, the wind in trees adds background ambience and provides continual, often subliminal information about weather conditions.

On a more intimate scale, bamboo, reeds and long grass respond quickly to the lightest air movements. Running water, trickling over pebbles and stones, adds soothing rhythm and harmony. Trees, flaxes and a feeding table

attract small song birds. Watery spots — ponds, streams, stormwater ditches,
mangroves — draw water birds and wild fowl. A patch of bush provides cover
for night birds like kiwi, weka and morepork.

Courtyards and entrances, decks and patios can be enhanced by wind
chimes and water sculptures. Gravel paths and
bamboo curtains gently announce the arrival of
visitors. A hand-rung bell or door knocker is
acoustically more harmonious than an electric
chime or buzzer.

Furnish quiet, intimate indoor spaces with
absorbent surfaces — heavy curtains, thick rugs,
wall hangings, luxuriant furnishings, screens and
plants to soften the sounds. Where you want to
create a feeling of space, a room with bare floors
and hard surfaces will reverberate and feel
larger as a result.

> ### *TOP TIPS FOR QUIET LIVING*
>
> ✓ Choose a quiet location.
>
> ✓ Orientate living areas towards peaceful spaces.
>
> ✓ Install laminated noise-control glass.
>
> ✓ Install sound-rated walls to isolate noisy spaces.
>
> ✓ Source quiet appliances.

Part Three

The Life Cycle

Chapter 13

Food

A MATTER OF CHOICE

Food is an area that arouses strong passions. A careful weighing of factors is needed to make informed eco choices. Traditionally, our dietary choice has been dictated by the local environment, the seasons and the climate but the last 30 years has seen an explosion in availability of foodstuffs. The global economy has brought a global menu with most fruits and vegetables available all year round. Fertilisers, pesticides, veterinary medicines, preservatives and processing aids are used to boost productivity and control plant disease. However, this choice and abundance comes at a cost – in the quality of food and in pressure on the environment. Maintaining food supply and food safety entails a careful balancing of risks. There are two main branches of concern: damage to ecological systems and damage to human health.

In producing our food, we compete with other creatures who also need a feed – bacteria, fungi, insects, birds ... and the plants too, who want to live, so produce their own toxins to protect themselves from predators.

Agrichemical production seeks to manage and control these living systems using chemically synthesised substances, in the main, for human benefit. 'Organic agriculture' or 'sustainable agriculture' seeks to work in harmony with natural ecosystems without the use of synthetic fertilisers and pesticides. By choosing to eat food produced by one or the other method, we indirectly affect the greater environment.

HEALTH

Neither agrichemical nor organic production can guarantee non-toxic food for humans. Both synthetic and natural pesticides can leave residue on food.

There is a risk that whatever is toxic to 'pests' may also be harmful to humans, bearing in mind that substances that have lethal effects on small creatures may have little effect on large creatures (us); and that substances that are toxic in large doses may be harmless in minute doses. In the end, the choice may be between residue from a pesticide developed by people or residue from a pesticide developed by a plant with which we have coexisted for thousands of years, such as the garlic plant. Perhaps the devil you know (the plant) is better than the devil you don't (the pesticide).

There are also natural insecticides and fungicides produced by plants and organisms that can affect humans; for example, the carcinogenic aflatoxins produced by moulds growing on peanuts. Because of the extreme toxicity of these natural substances, these foods are subject to strict monitoring in New Zealand. Organic production, while shunning artificial pesticides, cannot guarantee there will be no natural toxicity. But it can be argued that it is less likely to create an unnecessary imbalance in the environment, causing stress and toxic reactions in the plants; and that by working in harmony with living systems, there will be less need for plants to protect themselves from disease and predation and consequently less natural toxicity in the plant. It could also be argued that it is safer to choose one source of toxin (plant-based) rather than two (plant-based and synthetic).

RISKS TO THE ENVIRONMENT

In reducing competing organisms (pests), we also risk inadvertently reducing beneficial organisms, such as the microscopic life forms that help plants access nutrients from the soil. As well, decimating one population may have a flow-on effect to other populations in the food chain, and upset the natural ecological balance. For example, pesticide use on fruit to reduce fungal and insect damage may also reduce the bird population that feeds off the fruit and insects. As the bird population declines, the insect population expands, necessitating the use of further insecticides.

Artificial fertilisers

Most artificial fertilisers contain nitrogen and potassium but few or no trace minerals, humus, organic acids or microbes. High-nitrogen fertilisers are especially hard on earthworms, fungi and other beneficial microbes, which allow plants to access nutrients in the soil.

A further concern is that, because artificial fertilisers dissolve in water, they release nutrients more quickly than organic fertilisers. The fast release causes a glut of nutrients and unnaturally fast plant growth, making the plants more vulnerable to infestation and disease.

In the long term, heavy use of artificial fertiliser adds nitrates and salts to the soil, affecting soil fertility. And when washed into waterways, fertiliser phosphates cause eutrophication by providing an abundance of food for algae, which bloom, consume the oxygen in the water, and cause conditions that suffocate other marine organisms.

Single crops

Agrichemical farming favours single-crop farming: it is easier to manage and, initially, more productive. But just as you are more likely to catch a cold in crowded places, plant disease is more likely in monoculture. Even growing plants of a similar type, such as tomatoes and potatoes, in close proximity increases the likelihood of a plant disease spreading. Managing the increased risk, while at the same time pushing for a quicker crop turnaround, requires greater use of pesticides and fertilisers with subsequent loss of insect, bird and soil life. This cycle of depletion provides diminishing returns and increases the chance of plant disease over the years.

A variety of plants — which is where the idea of 'companion planting' comes from — is a more robust ecosystem. Organic agriculture, by focusing attention on soil-building using compost, enhancing plant health and coexisting with insects and microbes — looks to create a natural spiral of fertility and health, with increased production and resistance to disease over the years.

Genetically modified (GM) crops

Genetic modification is highly contentious. Again, there are two areas of concern: the health effects on humans and irreversible changes to the environment and the gene pool. There are also two branches of GM: GM confined to the laboratory or a strictly confined environment such as GM cows that secrete milk for the treatment of cystic fibrosis, and GM that is released into the field.

The first would seem to confer health benefits with few risks for the wider environment or gene pool. The downstream effects of the second (release into the field) can only be guessed at: we don't yet have a sufficient knowledge base to assess the impact of intended or unintended changes. However, we do know that transporting genes across the divide between the plant and animal kingdoms will effect changes that could not occur naturally through mutation and natural selection. We can't guarantee that genetic modification won't produce unexpected features as side effects of the manipulation or that unplanned cross-contamination with other crops won't unintentionally alter or obliterate present strains. Liability for unforeseen consequences will likely be impossible to determine and enforce.

With the release of GM crops into the environment, there may be only one
moment of *collective* choice. If GM crops cross-pollinate with other crops, the
irreversible nature of this step will take away any ongoing choice from the
individual.

~ *GM labelling* New Zealand's GM labelling requirements on food are
stringent by international standards. The Australia and New Zealand Food
Standards Council (ANZFSC) requires mandatory labelling of foods containing
0.1% or more genetically modified DNA or protein, with a 1% threshold of
'accidental mixing' of GM and non-GM material. Processing aids are included
in this regime but highly refined additives such as sugars, oils and starches,
which no longer contain GM material, are exempt from labelling, unless they
are significantly different nutritionally or in their end use from their non-GM
counterparts.

CONTROLLING THE RISKS

To minimise risk to health or the environment, there are strict governmental
controls on food production and processing. There is also a requirement to
disclose food content and processes. The dietary choice is handed to the
consumer. This is a powerful incentive for vigilance and caution among food
producers.

Food safety

Food Standards Australia New Zealand (FSANZ) monitors the safety of chemicals
in food production. It sets maximum chemical residue levels on food for
consumption and monitors chemical additives to food, such as processing
aids, colouring, preservatives and food contaminants such as metals and
natural toxicants. It is also responsible for setting labelling requirements on
food for sale.

Residue on food

Before a pesticide is allowed to be marketed and used in New Zealand, it
needs to provide a toxicological data package containing extensive detailed
research information on its potential human health impact, and also
increasingly on its ecological impact.

The four-yearly New Zealand Total Diet survey measures pesticide residue
in food and assesses the risks for human health. This provides a check that
FSANZ requirements are being met and is an avenue for scientific concerns to
be investigated. There are also interest groups, such as the 'Safe Food
Campaign', which pursue issues and bring them to public awareness.

Food additives

Food additives are grouped into preservatives, colourings and flavour enhancers. Most food additives have code numbers that are part of an international numbering system. To be sure of what you're eating, check the (E) code number. Euphemisms for unpopular substances are sometimes used, such as 'modified starch' or 'flavour'.

Most additives appear to be relatively harmless. However, there are some areas of concern: sulphites used in preservatives can cause allergic reactions in susceptible people; food colourings have been linked anecdotally to attention and hyperactivity disorders; and monosodium glutamate (MSG), which is used to heighten the perception of flavour and suppress the perception of bitterness, has been linked with varying adverse reactions in some individuals.

Artificial ripening

Ethylene is a hormone produced naturally in small quantities by most fruits and vegetables. It affects the growth, development and ripening of plants. (This is why kiwifruit ripen when placed inside a closed paper bag with an apple for a few days.) Commercially, ethylene gas can be used to artificially promote ripening in fruits such as bananas, citrus, pineapples, dates, persimmons, pears, apples, melons, mangoes, avocados and papayas.

Imported food

The transport of imported food, especially the airlifting of high tonnages of out-of-season fresh foods, places significant costs on environmental resources. Not only is there the environmental degradation associated with its transport, but also the adverse impact of fumigation procedures, plus the possibility of a biosecurity breach.

Both imported and domestically produced food sold in New Zealand must comply with the New Zealand regulations (Maximum Residue Limits of Agricultural Compounds). Our biosecurity regulations also demand that imported food be free of pests.

In the past, ethylene oxide and methyl bromide have been used in fumigation. Ethylene oxide leaves undesirable residues and is now banned. Methyl bromide is being phased out worldwide due to its implication in ozone depletion. Irradiation has been a controversial option but is now used in a limited way.

Food irradiation

Irradiation of foodstuffs — exposing the food to a source of ionising energy — is used as a food-preservation process and a quarantine safeguard. It destroys the bacteria that cause food decomposition and food poisoning. Under the standard covering the irradiation of food in Australia and New Zealand, this energy can be in the form of cobalt 60-sourced gamma rays, machine-generated X-rays, or an electrically generated electron beam.

Irradiated food doesn't become radioactive. When the treatment stops, energy does not remain in the food and there is no direct contact between the energy source and the food, so radioactive contamination is not possible.

The advantages of food irradiation are protection against harmful bacteria, longer shelf life and protection against imported pests without chemical fumigation.

There is concern that irradiation creates free radicals in the cells it penetrates. Free radicals are implicated in heart disease, cancer and premature ageing. (Antioxidants in fruit, vegetables, whole nuts and seeds and vitamin E protect against free radicals.)

A second concern is that new compounds — radiolytic products — previously not encountered by humans, are formed. Their effects are unknown, although similar compounds are produced in other forms of food processing.

A further concern is the depletion of some B group vitamins and A, C, E and K vitamins with irradiation. Storage and food preparation add to this depletion.

The disposal of the waste material — semi-spent radio nucleotides — is also problematic. Because of its long life, the burden of disposal is likely to fall on future generations. If irradiation becomes widespread, bacterial resistance may also develop.

In New Zealand, the stated policy is that food can be irradiated only if there is no other safe method available. Any irradiated food must go through a strict safety assessment by Food Standards Australia New Zealand and, if approved, labelled as having been treated by irradiation. In Australia and New Zealand, only herbal infusions, herbs and spices and more recently tropical fruit from Queensland have approval to be irradiated.

Food labelling

Food labelling must show:

> - the nutritional content of the food
> - the percentage of the characterising ingredient in the product
> - all the main ingredients in descending order
> - potential allergens in foods
> - GM material
> - irradiation
> - food additives and their E code number so that they can be identified.

Takeaway and restaurant food and fresh produce are presently exempt from labelling requirements.

Food preparation

In these days of fast foods, even with quite stringent labelling requirements, we often have little idea of the condition of the food before it was processed, the level of hygiene or the method used to prepare it before reaching us. The time lapse between picking and eating fruits and vegetables is critical to taste and nutritional value: vitamins decline with time following harvest. Cutting, shredding and cooking leads to vitamin loss, especially of the water-soluble vitamins, vitamin B complexes and vitamin C. Buying fresh, unprocessed food and preparing it at home, in ways that retain nutrient content such as a quick stir fry or fresh fruit or vegetable salad, is a sensible option.

Food preserving

Old-fashioned methods of preserving foods such as bottling fruit and making jams and pickles are time-consuming but satisfy an ancient urge to store food in the time of plenty for the time of need.

There are two main methods of bottling fruit and pickles (see opposite). The first — the overflow method — is fast and easy but not always reliable. The second — the water-bath method — takes longer but is more reliable.

~ *Deep freezing* Place the food item in a plastic freezer bag. Expel the excess air. Close with a tie and place in the freezer. (Note: never refreeze frozen food.) Blanching vegetables in a large volume of boiling water before freezing is sometimes recommended (a process used by most commercial manufacturers), but results in further loss of nutrients.

Food storage

Cool, dark storage slows deterioration: 10°C is ideal but less than 20°C is essential.

Dried, frozen and canned foods have a recommended shelf life of between six months and two years depending on the item. Commercially canned food is labelled with a use-by date. It does not become inedible on a particular day or week, but nutritional value and appearance deteriorate rapidly. Canned fruit can lose up to 20% annually of its nutritional value in the years following its use-by date.

If home-bottled fruits go mouldy or bubbly or if the lid unseals, the food is not safe to eat or even taste. Acid foods, such as pickles and tomatoes, will eventually interact with the metal of the tin. Food in cans that show signs of rust should not be eaten.

Preserving fruit

The overflow method

The fruit is completely cooked before being put into sterilised jars and sealed. Fast work is essential so that the jar is sealed while still very hot.

- Make a light sugar or honey syrup and bring to the boil.

- Add prepared fruit and cook until tender.

- Sterilise jars and seals with boiling water.

- Fill one jar at a time using a sterilised spoon or jug.

- Work any air bubbles out of the jar with a sterilised knife.

- Top up the jar — to the point of overflowing — with boiling syrup.

- Wipe the rim with a sterilised cloth.

- Place a sterilised lid in place and screw the metal band down tightly.

- Leave to cool. Do not retighten the metal band.

As the bottled fruit cools, the lid will compress, indicating an air-tight seal has been achieved.

The water-bath method

- Place cloth or wood rack in the bottom of a large pan with enough water to cover the jars by at least 25 mm.

- Heat the water bath to nearly boiling.

- Pack the prepared raw fruit into jars and cover with boiling syrup or water.

- Place seals on jars and screw lids on firmly.

- Place the jars in the water bath.

- Bring the water to the boil as quickly as possible. (Boil for a set time — pears 35 minutes, apples 15 minutes, stone fruit 25 minutes, tomatoes 40 minutes.)

- Top up water level to keep it above jars if necessary.

Note: It is possible to preserve non-acid vegetables by the water-bath method but this is not recommended unless they are pickled, with vinegar acting as an added preservative. (Tomatoes, though thought of as a vegetable, are an acid fruit and are therefore safe to preserve.) It is much safer and easier to deep-freeze meat and vegetables.

Hydroponics

Hydroponics is the growing of plants in water rather than soil. Nutrition — chemical or natural — is carried in the water. Some people claim that hydroponic produce fed with natural substances is organic. Others argue that growing plants in water is not in harmony with natural ecosystems ... which leads us to 'organics'.

Organics

Organics is easier to define in theory than in practice. The meaning of 'organics' or organic agriculture in an eco context is quite distinct from the scientific definition of 'organic', meaning simply 'carbon based'. For marketing purposes anybody can call their produce organic, eco friendly or green, but to be credible they need certification. However, even organic certification varies, with some agencies being more rigorous than others.

All have a code of practice, defining allowable practices, substances and so on. However, some also adhere to a 'holistic' philosophy where, as far as possible, the farm forms an integrated, self-contained unit, with diverse planting of crops and trees, and livestock that are able to perform all aspects of their innate behaviour.

For example, in organic egg production, a certification agency whose emphasis is practical may require that hens be fed with organic mix, treated with natural remedies and be able to range freely in a hen house or fixed yard.

An agency whose emphasis is philosophical as well as practical may also require that the poultry have free access to diverse, well-vegetated terrain through moveable housing or rotational ranging, and that roosters be part of the flock.

~ *International certification* For export purposes, international certification is needed. There are a small number of international organic certification agencies which adhere strongly to organic principles and standards. Those most frequently used in New Zealand are IFOAM (International Federation of Organic Agriculture), and ISO 65 (the European Union import standard requirement).

~ *New Zealand certification: Demeter, Bio-Gro and AgriQuality* In New Zealand, there has recently been progress in forming a national, government-sponsored organic standard, which aims to be at least equal to the international standard required for export (IFOAM).

New Zealand currently has three organic certification agencies that provide licensing for organic growers: Demeter, Bio-Gro and AgriQuality.

The Demeter trademark was created in Germany in 1928 and has been adopted in New Zealand by the biodynamic movement based on the Rudolf Steiner philosophy. It is a small organisation with challenging standards and a strong focus on the philosophy of organics.

To gain certification, properties need to be audited for at least three years to ensure that the land is (virtually) free of pesticides and fertiliser residue. Parallel production where inorganic and organic products can be grown on the same property is accepted only as a transitional stage.

Because of its small size Demeter has not gained ISO 65 registration but is a member of IFOAM.

Bio-Gro started in 1984 with a group of people who were involved in the organic movement, either in the Soil and Health organisation, or the biodynamic movement. It grew quickly from a small non-profit organisation to a professional, internationally recognised body. Like Demeter, it emphasises standards and philosophy and accepts parallel production as a transitional stage only. Properties are audited for three years before certification. It is ISO 65 approved and a member of IFOAM.

AgriQuality has grown out of the Ministry of Agriculture and Fisheries. In 1998 it became a state-owned enterprise, with organic certification just one branch of its work. AgriQuality emphasises standard compliance and methods rather than philosophy. It has the option of reducing the audit period to one year, dependent on the history of land use. AgriQuality allows parallel production indefinitely. AgriQuality has ISO 65 approval.

~ *Buying organic produce*   Organic produce is a growing trade but there are some problems with authenticity, quality, cost, range and availability. Organic fruit and vegetables often lack visual perfection and uniformity. Because of the intensive labour costs involved in organic production, the price of produce is generally (although not always) higher than non-organic produce. Supermarkets sometimes have a small organic section but in terms of display, levels of freshness and product range, it is usually treated as the poor cousin of the mainstream fruit and vegetable section.

Increasingly, supermarkets are carrying organic milk, bread, eggs, cereals, nuts, pastas and rices, and some stores dabble in organic meat. Specialist organic butcheries, produce outlets and health food shops often establish a wide and loyal customer base, even though the product range can be small.

Some organics customers prefer to buy produce direct from the grower or farmer. This can be time-consuming, so shared 'community' systems have evolved. Typically, a box of seasonal organic fruit and vegetables is provided for a set price once a week. Many of these schemes run on a voluntary basis and are short-lived. However, there are a number of commercial schemes running throughout the country — some with on-line ordering — which offer regular home delivery on a more formal business basis.

Despite the drawbacks, organic production is gathering strength. As organic produce grows in popularity, turnover will be quicker, produce will be fresher and the cost lower.

FISH FOR DINNER

Fish farming, or aquaculture, is the fastest-growing sector in the world food economy but fish farming, in particular the sea cage farming of finfish, has outstripped adequate environmental safeguards and is proving incompatible with the sustainability of wild fisheries.

The New Zealand fish-farming industry is a growth industry and concerns over its impact on the environment and coastal ecology are now being voiced and addressed here. One major New Zealand salmon farmer has already experimented with genetic modification of fish but pulled back from further experimentation in the face of adverse public opinion.

Shellfish farming is considered relatively benign compared with intensive fish farming, but both have potential to radically alter the coastal environment and change natural coastal processes. This can involve the build-up of shell and waste material below farms, the loss of natural character and amenity value, adverse effects on water quality, coastal and marine plants and animals and the exclusion of other potential uses from marine farm areas (such as water skiing and boating).

In New Zealand, the government imposed a two-year moratorium (expires November 2003) on new aquaculture activities in coastal marine areas to give regional councils time to develop provisions in their Regional Coastal Plans for zones where aquaculture will be either undertaken with a coastal permit or prohibited.

Wild ocean fish and shellfish are a good source of organic food but the overfishing of certain species, if not adequately monitored and controlled, can lead to serious, if not irreversible, damage to fish stocks as demonstrated in our crayfish, paua, snapper and orange roughy fisheries.

In Europe, the Mediterranean, North America and Asia, the response to overfishing of wild fish stocks has been to develop intensive industrial-scale aquaculture, but this has quickly become synonymous with pollution and destruction of the coastal marine environment.

The five fundamental flaws of finfish farming are:

➤ WASTES: Untreated fish faeces are typically discharged directly into the sea. This untreated nutrient-rich waste is a potential trigger for toxic algal

blooms (which poison and shut down shellfish farms), and eutrophication,
the dying-off of marine organisms in inland waterways through lack of
oxygen.

➤ MASS ESCAPES: Escaped fish have the potential to spread infectious
diseases to wild populations, and through interbreeding, hybridising and
competing with wild fish, of displacing and depleting natural fish stocks.

➤ DISEASES AND PARASITES: New infectious and parasitic diseases are
appearing all the time. As with battery chicken farming, disease is a
function of overstocking, which is itself a function of farm economics.
There is an established link between parasitic and infectious diseases in
farmed fish and the destruction of wild fish populations. The most
common response to disease and parasitic infestation is control by
antibiotic and other chemical intervention.

➤ CHEMICALS: Used to maintain fish health and (in salmon) to impart a
desirable colour to fish flesh, chemical treatments of farmed fish
adversely affect other non-target marine organisms. The phenomenon of
'bioaccumulation' — the accumulation beneath fish farms and in fish
themselves of a wide range of toxic organochlorines and heavy metals,
which accumulate through fish feed — is also a concern.

➤ FEED/FOOD: Intensive fish farming depends on a fast-diminishing supply
of wild fish to provide feed stock in the form of fish meal and fish oil. The
production of one tonne of farmed salmon requires the capture and
conversion of three tonnes of wild fish (with farming other sea fish this
factor rises to five tonnes). The serious imbalance this causes to wild fish
stocks, many of them small or deep-sea fish that would otherwise not be
targeted, makes carnivorous finfish farming unsustainable. The fact that
the world's oceans cannot continue to supply the food needed to farm
fish in this way is expected to collapse the world marine aquaculture
industry in a matter of years. In New Zealand, fish farming is not yet a big
enough industry to heavily impact on wild fish stocks, but our oceans are
already being fished to supply feedstock for northern hemisphere fish
farmers.

In New Zealand there are ocean farms and land-based fish farms. Some
fish are farmed conventionally, others organically, and there are farms where
the utmost care is taken to preserve the ecology of the local environment.

The alternative to farmed fish is store-bought wild fish, or catching your
own, but be aware there is a recognised health risk associated with the build-
up of heavy metal and pesticide contamination in all marine fisheries. Health

experts advise that the smaller, younger and faster-growing fish is less likely to carry reserves of these contaminants.

A 'good fish' for dinner is:

➤ fast-growing
➤ abundant
➤ sensibly managed.

Good fishing practice causes:

➤ minimal bycatch (other species caught but not wanted, and therefore dumped)
➤ minimal damage to the ecology (trawl nets can cause massive damage to the sea floor)
➤ minimal pollution in a farm environment.

TOP TIP FOR AN ECO-FRIENDLY DIET

✓ Source seasonal, organic food produced locally or grown in the backyard.

Chapter 14

Gardening

ORGANIC GARDENING

One solution to the high cost of organic produce is to grow your own. Organic gardening can range from a few herbs grown on the window sill to a certificated commercial operation. An ideal site for an organic garden is sunny, sheltered, well drained, flat or north facing and free from competing root systems of trees and hedges. Community gardens can provide plots for lease — there are presently around 16 community gardens throughout the country run on council land, and many more on private property. However, the leases are not always renewable and as once-idle land becomes more valuable, well-established community gardens sometimes have to be disbanded.

CONTAINER GARDENS

Most vegetable crops and small fruit trees can be grown in containers.

The versatility of container gardens makes them ideal for apartments, city sections and transient lifestyles. But they are vulnerable to extremes of temperature and moisture level, and the depletion of soil nutrients. As with all plants growing under unnatural conditions, they are prone to infestation and disease.

The larger the container, the less care is needed in watering and feeding. Unglazed pottery will breathe more easily than glazed pottery or plastic. Pots need good drainage holes and a tray underneath for water.

Container gardens need a semi-protected position out of the full force of the sun and wind. Once positioned, the plants orientate themselves towards the sun so it is best not to move them unnecessarily.

GARDENING OUTSIDE

Conventional beds

The conventional method of preparing a garden bed is to break up the soil to a spade's depth, then to add a generous amount of compost until it forms a light friable mix — crumbly rather than sticky or sandy.

Raised beds

A raised bed provides better drainage and heats up more quickly in the spring than a flat bed. You can simply mound up the soil and compost to a height of 30–50 cm, or for a permanent bed, enclose the garden in a frame. When choosing a frame avoid treated timber, as it contains chromium, copper and arsenic. Durable, eco-friendly frames are difficult to find. Jarrah (Australian hardwood) railway sleepers or totara fence posts are good but are now scarce and expensive. Macrocarpa, ponga logs and manuka are locally available but have a shorter lifespan. Be aware also that slugs and slaters love to live between soil and wood. If you're innovative, concrete blocks, bricks, stones and tyres can be used.

No-dig gardens

A no-dig garden bed is a variation on the raised bed. It can be built over existing garden beds, lawns and even on hard or rocky ground.

Frame in the usual way. Lay down a thick layer of wet newspaper or cardboard, coconut fibre, natural carpet underlay or other natural porous material as a weed barrier. Ensure the weed barrier completely covers the enclosed area. It should be at least 6 mm thick to stifle weeds. For a growing base, use a rich, sterile compost. Add organic fertilisers but cover with a top layer of 10 cm of well-rotted compost or worm castings for planting. Top with mulch. Water well and allow to settle before planting.

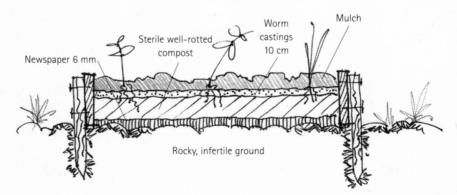

Worm castings 10 cm

Mulch

Sterile well-rotted compost

Newspaper 6 mm

Rocky, infertile ground

The no-dig garden

COMPOSTING

The secret of organic gardening is compost — the transformation of organic waste to provide fuel for new life. The easiest form of composting is to apply organic waste directly to the soil, either on top (mulching) or underneath (soil incorporation).

Mulching

Mulching suppresses weeds, conserves moisture, reduces soil erosion and protects plants from cold. Eventually the mulch breaks down, providing nutrition for plants.

Simply place garden waste — grass clippings, leaves, straw, sawdust and wood chips — around plants, trees and shrubs. Leave a few centimetres around the trunks of trees mulch free, so the trunk can breathe. Pressing mulch against the trunk can encourage fungal decay.

Woody mulches are slow to break down and in the process deplete the soil of nitrogen, leaving the plants they are meant to nourish stunted and yellowed. Pine mulch acts as a natural pesticide.

The solution is to mix woody material with high-nitrogen material such as green, leafy mulch. The green mulch will be exhausted more quickly than the wood so will need replenishing occasionally.

Mulching doesn't generate the heat needed to destroy seeds and disease so avoid diseased plants, weeds or grasses that have gone to seed, or cuttings and tubers. Also avoid kitchen waste.

Soil incorporation

Organic material buried deep in the soil is a safe way of composting pungent waste (meat, fish, vegetable and fruit scraps) but because of the absence of air, some nutrients will be lost. Take care that meat and fish scraps are not buried near waterways. By preference feed these scraps to animals or make into liquid manure.

A composting heap

Mulching and soil incorporation are easy composting methods. However, to produce fast, sterile compost requires knowledge, skill and experience.

An ideal compost is sterile, sweet smelling, rich and crumbly, like black, gold nuggets. To effect this alchemy you first need to reduce the process to its base elements.

Compost needs air, water, microbes, insects, nitrogen and carbon. Compost piles trap heat generated by the activity of billions of micro-organisms. Bacteria are the first, most numerous and most effective decomposers on the

scene. Fungi and protozoa soon join the bacteria and later, centipedes, milli-
pedes, beetles and worms complete the composting process.

An open-air environment provides airborne oxygen, nitrogen and water;
open ground provides the microbes and insects; and organic material provides
nitrogen and carbon in solid form. Applying heat accelerates and purifies the
composting process.

The secret is to allow these elements to come together in roughly the
correct proportions. Too much water and the compost turns to slime and its
goodness leaches away, too little air and the compost suffocates.

~ *Open-air heaps*   A pile is all that is necessary to make compost but a
contained heap is tidier. A simple open-air container can be made of wire
netting, old fencing, wooden pallets, or wood and wire. Open-air heaps drain
freely and are easy to aerate but may attract vermin and flies. Burying fresh
scraps deep in the heap limits attempted scavenging.

~ *Closed compost bins*   Closed bins are difficult to aerate. Frequent turning
and the inclusion of artificial air funnels (such as perforated piping) into the
heap can help maximise aeration. Wire netting on the bottom of the bin will
repel rats and mice without excluding worms. Commercially manufactured
compost tumblers provide a convenient means to turn and aerate compost
and pest-free decomposition, but prevent direct contact with the ground.

~ *Materials*   Anything organic can be composted: nature has no favourites
but it is better to avoid meat, fat, fish, milk and cereals. Shun also seed heads,
cuttings or tubers and diseased plants. It is possible to include these but only
if a temperature of at least 75°C is achieved to destroy seeds and disease.
Otherwise, most kitchen scraps and garden waste can be composted; also hair
clippings, seaweed (rinse excess salt off first) and animal manure (but not
from meat eaters or animals that have been dosed or wormed).

Chopping or shredding garden debris provides more surface area for
microbes to feed on, which helps it decompose faster.

~ *Size*   A compost pile 1–2 metres square is the optimum size for hot, fast
composting. Smaller piles cool off too quickly to generate enough heat,
because they have too high a proportion of material exposed to the air; larger
piles don't allow enough air to reach the micro-organisms at the centre of the
heap.

~ *Layering*   To achieve the best nitrogen/carbon balance, layer materials two
parts brown (high carbon) to one part green (high nitrogen).

➤ For microbes — add thin layers of dry leaves every 20–30 cm.

➤ For insects — loosen soil beneath the heap.

➤ For worms — loosen the soil beneath the heap. Add a handful from the worm farm (see page 169) in the compost cooling stages.

Rotating barrels will need added earth and worms to compensate for the compost's lack of contact with the soil.

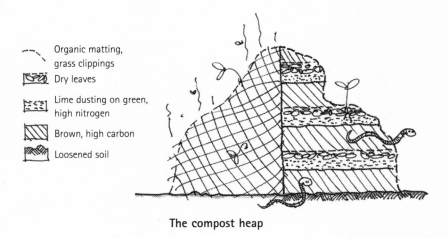

Organic matting, grass clippings

Dry leaves

Lime dusting on green, high nitrogen

Brown, high carbon

Loosened soil

The compost heap

~ *Aeration*   Turn four to seven days after the heat has dissipated, for aeration. You may need several heaps to effect a rotating system.

~ *Moisture*   The compost should be just slightly damp — like a wrung-out sponge. If it is too wet the micro-organisms will not thrive and the nutrition will leach away. Protection from the rain is preferable. Choose sheltered situations for open systems such as under trees or on the sheltered side of the garden shed. Organic matting or grass clippings thrown on top can provide some protection from the weather. If the heap is too wet, add brown matter, if too dry, add green.

~ *Temperature*   The most efficient decomposing bacteria thrive in temp-eratures between 55 and 80°C. The hotter the pile, the faster the composting. If you achieve a good balance of carbon to nitrogen, use shredded material and maintain adequate moisture and aeration, the temperature will rise steadily over several days. Fresh grass clippings on top will turn up the heat. The hottest part is always in the centre so when turning the heap, throw the outer layer into the centre.

THE EFFECT OF DIFFERENT ELEMENTS IN COMPOST

Element	Effect	Deficiency	Natural sources
Nitrogen	Contains proteins Stimulates green growth	Yellowing of leaves, spindly, or stunted growth, older leaves drop. Plants flower or mature early	Grass clippings, green vegetables, bird manure, fish, blood and bone, legumes (nitrogen-fixing plants)
Phosphorus	Stimulates root growth and seed maturation	Purple leaves, brittle roots and skinny stems, late fruit set	Comfrey, seaweed, horse manure, blood and bone
Potassium	Promotes plant vitality and health	Leaf margins brown, scorched, cupped downward. Leaf spots appear: dark centres, yellow edges Poor root growth	Wood ash, comfrey, horse manure, seaweed
Calcium	Cell walls, root development, leaf growth	Deformed leaves and branches, weak stems and roots	Dandelion, lucerne, comfrey, horse manure, seaweed, blood and bone
Magnesium	Chlorophyll and green leaf development	Margins yellow or blotched. Leaves yellow, red, purple (chlorosis)	Grass clippings, seaweed

~ *Timing*   It is possible under ideal conditions in the New Zealand climate to effect a transformation in six to 10 weeks. Compost should still be working when placed on the garden.

LIQUID MANURES

Compost will supply most garden needs but for a quick fix, apply liquid manure. Liquid manure is obtained by soaking source material in water. The nutrients are released into the water for easy absorption by plants. Here are three recipes: two from the land — one plant-based, one animal-based — and one from the sea.

Element	Effect	Deficiency	Natural sources
Sulphur	Lowers pH, in small amounts is stimulant for microbial life	Leaves yellowish, pale. Poor spindly plants	Cabbage leaves
Boron	Assists transport of sugars, pollen formation and cell wall growth	Leaves die or distort. Stems split (cabbages) or crack (celery)	Beetroot leaves, horse manure, compost, seaweed
Copper	Enzyme activator	Leaves wilt then die. Undersized onions, peas in pod match-head size	Yarrow, dandelion, chick weed, horse manure, untreated sawdust, seaweed
Iron	Catalyst to chlorophyll formation	Interveinal leaf yellowing (chlorosis)	Dandelion, horse manure, spinach, seaweed
Zinc	Essential to growth-control hormones	Small leaves, stems shortened, growth retarded (mainly beans and sweet corn)	Horse manure, corn stalks, untreated sawdust, seaweed
Oxygen	Stimulates microbial activity, allows free root growth	Overall poor growth	Humus, pear moss, worms, tillage

~ *Liquid plant manure (or tea)* Place the harvested plant material (comfrey is ideal) in a bucket and cover with water. Put a lid on the bucket and leave the tea to brew. After several days you will have a weak but useful brew that can be used undiluted. The brew can be left to stew for as long as you like — or as long as your nose can stand it — provided you stir it regularly to keep it from going stagnant. After two to four weeks the brew will be noticeably stronger and will need to be diluted to the colour of weak tea before use. Use it as a plant food (diluted 1:10 with water) every two weeks, or as an occasional foliar spray (diluted 1:20). Dump the material waste in the compost heap.

~ *Liquid animal manure* Half-fill a sack with manure from organically raised animals or birds and suspend it in water in a large container. After two weeks, ____

dilute the brew 50:50 and use it on the garden. Throw the soggy manure on
the compost heap.

~ *Liquid seaweed manure* Collect seaweed from an ocean beach after a
storm. The large, rubbery sort is best. Rinse in fresh water or leave in the rain
to remove most of the salt. Suspend in a sack in a container for several weeks.
Dilute the resulting brew 50:50 with fresh water and apply to crops. Dig the
seaweed into the garden. This brew, like the nettle and comfrey brew, is rich
in potash and is good for potatoes and tomatoes.

Other fertilisers

Organic compost and liquid manure are also available commercially. But
check their organic credentials first. Some 'organic' composts simply signify
they are 'carbon based' (they meet a scientific definition of the word 'organic'
but are not certified by any of the recognised organic authorities) and may
consist of plant or animal material which contains pesticides.

Commercial mixes have usually gone through a very hot composting
process to be completely seed and weed free. This creates nitrogen losses and
so most commercial composts are low on nitrogen. Unless some form of nitrogen
is added, they play more a soil-conditioning role than a fertility-boosting one.

Other materials commonly used in compost, dug into the soil or applied
as a side dressing are listed below. Composting is the safest method, as plants
can be 'burnt' by direct application. If the materials are dug into the soil,
allow several weeks before planting. If applying as a side dressing keep 30 cm
away from the plants.

~ *Blood and bone* Blood and bone — the dried and powdered waste from
meat processing plants — is an easy source of rich, slow-releasing manure for
organic gardeners.

~ *Ash* Ash from untreated timber is a valuable source of potash, although
coal ash and ash from treated timber are very toxic.

~ *Seaweed* Seaweed can be applied as side mulch. Some seaweeds contain
more nitrogen and potassium than animal manures. They are free from plant
disease and seeds, are a source of natural antibiotics and provide a good conditioner for sandy soils. Rinse or leave in the rain first to remove excess salt.

~ *Lime* Lime is a naturally occurring mineral which sweetens the soil and
reduces acidity. Acidity (pH) ranges from 1 (very acid) to 14 (very alkaline). The
best range for plants is from 5.5. to 7.5. Within this range, plants vary in their

pH preferences. Soil test kits can be purchased quite cheaply. To correct a soil that is too low in acidity, add flowers of sulphur.

CHOOSING CROPS

In selecting crops to grow, position, sunlight, moisture, nourishment and timing are critical. Companion planting — choosing plants that enhance and protect others — also needs consideration. The preferences and needs of some popular crops are indicated in the table on the next three pages.

Diverse planting provides food and cover for a variety of living things, including beneficial insects, which help the garden's ecosystem. Crop rotation helps maintain a healthy balance of nutrients in the soil and reduces the risk of disease. Rotate the following crop families, preferably on a two- to three-year cycle.

CROP ROTATION

Rotate the following crop families on a two- to three-year cycle

Legumes and pod	Alliums	Brassicas	Solanaceous, root, and tuberous crops
Beans, peas. Legumes fix nitrogen in the ground so are good also as a green crop	Onions, leeks, garlic	Cauliflower, cabbage, brussels sprouts, broccoli, kohlrabi, turnips, radishes, bok choy	Peppers, tomatoes, eggplant, potatoes, kumara, celery, beets, carrots, parsnips

If space is limited, think about plant yield. One corn plant produces just one good cob, with maybe a small secondary cob, but a cherry tomato vine bears fruit by the hundred.

If time is limited, you may choose permanent or semi-permanent beds of asparagus, globe artichokes or strawberries, or crops that need little attention like broccoli, garlic and silverbeet.

PLANT HEALTH: DEALING WITH DISEASES AND PESTS

Happy plants are healthy plants. If you practise good organic gardening keeping in mind each crop's preferences and needs, choose disease-resistant varieties and practise crop rotation and companion planting, disease and infestation will be rare.

CROP GUIDE

Crop	Plant	Harvest	Likes	Dislikes	Companions	Effort
Asparagus	Spring to early summer	Early spring to early summer	Permanent spot, seaweed	Weeds	Calendula, basil, parsley, tomatoes	Easy
Basil	Spring to early summer	Summer to autumn	Sun	Crowding	Tomatoes	Easy
Beans	Spring to early summer	Summer	Sun, frequent picking	Shade	Marigolds, cabbage, carrots, cauliflower	Easy
Broccoli	Summer	Autumn to winter	Rich soil, staking, frequent picking	When young, white butterfly	Celery, rosemary, sage, thyme	Moderate
Cabbage	Spring to autumn	All year but best as winter crop	Rich soil	White butterfly (when young), water logging, slugs		Moderate
Carrot	Spring to autumn	All year	Deeply dug, sandy soil	Carrot fly, compacted ground	Leeks, tomatoes, lettuce	Moderate
Cauliflower	Spring to autumn	All year but best as winter crop	Very rich soil	White butterfly (when young), water logging, slugs	Celery, rosemary, sage, thyme, onion	Moderate

160

Crop	Plant	Harvest	Likes	Dislikes	Companions	Effort
Cucumber	Spring to early summer	Summer, autumn	Compost, sun, support, space	Shade, drying out	Zinnia, beans, carrots, corn	Easy
Garlic	Shortest day traditionally but early autumn OK	Longest day or when leaves dry at the tips	Anything	Water logging	Good friend to other plants	Easy
Leeks	Spring sowing, early summer for seedlings	Autumn and winter	Rich soil, long season		Celery, carrots, onions	Easy
Lettuce	Spring to autumn	All year	Compost	Water logging, scorching, slugs	Carrots, cucumber, strawberries	Easy
Mesclun	Spring to autumn	Spring to autumn	Frequent picking	Water logging, scorching, slugs	Carrots, cucumber, strawberry	Easy
Onions	Spring	Mid to late summer when the leaves dry off	Good drainage	Drying out, water logging, thrips if dry	Cauliflower, cabbage, carrots, lettuce	Moderate
Parsley	Spring to autumn	Summer to winter	Sun	Over-picking		Easy
Peas	Spring	Summer	Support, frequent picking	Crowding, shade	Beans, carrots, corn, tomatoes	Easy
Pumpkin	Late spring, early summer	Late autumn when the stalks dry off	Compost, space, water	Starvation/poor soil	Corn	Easy

Crop	Plant	Harvest	Likes	Dislikes	Companions	Effort
Potatoes	After last frost, late winter	Early spring to late summer	Food, air, space, hoeing up	Cramped conditions, damp, blight, exposed tubers	Garlic, beans, cabbage, cauliflower, corn, peas	Moderate to hard
Silverbeet	Spring to late summer	All year but static in mid-winter	Anything		Strawberries	Easy
Strawberries	Autumn	Spring to summer	Rich soil, permanent bed	Slugs, birds, ants	Marigold, beans, spinach	Moderate
Sweet corn	Spring to mid-summer	Summer	Rich soil, grown in clumps for support	Drying out	Beans, cucumber, zucchini, peas, pumpkin	Easy
Tomatoes	Spring to summer	Summer to autumn	Rich food, fresh ground, support, sun	Water logging, drying out, birds, slugs, damp, crowding, blight	Marigold, asparagus, basil, carrots, chives, garlic, onions	Moderate to hard
Zucchini	Spring to summer	Summer to autumn	Rich soil, compost, sun, space, water	Damp, crowding	Tomatoes	Easy

If a problem arises it can often be nipped in the bud by removing and burning diseased leaves and squashing harmful insects — this discourages their relatives from sticking around (not recommended for eco-sentimentalists).

You can also use natural predators to eliminate unwanted insects.

Other specialised biological controls are available commercially.

COMMON BIOLOGICAL CONTROLS

Predator	Prey
Ladybird	scales, thrips, mites, aphids
Praying mantis	eggs, scales, grasshoppers, moths, aphids, beetles, ants, grubs

To catch slugs and snails, provide attractive places for them to congregate, for example, lay a plank or piece of heavy sack on the earth, or half-bury a container with a little beer at the bottom in the garden (even slugs like a good night out).

However, sometimes, despite the best care in the world, disease strikes and you do need to use remedies.

Chemical pesticides have many adverse side effects: they kill beneficent soil life and encourage the evolution of resistant pests. Residues from yesterday's 'safe' pesticides, such as DDT, cause ongoing health problems.

Some 'natural' remedies commonly used by home gardeners in the past are also harmful. Tar oil and petroleum leave residues of sulphur and highly poisonous phenols; copper, lead arsenate, mercury and arsenic fungicides deposit heavy metals in the soil.

Organic sprays
Organic sprays and applications include the following.

~ *Water* A heavy stream of water won't necessarily kill but it will dislodge many small insects. Use to discourage aphids, white butterfly, caterpillar and codlin moth.

~ *Liquid seaweed* Spray at the first sign of disease. Frequent, light applications over a number of years are the most effective. Use on fungi (tomato blight, grey mould on strawberries) and nematodes.

~ *Milk*   Spray a 50:50 milk and water solution to control mildew on cucumber, zucchini, peas and pumpkin.

~ *Pyrethrum*   Frequent spraying is necessary as it is rapidly broken down by light. Use against aphids, leafhoppers, codlin moth, slugs, ants and woolly aphids. It is toxic to beneficial insects such as ladybugs and wasps as well, so use with caution.

~ *Garlic and onion sprays*   Soak 75 grams of garlic bulbs in 2 tablespoons of mineral oil for 24 hours. Later add a half-litre of water in which 10 grams of soft soap has been dissolved. Strain and store. To use, dilute 1:20 with fresh water. Spray for onion flies, slugs, moth, caterpillars, codlin moth and pea weevils.

~ *Rock and wood ash, crushed egg shell, crushed sea shell*   These sharp, very fine particles are injurious to insects and slugs. They can be used as a spray mixed with a small amount of flour, water and soap, and sprayed onto leaves (but not ones you are about to eat) or in a protective ring around tender seedlings that are munched on by slugs and snails.

Competing weeds

Even weeds have their place in an organic garden. Weeds can break up and condition the soil, and conserve moisture and heat, but can also smother and starve crops. Moderation is the answer. Hoe in the weeds before they grow too large, or go to seed. Weed eaters, line trimmers, hot water and gas-fired weed burners are a non-chemical way of keeping tidy edges and paving. A pinch of salt will cause weeds to wither and die but it should be used sparingly to avoid salt build-up in the soil. Organic commercial weed killers are also available – some made with natural herbicides such as pine oil.

Organic seeds and seedlings

To be truly organic, you need organic stock. If you save your own seed stock it will have the added advantage of enhancing adaptation to your garden's conditions.

---

*TOP TIPS FOR ORGANIC
GARDENING*

Happy plants are healthy plants
– they like the:

✓ right time

✓ right place

✓ right climate

✓ right food

✓ right companions.

Chapter 15

Permaculture

The term permaculture (permanent culture) describes a farming philosophy that integrates natural flora and fauna, diverse planting, livestock, water, energy and recycling systems. Developed in the 1970s by two Australians, Bill Mollison and David Holmgren, the concept now includes social and cultural elements as well. The effective practice of permaculture entails long, thoughtful observation of nature to develop systems that benefit all life forms. General principles include:

➤ implementing the least possible change to gain the greatest possible effect, for example, a no-dig garden

➤ multiple functions for every system, for example, bees used for pollination of crops and honey for the table

➤ multiple ways of fulfilling every function, for example, recycling by using community recycling bins, worms, chickens, compost.

A fuller description of permaculture philosophies and systems are in Bill Mollison's manual (*Permaculture: A Designer's Manual*, 1988).

In earlier times, permaculture was an accepted way of life. Many households ran chickens in the backyard, which disposed of scraps, provided manure for the garden and eggs and meat for the table. An orchard out the back supplied fruit in season, nectar and pollen for a beehive and wild places in which small creatures (and children) could play and thrive.

Today, there is often a sense of *dis-integration*. Commonly, food comes from the supermarket, scraps go to the tip and childhood exploration is confined to a small screen.

However, it is still quite possible to run an integrated, eco-friendly household in the suburbs and cities. Organic gardening lends itself naturally to permaculture. Livestock add an extra dimension. The key principle is that each element contributes and gains from the whole, creating ever-expanding possibilities as more and more is encompassed.

CHICKENS

There are no restrictions on keeping roosters, hens or other poultry in rural areas but in urban areas, roosters are permitted only on properties greater than 2000 square metres (half an acre) and the number of poultry that may be kept without council consent is restricted to 12. (Half a dozen is a manageable number for most families.) Poultry housing must be weatherproof, easily cleaned and further than 2 m from a boundary and/or 10 m from a dwelling. Written application to the council can be made for exemptions from these rules.

Shelter

Chickens need a dry place to nest, shelter, scratch for food and dust their feathers for lice. Unless they are sheltered from the rain they will quickly turn an enclosed space into a putrid mud bath. Their hut need not be large but must have perches and nesting boxes. They will also require a sheltered scratching pen under trees, bamboo or other cover.

To pen chickens, use 19 mm wire netting at least 2 m high. It is best to bury it 20 cm into the ground to stop the hens scratching their way out and dogs, rats, stoats and ferrets digging their way in.

Moveable pens are sometimes used but need to be large, sheltered and readily mobile. Chickens are natural scarifiers. In no time flat, a flock of chickens will turn pasture into bare soil. To conserve pasture, they need to be moved two or three times a week.

Conversely, in line with permaculture principles, you can make good use of their scratching. A moveable pen can be used to break in new ground for a garden or orchard. A 'chicken tractor' (a pen with wheels — see Bill Mollison's manual) can fertilise half a dozen garden patches on a rotation cycle of about 18 months (three months on each patch).

Foraging

Chickens like to range freely for food, the problem being that they soon find secret nesting spots and make short work of your, and your neighbour's, garden.

Chickens mostly lay their eggs early in the day so having an enclosed area where they spend the morning and night is helpful. A hen's distinctive cackle after laying can help you locate secret nests.

It is essential to keep chickens out of gardens, as they will demolish seedbeds, young seedlings and tender leafy crops very quickly. You can fence the garden in or fence the chickens out. If you have a lot of space, keeping them somewhere infinitely attractive like an orchard, or letting them out for just a few hours each day can work.

In the city, the only solution may be to keep them penned in and to bring the greens, the grain and the water to them.

Food and water

Chickens need a handful of grain a day, supplemented with mash or scraps, greens and grit (ground up shell). In the first six months of life, when their egg-laying capacity is set, they require a high-protein diet. For organic eggs, use organic stockfeed.

Second only to pigs as waste devourers, chickens make quick work of protein food scraps that might otherwise attract vermin and flies if composted. Meat and fish are on their menu but avoid dairy products (birds don't drink milk) or eggs and chicken scraps (cannibalism) and never give them decaying or mouldy food.

Greens are essential for rich, orange egg yolks. If free ranging is not possible, bring them puha, dandelion, silverbeet, the outer leaves of cabbage and cauliflower, and slugs and snails trapped in the garden. You can also plant food in the run — coprosma, mulberry trees and passion-fruit vines provide fruit and berries — but young plants will need to be protected to grow. Comfrey planted along the fence line will provide extra greens.

Chickens must have a constant supply of fresh, clean water to produce eggs. A container, open at the front but covered on top and raised 30 cm off the ground, gives access for drinking but not paddling or falling debris. A plastic drum with one side cut out works well, especially if it is hooked up to water catchment from the hutch roof.

Health

The main health hazard for chickens is mites. Mites in the feathers are kept under control by dust baths but of more concern are the scaly mites, which build up an encrustation on the legs. The most effective way of controlling scaly mite is to keep the coop clean with clean, dry litter on the ground to absorb droppings, which is removed every few weeks for the garden. Avoid closely placed perches or perches placed directly one above another, as this allows the birds to mess the perches and spread infection. It also avoids nightly squabbles as each hen tries to gain the highest perching position!

Company

Chickens are social birds — you need at least four to form a group. Hens are healthier and happier with a mate. A rooster will foster, protect and herd his hens. (He also happens to be a requirement among some organic certifiers.) He will sort out their quarrels and avert vicious pecking regimes. Roosters like to crow around 4 am. You'll soon discover which of your neighbours is also keeping chickens, but won't hear them after the first few weeks. Your chickenless neighbours may.

Egg laying

The nest box needs to be off the ground, a comfortable size for one or two hens — it is friendlier to lay in pairs — and half-filled with clean straw. If the hens are reluctant to use the nest, try a plastic egg to start the clutch. Given sufficient perching space they generally won't mess the nest. Never leave a broken egg in the nest. It is unusual to find an egg-eating hen, it is more likely to be a rat but, to be sure, give them enough grit so the shells are strong, and give them enough food so they don't go hungry.

Hens start laying at about six months of age. Young hens will lay six eggs a week about nine months of the year. This reduces after the first year but even a very old hen will produce the odd egg. Wipe but do not wash dirty eggs as water removes their protective covering. Store at room temperature. Fresh eggs should last for about six weeks.

Stock

White, red and brown shavers are common breeds in New Zealand. Bantam hens are attractive but tend to be more feisty and higher flyers. Their eggs are very small. However, they are excellent mothers and will brood eggs from other hens.

You can purchase day-old, sexed chicks or raise your own if you have a rooster. Fertile eggs take 21 days to incubate and hens will raise their own given half a chance. In fact, broody hens can be a problem as they stop laying and virtually stop eating, even if the eggs are infertile. The only cure is to send them 'cold turkey' by removing access to eggs for several days. Confinement in an uncomfortable, draughty box hastens this process. Shavers are less inclined to go broody than bantams.

Chicken manure

Chickens provide organic manure for the garden. Their droppings are rich in potassium and nitrogen, which promote rapid leaf growth. The manure is usually mixed with litter or sawdust but can easily burn plants if applied directly to the ground. It is better composted or made into liquid manure.

> ### *Liquid chicken manure*
>
> ➤ Suspend a hessian bag half full of chicken manure in a drum.
>
> ➤ Cover with fresh water.
>
> ➤ Shake the bag occasionally.
>
> ➤ The brew will be ready for use within a fortnight.
>
> Diluted 1:5 with water, it can be used as side dressing, a foliage spray and pest control.

With some dedication and planning, chickens can play a valuable part in eco living. They are decorative, productive and great waste disposers!

WORM FARMING

A worm farm is a great way to turn organic waste into compost. Worms create superb liquid fertiliser (worm wee) and vermicast (worm castings), products that are among the best-balanced and most nutritious additives for outdoor gardens and indoor pot plants. Anyone can farm worms but they are an especially good means of reducing waste for people who live in units or high-rises (stick one on your balcony), where there isn't room for a backyard compost heap. Tiger worms are the breed best suited to New Zealand conditions.

The container

You can either build your own from recycled materials or buy one. Commercially manufactured worm farms (and a starter pack of worms) can be bought from most garden centres, or eco stores. They are also available via mail order and the Internet. For indoor use, the most convenient and self-contained systems are made from recycled plastic. If you have the space, a bigger outdoor worm farm can be easily made from recycled materials as diverse as masonry, corrugated iron, washing machine bowls, plastic barrels, 44-gallon drums (split sideways), car tyres and bathtubs (avoid treated timber). If possible, place the worm farm somewhere where it will get the sun in winter but be shaded in summer — they like a temperature of 15–25°C and slow down their activity in cooler weather.

Keep these factors in mind:

➤ Worms like a quiet, dark environment free of excessive vibration.

➤ Worms need to breathe but also need to be protected from pests — both from above and below — which might be attracted to food scraps.

➤ The farm must be kept moist and good drainage is needed, particularly if exposed to the weather.

➤ Some means of collecting the liquid fertiliser that drains from the farm is worthwhile.

The surface area of the farm is more important than its depth. A container that is shallow and has a large surface area will work better than a deep container with a small surface area. As a rough guide, a container 1 cubic metre in size (e.g. 750 mm x 750 mm x 500 mm) will support all the worms needed to munch through all the organic waste produced by a family of four.

Bedding

Start with soaked, shredded newspaper (not coloured) 10–15 cm deep. Add a few spadefuls of garden soil, leaves and finished compost, and a couple of crushed eggshells to provide the calcium needed in reproduction. Introduce the worms to their home, allow them to burrow into the bedding and leave them to settle in for a few days before feeding. Cover the bedding with matting (organic) to keep it warm and dark. The worm farm should be room temperature and moist but not wet.

Feeding

You can feed worms vegetable and fruit scraps and starchy leftovers such as bread, oatmeal and pasta. Wrap starchy food in damp newspaper to contain any mould forming. Avoid acidic fruits such as citrus, or onions, garlic, meat,

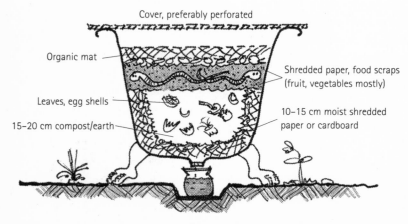

Cover, preferably perforated

Organic mat

Shredded paper, food scraps (fruit, vegetables mostly)

Leaves, egg shells

10–15 cm moist shredded paper or cardboard

15–20 cm compost/earth

The worm farm

dairy products and salty or fatty foods. Worms enjoy soaked and shredded fibrous materials such as egg cartons, cardboard and newspaper. Frequent but moderate feeding is best. As a rough guide, worms can process about their weight in scraps each day — add more food only when the first lot is partly eaten and don't let the scraps build up more than 50 mm in depth. Be careful not to feed them anything treated with pesticide — it kills them!

A worm farm should not smell unpleasant — vermicast does not support odours and is quite hygienic. The only odour a farm should have is that of fresh, unprocessed waste. An unpleasant smell indicates a problem: the worms may have died because the compost is too hot (it should not feel hot to the touch) or wet (there's a drainage problem). If the system appears to be overloaded with waste, stop feeding and wait for the worms to catch up.

Other critters

A worm farm is a living system, which means it is likely to host organisms other than compost worms, especially if it is outdoors. Most creatures (earwigs, beetles, slugs and slaters) live in the top few centimetres of the compost and help the breakdown process. They are generally harmless and if the lid is left on, will not be a problem.

The tiny white worms which often appear in the compost are not compost worms, but a related earthworm that thrives on acidic material. Don't deter these, as they help maintain the right pH balance for other worms.

If at any stage you want to 'cleanse' the system of freeloaders, cover the compost with 10 cm of light earth and let it rest for a week. As a last resort, a persistent pest problem can be fixed with a sprinkling of agricultural lime.

Harvesting

As the worms multiply, small whitish egg sacs or cocoons will become visible. This is a sign the worm farm is working well. The liquid that drains from the bottom, diluted 50:50 with water, provides a potent liquid fertiliser.

Commercial worm farms supply instructions on how and when to harvest vermicast. In a home-made worm farm, you can harvest the castings once the bedding is no longer identifiable. In a new system this might take some months, but castings can be regularly removed as long as enough is left for bedding. If your container is big enough the easiest method is to feed at one end of the container only, for about two weeks. Most worms will migrate to the food end, allowing you to remove castings from the other end.

If your container is too small for that to work, just lift out the top 150 mm of material and put it aside. Remove a layer of castings for your garden, and replace the top layer.

Another method involves starting a new farm in a second container. Like most primary producers, worm farmers have a tendency to want to expand! Move aside the fresh food scraps in the first container and remove the cooled 'live castings' for use as bedding in the second container. These castings will contain enough worms and eggs to 'seed' the new farm. Replace the food waste in the retired farm and cover it with a layer of clean waste material (grass or shredded paper). After some weeks the worms will have eaten all the remaining waste and will be near the top looking for more. Take off the top layer containing the worms and put it in your second farm to boost the population. What's left is your vermicast harvest.

The pH of finished vermicast is neutral, and it commands a premium as a plant-bedding medium and as a side dressing for growing plants. Use it to boost the health of the plants in your own garden, or give it to someone with green fingers.

BEES

Bees provide pollination for crops and honey for the table. You need knowledge, equipment, protective clothing and a spot not too close to neighbours. Both amateur and professional hives need to be registered with the Ministry of Agriculture and Fisheries (MAF). This is a free service and hives may be inspected for disease from time to time. Local councils can remove hives that are causing nuisance or injury.

Lifestyle

Bees form complex, highly organised societies. Individuals are bred for clearly differentiated roles — each colony has one queen, a small number of drones (males) and many workers. The queen provides the hive with eggs. The workers feed and nurse the young (and in doing so determine which shall belong to each social grouping) and collect and store honey and pollen. The drones are indolent layabouts tolerated for one reason only — reproduction.

In spring, when the queen increases her egg laying and the hive expands, the nurse bees nurture new queen cells and as soon as one hatches, the old queen leaves, taking most of the mature workers with her. The swarming bees circle the old queen in a dense cluster before settling somewhere — usually on the branch of a tree, where they hang until bee scouts find a new and suitable home. A swarm of bees in flight often creates alarm among bystanders, but this is needless because bees are invariably placid and will not sting when swarming.

Meanwhile, at the old hive, the young queen flies high to mate just once with a single drone. This sets her egg-laying capacity for life. After this, the drones are dispensable but are tolerated until honey supplies become short at the end of the summer, when they are unceremoniously biffed from the hive and barred from returning. They die overnight.

Managing bees

The beekeeper controls the bees' natural tendency to swarm by regularly inspecting hives, removing developing queen cells, and replacing worn-out queens every second year with a new, young, cultivated queen. The queen is confined during the spring breeding season to the lower brood boxes by a wire excluder. The worker bees, being smaller than the queen, pass through the excluder to store honey in the honey supers above the brood boxes.

The beekeeper will need several supers full of prepared frames to store honey, as well as gloves, veil and a 'smoker' to calm the bees. The smoke mimics a forest fire, causing aggressive bees to turn back into the hive to gorge in readiness for sudden departure.

Bee strains vary in their temperament and industriousness, which affect ease of handling. It pays to start with a queen from known stock rather than chance a wild swarm.

The harvest

Bees will improve the set of fruit in your orchard and pollinate garden flowers for miles around. But the real reward is honey. Honey removal and extraction follows the main honey flow, which follows the flowering of the predominant crop. You can use an extractor to spin the honey from the frames before reinserting them for the bees to fill once more (spinning doesn't work for thick honeys such as manuka) or you can scrape the wax and honey from the frame, then return the scraped foundation to the hive for the bees to rebuild. Honey sections — the small rectangular frames designed to contain comb honey — can be used at the height of the season to produce comb honey.

If bee pollination is your main concern, local beekeepers will place hives on your property for a fee.

Disease

Unfortunately, disease is now a nationwide concern with the arrival of the varroa mite in mid-2000. It is presently confined to the North Island but may well cross the Strait and become a nationwide pest. Symptoms include disfigured adult bees with deformed legs and wings, mite-infested capped drone brood, discarded larvae and pupae, spotty brood pattern, reddish brown spots on white pupae and cells uncapped and destroyed. Foul brood symptoms are similar but have an unpleasant odour as well. Disease should be reported immediately to MAF.

Bees are enjoyable and benefit fruit trees, shrubs, flower beds and vegetable gardens but require investment, dedication and skill. In particular, backyard beekeepers must be prepared to inspect their hives no less than once every 10 days during the period when hives are likely to be creating queen cells — usually in October–November. To miss an inspection risks having a hive swarm just at the time when it should be building up strength for honey gathering.

NATIVE PLANTS, BIRDS AND SMALL CREATURES

Nearly 80% of native plants are unique to New Zealand; some are facing extinction. If possible, set aside wild areas on your property where native plants, birds and other small creatures can thrive.

Regrowth occurs in several phases, with one generation of plants providing nursery conditions before being superseded by the next. Pioneer plants — hardy natives that will withstand varying conditions — are the first colonisers. Common pioneers include toetoe, carex, flax, karamu, houhere (lacebark), mahoe and manuka. The sheltered conditions and filtered sunlight provided by their canopy provides a perfect nursery for larger broadleaf trees such as rata and rewarewa. These in turn overtake the pioneer plants and the canopy closes over further, allowing shade-loving ferns, palms, mosses, algae and fungi to proliferate on the forest floor. This provides rich pickings for the birds that bring seeds from local forests. Eventually slow-growing trees arrive and create a high but not impenetrable canopy, letting through just enough light to support life below.

Clearing

Occasionally the existing scrub — perhaps gorse or wattle — can provide protection for hardy, shade-tolerant pioneer plants such as karamu, houhere and mahoe, and prevent the invasion of noxious weeds. As the pioneers grow, the scrub is starved of light and subsides. Old gorse, which is dry and sparse with open spaces at its base, provides good nursery conditions for other plants, but holes or rows will need to be cut in young green gorse to give pioneer plants the room to develop.

New Zealand Ecological Restoration Network (NZERN)

NZERN is a non-profit, community-driven, membership-based organisation dedicated to sharing knowledge and experience of ecological restoration. It provides information about community initiatives and groups, local plant selection and guidelines and local resources. Check it out at www.bush.org.nz

---

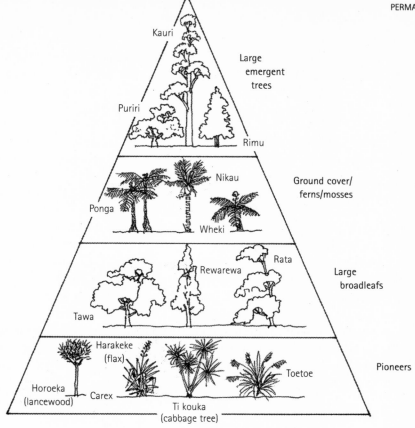

Kauri

Large
emergent
trees

Puriri

Rimu

Nikau

Ground cover/
ferns/mosses

Ponga

Wheki

Rata

Rewarewa

Large
broadleafs

Tawa

Harakeke
(flax)

Toetoe

Pioneers

Horoeka
(lancewood)   Carex

Ti kouka
(cabbage tree)

Order of arrival

Often, introduced weeds will completely suppress regeneration and the only solution is to clear the ground before planting.

Noxious weeds — those which suppress the regeneration of native plants — usually take a few decades to gain a foothold in a new land. Seventy-five percent of our noxious weeds are ornamental plants that have escaped from residential gardens, slowly gathered strength, and turned a tenuous foothold into a stranglehold. Recent examples are agapanthus and the Mexican daisy. Be wary of what you plant: there is a brief opportunity to contain the pest between the recognition of the potential danger and the point of no return. Mature trees and plants can often survive the invasion of noxious weeds but new growth can be completely suppressed. Without new growth, the lifespan of invaded ecosystems is limited.

In clearing the ground of noxious weeds, always target outliers — isolated plants colonising fresh ground — before tackling the main clump.

Local councils provide 'Pest Fact Sheets' explaining effective means of identification and removal. Top of the hate list are wandering Jew, wild ginger, old man's beard and asparagus fern.

You may also need to cull the local, introduced wildlife, such as possums, ferrets and stoats. Traps are on the market. Check with your local council or DOC for the most effective pest-control strategy in your area.

Planting

First plant or sow the small, hardy 'pioneer' native plants that provide nursery conditions for larger trees. Because local conditions vary, note successful local species or check with your council for a planting guide. It is best to source local seed — native plants have natural distribution areas and even within species there are subtle, local genetic differences. The 'eco-sourced' label in garden centres specialises in local seed.

Common planting plans are as follows.

~ *Stream banks*   Start with small pioneer plants — toetoe (not the introduced pampas grass), ti (cabbage tree) and carex (native sedge), planting right down to the water's edge. This helps stabilise the stream banks. Once established, plant larger pioneer plants — karamu, manuka, flax, houhere and mahoe — but not too close to flowing water where they may slip in. Later, introduce larger trees such as kahikatea, totara and puriri.

~ *Farmland*   Flax and toetoe can provide a cheap, stabilising cover especially in exposed or eroding areas. Flax provides a good edging to keep out invading plants or browsing animals.

On cleared grassland, first plant manuka and kanuka with toetoe as fillers in between the seedlings. The toetoe conserves moisture and suppresses competing plants, accelerating the growth of the young trees by up to four times. Once the manuka and kanuka form a canopy, underplant with shade-tolerant natives like puakou (five-finger) and lacebark in damp, sheltered, shady, south-facing situations and karamu and mahoe in sunnier positions.

Native toetoe or South American pampas grass?

The South American pampas grass has purple-pink seed heads, although these fade to creamy brown in the later stages. Toetoe seed heads are a creamy white. The pampas seed heads stand straighter and the leaves are stiffer and narrower than toetoe. Their dead leaves curl into spirals whereas toetoe heads hang straight down.

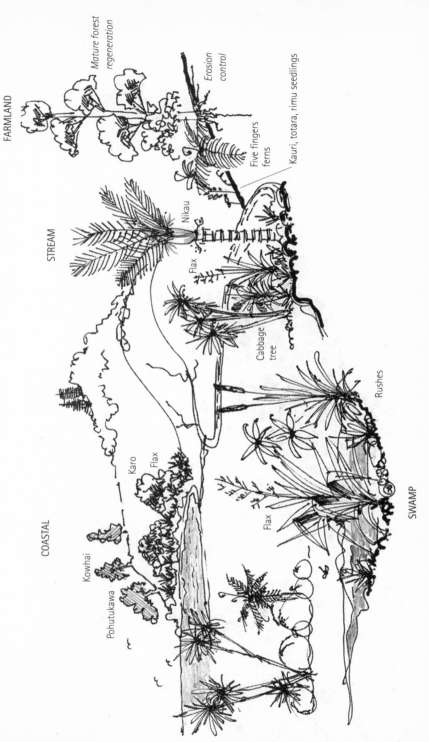

FARMLAND

Mature forest regeneration

Erosion control

Five fingers
ferns

Kauri, totara, rimu seedlings

STREAM

Nikau

Flax

Cabbage
tree

Rushes

COASTAL

Kowhai

Pohutukawa

Karo

Flax

Flax

Flax

SWAMP

Regeneration

When well established, remove the scrub canopy and plant larger trees such as kauri, totara, kahikatea and rimu.

If land is gorse-covered, sow or plant mahoe, houhere, cabbage tree, hangehange and kawakawa in gaps within the gorse, before introducing larger trees.

~ *Swamp* In standing water, plant rushes — different varieties for varying water depths. On the edge and in shallow water and ditches, raupo does well. Behind in swampy ground, introduce toetoe, flax and further back again, cabbage trees. Underplant with kahikatea — this will need shade when young but will tolerate sun when older. In especially shady, damp areas, plant the slow-growing nikau palms — these need a sheltered, shaded spot throughout their lifespan. Plant mamaku (black tree fern) in the dampest spots and ponga (silver fern) in drier places.

~ *Coast* Rocky areas need to be planted with the hardiest of pioneers — native ice plants do well. On dunes and back dunes, start with small pioneer plants — flaxes, toetoe and carex. Underplant with larger pioneers such as the pittosporum karo. On dry, exposed coastal areas, ridges and cliffs, introduce kowhai and pohutukawa. (These should ideally be part of a forest ecosystem. They are not really stand-alone trees.)

~ *City* In small plots and in the corners of city gardens, start with coarse mulch to provide groundcover, and stones to provide shelter for geckos and skinks. In sunny spots, the smallest of pioneers — carex — will provide quick grass cover. As a central feature you can use small decorative natives such as miniature kowhai (*Sophora prostrata* grows about 2 m high), miniature pohutukawa (2–3 m in height) or varietal manuka, whose flowers range from deep red to crimson to purple.

Where there is a little more space, pittosporum and cabbage trees do well. In shady spots, underplant with native ferns.

Planting for birds

The nectar of kowhai, cabbage trees, pohutukawa, rewarewa, rata, puriri and flax flowers and the fruit of totara and kahikatea attract tui and bellbirds.

New Zealand pigeons love the fruit of the miro tree, the berries of the karaka and the flowers of the kowhai. Grey warblers, silvereyes (tauhou, also known as waxeyes and white eyes) and fantails feed mostly on flying insects, so are attracted to gardens with rich vegetation and insect life.

Wet areas attract pukekos, ducks and herons, which feed on slugs, snails, insects and plant matter.

Encouraging the accumulation of loose bark, rotten branches, soft soil and fallen leaves as groundcover for insects, worms and other small native creatures, will attract birds such as shining cuckoo and morepork.

To encourage geckos and skinks add loose rock, which provides hiding places from predators and sun basking spots.

'Do nothing' farming

In an island in the south of Japan, Masanobu Fukuoka has spent over 50 years perfecting the art of non-interference in farming. He grows his vegetables and fruit trees as if they were wild plants, broadcasting the vegetable seed in straw and clover mulch in the orchards before the spring rains. Roaming poultry supply the fertiliser.

Fukuoka's method is the ultimate in simplicity and permaculture. He starts with bare red earth and creates a wild, edible, bountiful garden.

Fukuoka seedball

Seeds — local if possible
Compost from beneath desired trees
Weed-free clay (dig deep — red terracotta is best)

➤ Clean, dry and store seeds.

➤ Mix seeds together in natural combinations.

➤ Sieve compost to remove stalks and leaves, and dry it in the shade.

➤ Dry and grind clay to a lump-free consistency (use two bricks as a grinder). Alternatively, bentonite clay — a soft, fine-grained, cohesive clay — is available at garden centres.

➤ Take one part seeds, three parts compost.

➤ Add five parts powdered clay and mix well.

➤ Add a little water until dough-like consistency.

➤ Pinch off a small amount, compress between fingers and roll in the palm of the hand. The seedball should be the size of a small marble.

➤ Dry the seedballs in a shaded spot.

➤ Disperse by hand, helicopter or sling shot!

Chapter 16

Cleaning

In the name of hygiene we are encouraged to wage chemical warfare on anything we suspect isn't clean. We swab household surfaces with toxic chemicals, drench our clothes and fabrics in phosphates, blast troublesome smells and insects with aerosol poisons.

Yet it isn't possible to survive in a sterile, microbe-free world. It is better to seek cleanliness not sterility, order not devastation. An appropriate level of cleanliness can be maintained using eco-friendly substances and routines that do not damage other living systems.

CLEANSERS — WHAT'S IN THEM?

Cleansers contain a range of ingredients — some common, some mysterious. Here's what they do.

Soaps

Soap is a cheap, mild, biodegradable product derived from renewable resources. It combines animal and vegetable fats or oils with either of two alkalis — caustic soda (lye) or potash. Soap works by lowering the surface tension of water, allowing it to penetrate the material, 'grab' the dirt and carry it away.

Natural soaps do have drawbacks: they gel readily and may clog drains and sewage systems. They also react with the calcium and magnesium ions found in hard water to form a curd-like precipitation that settles on whatever is being washed. The deposits gradually accumulate, causing an unpleasant smell and deterioration of the material. Even with soft water the same ions are present in the dirt on the clothes, so a build-up of deposits still occurs in the fabric.

Soap tends to deteriorate during storage and doesn't have the hard-hitting cleansing power of synthetic detergents.

Detergents

Detergents differ from soaps in that they contain synthetic distillates of petroleum rather than animal or vegetable fats and oils. It was to avoid the reaction between soaps and hard waters that synthetic detergent was invented, using the compound propylene, a waste product of the petroleum industry. As with soap, detergents work because each of their molecules has a hydrophobic (water-hating) part and a hydrophilic (water-loving) part. The water-hating part of the molecule attaches itself to the dirt — which is generally attached to materials by oil or grease — and the whole lot is carried away by the water-loving part. Common additives include bleaches, whiteners, water softeners and artificial fragrances.

Chlorine

Chlorine in its natural form is a poisonous gas. In cleaning compounds it is liquefied and used as a bleach, antiseptic and disinfectant. Chlorine's powerful disinfectant qualities come from its ability to bond with and destroy the outer surfaces of bacteria and viruses. Breathing chlorine fumes can irritate the lungs, and is especially dangerous for people with heart conditions or chronic respiratory problems.

Ammonia

Ammonia is a colourless gas or liquid with a sharp, irritating odour. Liquid household ammonia contains 5–10% ammonia and is an irritant more than a corrosive hazard. However, it should not be used in enclosed spaces or by anyone with respiratory problems. Vapours, even in low concentrations, can cause severe eye, lung and skin irritation. When ammonia and bleach are mixed, a chloramine gas results that can cause coughing, loss of voice, sensations of burning and suffocation, and even death.

Cloudy ammonia is a mixture of an ammonia solution and liquid soap.

Surfactants

Surfactants are the active ingredients in soaps and detergents that give them their unusual cleaning power. Surfactants lower the surface tensions of water, allowing dirt or grease adhered to material to be washed off. There are several types: oil penetrating, thickening, foaming, water softening, conditioning and antibacterial.

Synthetic surfactants are derived from petroleum and will cause skin and other irritations in sensitive individuals. They break down slowly, particularly when released into aquatic environments. Some synthetic surfactants are banned on ecological grounds in parts of the United States and Europe.

Borax

Borax is a soft, whitish mineral salt crystal extracted from hot springs and the dry beds of salt lakes. It is a mild bleach and grease solvent, a natural deodoriser, stain remover and disinfectant, and an inhibitor of the growth of mould and mildew. It is also an insecticide and is toxic to many plants.

Baking soda

Baking soda (bicarbonate of soda) is the stuff that makes scones rise. It is made from soda ash (sodium carbonate). It is a naturally occurring substance which helps living beings maintain their pH balance. It also softens hard water and acts as a fabric softener and deodoriser. It cleans and polishes most shiny materials without scratching and removes some stains.

Washing soda

Washing soda (sodium carbonate) is a naturally occurring mineral whose alkaline properties soften hard water and cut through grease. Seaweed ash provided an early source and it is sometimes still called soda ash.

Vinegar

Vinegar is a mild (acetic) acid. It was made as a sour wine in Babylon, as early as 5000 BC. It can be made from a wide variety of fruit, vegetables and grains. White vinegar — made from fermented grain — can be used in cleaning. It dissolves and removes grease, traces of soap, mildew and wax. It is used in natural carpet-cleaning recipes as a stain remover and, when diluted with water, as a streak-free window cleaner.

Lemon juice

Lemon juice is acidic and has similar cleaning properties to vinegar. It deodorises, removes stains and is a mild bleach when used with sunlight.

ECO-UNFRIENDLY CLEANING

Synthetic cleansers

Environmental, ethical and health concerns are associated with the manufacture and use of synthetic cleansers.

~ *Environmental* In their production and use, synthetic cleansers release concentrated levels of chemicals into the waste stream, causing damage to the environment. Phosphates compose up to 30% of many laundry cleansers and detergents. Being nitrogen-based, they are a powerful fertiliser. When released into the waterways, phosphates over-fertilise algae, causing them to multiply, exhaust oxygen supplies in the water and rot. Other life forms in the water then suffocate and the waterways become clogged, putrid and incapable of supporting life.

~ *Ethical* Animal testing is used in the development of a wide range of cleansers, including polishes, oven abrasives, window cleaners, washing powders, dishwashing liquids, soaps and shampoos. Company use of animal experimentation is policy driven rather than product driven. Some companies go as far as 'green washing' — projecting a green image while using animal testing. Some use animal testing sparingly, others avoid it altogether. Most leading-brand household cleansers are manufactured by a small number of companies that insist animal testing is necessary to comply with international safety requirements. This is misleading. Animal tests are only required for new ingredients which have no known safety record. Companies that have abandoned animal testing meet the same stringent safety requirements by using existing ingredients that are already known to be safe.

~ *Health* The reason for testing cleansing products on animals is to ensure those products won't adversely affect humans. Even so, many people remain susceptible. There is a strong correlation between the increased use of synthetic detergents and the rising incidence of skin disease. The more severe effects of some chlorine compounds containing organochlorides is acknowledged but less understood.

Dry cleaning

In New Zealand, as elsewhere, the most commonly used degreasing solvent, perchloroethylene (perc), is recognised as an environmental pollutant because of its very slow biodegradation. Perc is a chlorine-based solvent. The International Agency for Research in Cancer (IARC) classifies perc, on the basis of tests on rats, as a 'probable human carcinogen'.

An older dry cleaning technology reliant on highly inflammable white spirits is still occasionally used but, like perc, it is an environmental pollutant that presents disposal problems. Another commercial alternative known as 'wet-cleaning' is used selectively by some dry cleaners to remove stains because stains in general respond better to water than chemical solvents. It relies on the carefully controlled use of a mixture of water, detergent and small quantities of solvents but is used less often. It too presents disposal problems.

Despite popular belief, hand washing is safe on almost all materials and many labelled 'Dry Clean Only' can be cleaned at home by careful use of soap and water. If possible, use fabrics that do not require frequent dry cleaning. If you do dry clean fabrics or clothes, air them thoroughly before use.

Personal cleaning

Consumer legislation and the Ministry of Health control cosmetics. There is no requirement in the medicines legislation for the ingredients of cosmetics distributed in New Zealand to be listed on their labels apart from those in hair dyes or containing hexachlorophene. However, to meet consumer demands, most manufacturers display a list of the chemical ingredients in their products. These are confusing for a lay person to understand and to add to this confusion, alternative names are sometimes used.

ECO-FRIENDLY CLEANING

Good planning is one of the easiest ways to reduce the need for cleansers. A house that has wood, cork or tiled floors, and rugs that can be shaken and aired, is much easier to keep clean than one with fitted carpets. So too are furnishings with cushion covers and slips which can be removed and washed. A house in which doors and windows can be opened wide is easy to keep fresh, and the use of insect screens keeps mosquitoes and flies at bay. Air extractors in kitchens and bathrooms minimise odours and reduce the build-up of grease and excess moisture.

Sensible household routines also play a part. Water is a universal cleanser but washing has a limited effect in removing microbes. To remove microbes you need to focus on drying — and drying thoroughly.

Surprisingly, the most bug-ridden object in the house is the cleaning aid we use most — the kitchen wipe, closely followed by the tea towel. The solution is to keep a stack on hand and launder them frequently.

The natural antibacterial properties of some timber — heart radiata in particular — have been shown to make it a better choice of cutting board than 'hygienic' plastic. Timber absorbs moisture better than plastic, and its faster drying surface makes it less supportive of bacterial growth.

Frequent and thorough vacuuming, and regular cleaning under and behind household appliances and furniture, discourages a wide range of household pests: mites, silverfish, fleas, cockroaches, ants and moths. The use of airtight food containers removes obvious sources of food for unwanted pests.

Granny's recipes

Planning reduces the need for cleansers but at times we feel we need more than common sense, warm water and elbow grease. It is relatively easy to make simple, natural cleaning products but caution is advised.

Naturalness does not preclude toxicity and care must be taken with powerful natural substances such as citronella, manuka oil and pyrethrum. Similarly, you can't assume that substances are eco friendly because they were commonly used in the past. Many of Granny's recipes used kerosene, turpentine, peroxide, camphor and carbolic acid, chemicals that are now regarded as harmful. Some, such as the pesticide DDT and the household fabric 'spot remover' carbon tetrachloride, are banned.

Granny's recipes aren't always tried and proven. Don't regard them as fail safe.

~ *Bleaches and stain removers*   The sun not only bleaches, it deodorises. Hang clothes in full sunshine whenever possible. Synthetic fabrics, which yellow in sunlight, should be dried in the shade or indoors.

~ *Soap*   Hard soap (cake soap) can be made using base ingredients or simple starter kits. The advantage in making your own is that you can add ingredients and fragrances of choice — oatmeal, kelp, lavender and manuka oil. Unlike commercial soap, whose glycerine is removed and sold back to the consumer in other skin-care products, home-made soap will contain at least 25% glycerine to act as a skin moisturiser and lubricant.

Making soap at home is not an activity to be taken lightly, falling somewhere between a craft and science. One of the key ingredients of soap is sodium hydroxide, commonly known as lye or caustic soda. As the name suggests, lye is caustic and toxic if ingested. Skin and eye protection is needed in handling it. Fortunately, lye loses its caustic properties during the soap-making process when it reacts with fatty acids to create soap and glycerine.

~ *Polish*   Commercial floor and furniture polishes typically contain aromatic phenols. Sometimes called carbolic acid, phenol is antiseptic but also toxic by absorption through the skin. Beeswax, natural (vegetable) turpentine and linseed, olive and cedar oil used singly or in combination are good home-made alternatives.

Laundry wash

5 litres of water
1 tablespoon of borax
1 teaspoon of white vinegar or baking soda
few drops of lemon oil to cut through grease
drop of coconut oil or palm oil for softness

Mix together and wash.

Laundry powder

Two-thirds soap flakes
One-third baking soda

Mix and use with warm water.

An all-purpose liquid soap

Old ends of bar soap (or grated slivers of soap)
Warm water

Dissolve soap in warm water.

Overnight bleach

Salty water, lemon juice or washing soda

Dissolve in one bucket of water.
Soak overnight.
Wash as normal.

(Don't use washing soda on silk.)

Stain remover

Several teaspoons of baking soda

Dissolve in pan of water.
Immerse article in water.
Bring gently to the boil.
Soak overnight.

(Especially good for stained tea towels.)

Dry cleansing powder

Equal amounts baking soda and borax

Use as an abrasive cleanser.

Liquid spray cleanser

2 litres warm water
1 teaspoon liquid soap
1 teaspoon borax
1 teaspoon white vinegar
few drops of pine, lavender, eucalyptus
*   or lemon oil for their antiseptic*
*   qualities and fragrance*

Spray and wipe.

Window/mirror cleanser

Half a bucket of warm water
A hefty squeeze of lemon juice or white
*   vinegar*

Apply with a scrunched up newspaper and
lots of elbow grease.

Dishwashing liquid

Plain liquid soap or plain soap in a shaker
Lemon juice or citrus oil to cut through
*   grease*
Camomile, calendula extracts or coconut oil
*   as a hand softener*

(For grease cutters and abrasives add citric
acid, milk whey, baking soda and sea salt.)

Automatic dishwasher powder

1 cup borax
1 cup washing soda
1 teaspoon baking soda in hard water
1 teaspoon white vinegar or lemon juice (in
*   rinse aid)*

(Note: will not clean heavily soiled items.
Extra attention is needed in rinsing and
stacking dishes.)

Burnt pots cleaner

2 teaspoons baking soda
1 cup of hot water

Mix together in soiled pot.
Heat on the stove until simmering.
Leave overnight.
Badly charred pots might need a second
soaking.

(Note: a small piece of pumice rock makes
an excellent abrasive for cleaning charred
pots and pans.)

Oven cleanser

2 tablespoons baking soda
Water to mix

Wipe away any residual grease.
Make a paste of baking soda and water.
Apply the paste and scrub.

Disinfectant

Half cup borax
5 litres hot water

Alternatively, lemon and thyme are natural disinfectants.

Toilet cleaner

One cup of white vinegar

Soak in the bowl overnight.
Scrub the next day.
Scrub stains with baking soda. Use lemon juice, eucalyptus oil or manuka oil to disinfect bowl and seat.

(For bowls stained with calcium residue in areas of hard water, half cup of washing soda once a fortnight softens the water and loosens the calcium deposits.)

Shower base and bath cleaner

Baking soda
Lemon juice
Manuka oil

Scrub with baking soda and a nylon scourer. Use lemon juice or manuka oil to disinfect the base.

Drain cleaner

Half cup baking soda
1 cup vinegar
Boiling, salty water

Tip baking soda down drain.
Follow with vinegar.
Cover until fizzing is finished.
Rinse the drain with boiling water and salt.
Repeat as necessary.

Air freshener

Sunshine is the best purifier. Open the windows and let the sunshine in. Otherwise try bowls of potpourri, a little essential oil in water, baking soda to absorb odours in the fridge, vases of fresh flowers and for desperate occasions boil cloves and cinnamon in water or burn a stick of incense.

Indigenous cleansers

Using cleaning agents that evolved in this land appeals to the eco-sentimentalist in all of us. Knowledge of Maori cleaning aids is scarce but a little remains.

Hot water is universally loved and valued. Maori used mineral hot pools for steaming, soaking and washing. They built simple steam saunas by slinging a low platform over fire-heated stones, which were splattered with water to create a steam bath. Soaking baths

Light furniture polish

Several drops of lemon oil
Half litre of mineral oil

Apply with a soft, damp cloth.

Rich furniture polish

50 g beeswax
120 ml vegetable turpentine
2 teaspoons linseed oil
2 teaspoons cedar oil

Melt over simmering water.
Apply with a soft cloth.

This is a heavy polish that conditions and protects wooden furniture and floors. Apply infrequently to avoid heavy build-up of wax.

were sometimes made in a length of hollowed tree trunk or in a canoe and kumarahou leaves and flowers were used in steam baths. The yellow kumarahou flowers, when crushed in the hand, form a soapy lather — 'gum digger soap'. Maori extracted anointing oil from titoki seeds (the fruit is poisonous) and for scented body oil added the crushed, sweet-smelling leaves of the mairehau plant.

Mosses or lichen — angiangi, kohukohu and waewae koukou — provided soft, warm and absorbent kope (babies' nappies), all held in place with a large leaf. As an added refinement, waewae koukou emitted a very pleasant scent. Kope were both disposable and biodegradable. Babies wore muka scrapings — the silky floss from the inner leaf of the flax. They called this silky gem kukukuku. It could be washed and dried and used again and again. Mothers washed and anointed their babies with titoki oil daily.

For clean oily hair or to add gloss and sheen to their tresses, boiling water was tipped over the young leaf tips from the ngaio tree and rubbed into the hair after washing. The young branches of the mairehau tree rubbed onto the body bestowed a sweet and pleasant fragrance.

Sachets from scented leaves and flowers of the mairehau tree were used for fragrance. Chemical analysis of the leaves reveals essential oils of citronella, phenol and camphene. Perhaps the sachets served a dual purpose as an insect repellant and perfume.

The gum of the miro tree or a potion of boiled, crushed titoki leaves were also used as insecticides. To keep away sandflies, ngaio leaves were rubbed on the skin.

For hangis, individuals ate from 'kono', small individual flax baskets that were thrown away after each meal. For simpler meals cooked on hot embers, they wrapped birds in clay and eels and fish in leaves. These 'dishes' were fast, hygienic and biodegradable.

Maori also used non-disposable dishes. For tribal feasts they served food in large, richly carved wooden containers and carried water in gourds. They reserved these vessels for food and water only and stored them in a separate place of their own, much as we reserve cutting boards and knives for special functions in the kitchen today.

Following the Maori example, early settlers found ways of using indigenous products to mimic the refinements of the old world. A manuka brush made an excellent broom for sweeping an earth floor. It was cheap, readily available, disposable and biodegradable. The antiseptic properties of manuka were a hidden bonus — bacteria disliked the astringent branches.

As an aid to another important function, the large, flat, soft and antiseptic leaves of the rangiora shrub, the 'bushman's friend' was — and undoubtedly still is — used as toilet paper.

Pumice provided a natural skin exfoliator; sea sponge a soft and absorbent cloth.

South Pacific recipes

A wave of natural cleansers based on New Zealand's unique flora provides new opportunities for research and development. Face cleansers, face creams, soaps, mouthwash, hair conditioners and antiseptic gel are all being made using the oil of the manuka tree. Flax is also a favourite in preparing toning gel, antiseptic gel and face cleanser.

> ### Hair conditioner
>
> *A few drops of manuka oil*
>
> Use in rinsing water to add sheen to hair.
>
> ### Disinfectant
>
> *3 tablespoons liquid soap*
> *2 cups water*
> *20–30 drops of manuka oil*
>
> Make a solution. Apply sparingly.

ECO-FRIENDLY INSECT CONTROL

Pyrethrum is a natural insecticide derived from the seeds of chrysanthemum flowers. It kills most insects and is commonly used in commercial fly spray.

Citronella is a natural insect and animal repellent derived from dried grasses. It is used in candles, lotions, gels, sprays, wipes and pet collars as repellents for mosquitoes, flies and fleas. It is also used in pellet form to repel dogs and cats in gardens. It can cause skin irritation but is otherwise considered safe.

Many aromatic herbs please us but repel insects. Strings of cloves, fresh-picked tansy, rue and pennyroyal hung inside and mint, basil, thyme and lavender planted close to the house or in window boxes can serve a dual purpose.

The following are some specific insect-control methods.

Ants

Ants could be considered beneficial because they like to eat other insects such as fleas, young silverfish and clothes moths. But they don't mix well with food. Borax and sugar mixed to a firm paste with a little water provides good control — the sugar attracts; the borax poisons. Bait systems like this are effective but work slowly, with the poison being fed by the foraging ants to all the unsuspecting members of the nest. If the nest can be located, a jug of boiling soapy water tipped into it will temporarily and quickly reduce a colony, and repeated flooding with a garden hose should encourage ants to move further from the house. Sprinklings of chilli pepper, black pepper or mint will deter ants from using a familiar indoor trail.

Cockroaches

Cockroaches enjoy warm, moist areas where food is readily available. Thorough sanitation is the best deterrent, particularly around and beneath appliances, sinks and other locations close to a food source where dark or humid conditions exist. Ventilating bathrooms, controlling humidity and water sources and increasing the light and air circulation in problem areas help control infestations. Borax mixed with rolled oats, honey or jam will poison cockroaches. If you want to trap them, smear Vaseline around the inner neck and halfway down the inside of a wide-mouthed jar. Put moist bread, cake or a drop of beer in the bottom of the jar. Cockroaches will climb in but won't climb out. Kill them by tipping them into soapy water, or put the lid on and place the jar in the freezer (leave at least 24 hours, or the cockroaches will merely cool off).

Fleas

An infestation of fleas can be alarming, and when it happens both fleas and eggs need to be dealt to. The flea that bites may have been deposited as an egg many months earlier, before hatching and causing trouble. After hatching from eggs, flea larvae can survive in unfavourable conditions for six months before entering a pupal stage. When conditions are right — it may be a rise in temperature or carbon dioxide concentrations — the flea emerges. Vibrations indicating the presence of a host also stimulate emergence. This explains why fleas in unoccupied homes become active as soon as humans or pets re-enter.

An aerosol pyrethrum spray will quickly knock down adult fleas and flea larvae but not flea eggs. Thorough vacuuming daily is the best method of removing eggs, larvae and adults. Important areas include carpets, under the edges of floor rugs, cushioned furniture, cracks and crevices on floors and along skirting boards. Steam cleaning carpets may also help as the hot steam and soap can kill fleas in all stages of the life cycle.

Pets are an obvious source of flea infestation. Wash all pet bedding (and family bedding on which pets lie) in hot, soapy water every two to three weeks to kill flea eggs and larvae. If an infestation is severe, discard old pet bedding. Flea combs are effective in catching adult fleas on pets. Comb where the most fleas congregate, usually the neck or tail area. Dunk caught fleas in hot, soapy water to kill them. Pets generally love to be combed.

Flea collars prevent fleas from biting pets but don't provide adequate control once an infestation has occurred. Some animals may develop a skin rash from flea collars. Herbal shampoos will discourage fleas and an occasional bath in soap and water will reduce a pet's flea population (dogs are generally more amenable to bathing than cats). Water containing a dash of pennyroyal, citronella, manuka or eucalyptus oil is credited with killing fleas. Badly infested dogs should be bathed every two weeks, cats once per month. If your pet doesn't like a bath, try vacuuming it — some pets enjoy it.

Garlic or brewer's yeast may also be added to the pet's daily diet to repel fleas.

Head lice

Head lice and their egg cases ('nits') are difficult to beat and for this reason insecticides are generally used if not as a first, then as a last resort. But pharmaceutical formulations need to be applied repeatedly and head lice are showing increased insecticide resistance. No product currently available kills all eggs. Whether or not you use an approved insecticide, consistent and frequent use of the 'conditioner and comb' technique is the best way of checking whether the treatment is working, by locating eggs, juveniles and adult climbers, dead and alive. Here's what to do:

➤ Apply conditioner to dry hair aiming to cover each hair from root to tip with a layer of conditioner.

➤ Detangle the hair using an ordinary comb.

➤ Immediately comb the hair with a fine-toothed nit comb. Both steel and plastic nit combs with conditioner are effective for detecting climbers.

➤ Wipe the conditioner off the fine-toothed comb onto a paper tissue and look for lice and eggs.

➤ Repeat the combing for every part of the head at least five times and examine the comb for lice and eggs.

Conditioner stuns lice for 20 minutes, so once the hair is properly covered with a layer of conditioner, comb the little suckers out. Many head lice infections cause no symptoms and probably less than half cause itch. So you have to look (and comb) carefully to find head lice.

If you find lice, treatment should follow. If you do not want to use insecticide treatments repeat the conditioner and comb method thoroughly — at first daily, then at least once a week.

Moths and silverfish

Discourage moths and silverfish by placing cloves, Epsom salts or dried lavender in bags in drawers and cupboards. Clean all clothes and bedding before storing and store in plastic bins or bags.

The use of mothballs for odour and insect control is inadvisable. Mothballs, which once contained camphor oil from the camphor tree, now contain ammonia and naphthalene, a volatile compound found naturally in crude oil and fossil fuels. Exposure to naphthalene vapour can damage and destroy red blood cells. Children are particularly at risk — mothballs look like sweets.

Weevils

Fresh bay leaves and whole cloves left on pantry shelving are credited with discouraging weevils but if grains, cereals and flour are stored in 100% airtight jars, infestation from within and without is prevented.

Flies

The use of fly screens and food covers are the best controls. A fly swat is excellent backup. Calendula and marigolds (pyrethrum family), and native ferns grown near doorways and windows help deter flies. Kitchen herbs such as mint, wild marjoram, basil and fennel are all repellents. So too are pennyroyal, tansy, rosemary and garlic.

ECO-FRIENDLY COMMERCIAL PRODUCTS

The alternative to using and experimenting with folklore recipes is to buy eco-friendly commercial products. The term 'eco friendly' means different things to different eco producers. Some concentrate on ethical production techniques; some on the low level of danger to human health; some on minimising downstream environmental effects; some on all of these factors. Some producers tell us what a product has, others tell us what it doesn't have.

Just because a product has a 'green' label doesn't make it eco friendly. If they are to be trusted, product labels should list ingredients clearly and state whether the perfumes, dyes, surfactants and preservatives used in their production are of natural origin. If ingredients are not specified the product is probably not eco friendly.

Eco-friendly commercial products use familiar natural ingredients such as sugar, salt, citrus acids, baking and washing sodas, chalks, clay and beeswax. They use oils from coconut, manuka and palm, herbal preservatives and resins and vegetable turpentine. While the ingredients are similar to those in Granny's recipes, commercial eco products have the advantage of being pre-prepared and packaged to maximise ease of use and effectiveness.

They are also surprisingly reasonably priced. Many are sold in concentrated form to reduce the need for containers and refills. If just a few drops are needed, concentrated eco-friendly cleansers are often close in cost to less-concentrated synthetically produced cleansers.

Eco-friendly dish-washing liquid, window cleaners and polishes are as easy and effective as the synthetic ones. Eco-friendly laundry and dishwasher powders are less effective but will work adequately if you make the effort to pre-soak heavily soiled clothes before washing, and rinse dishes before stacking them in the dishwasher.

Health shops and organic stores generally have the best selection of genuine eco-friendly cleansers and can explain their relative merits and philosophies. Some manufacturers run a catalogue mail-order service. Some supermarkets stock a limited range of eco-friendly cleansers but know little about them.

<table>
<tr><td>

TOP TIP FOR CLEANING

✓ Making small, incremental changes towards eco-friendly cleaning is easy, effective and economical and the environmental benefits far outweigh the effort.

</td></tr>
</table>

Chapter 17

Recycling

Around 500 BC Athens issued a law against dropping waste within a mile of city walls. Athenians then dumped their rubbish in heaps in the surrounding countryside — the open dump was officially born. In ancient China, townsfolk hauled their waste to the countryside to revitalise the fields — and composting became a viable business. Throughout history, anyone who set something down, thinking no one else could possibly find a use for it, woke to find it gone — thus was recycling invented.

Not too much has changed: we still have open city dumps, we still compost and we still recycle. What has changed is the complexity and scale of the waste. Our modern waste stream includes a wide range of complex manufactured materials — glass, plastic, metals, paints, pesticides and cleansing agents — many of them hazardous and taking centuries to decompose. With the explosion in population and the consumer opportunities offered by the technological age, the waste stream has now become an ocean of waste. It is obvious that the soil, air and sea can no longer absorb our rubbish. Leachate from landfills is linked to health problems; carbon emissions have far-reaching consequences for global warming; and persistent organic pollutants released in the soil, water and air are entering our food chain: the most vulnerable of earth's species are dying. There is now a very real danger that we will, as the Native American chief Seattle predicted in 1854, 'contaminate our bed and one night suffocate in our own waste'.

WHAT NOT TO DO

On an individual as well as global scale, we can be overwhelmed by the size of the problem — so many consumer goods for sale, so little thought given to their disposal. Computers fall into this category; their screens and electronic circuits contain quantities of the heavy metals mercury, cadmium and lead, yet truckloads of old computers are dumped daily in our landfills without any effort to separate or recycle these hazardous materials. (Not only are these minerals toxic, they are in short supply.)

The nickel-cadmium rechargeable batteries ('NiCads') commonly used in portable telephones, power tools, radios and video tape recorders are another problem in waiting. They pose little hazard in use (the cadmium is in a stable form) but are an environmental hazard in landfills. Cadmium is known to cause blood and reproductive damage, among other problems, yet no provision is made to collect or recycle it from these products. (NiCad batteries should not be thrown into regular rubbish collections but dropped off at a hazardous waste depot.)

Another bane is plastic waste. Three main disposal options exist: dump it, burn it or recycle it. Because they are non-degradable and therefore don't reduce in volume, plastics are becoming a disproportionate component in landfills. And the dumping of chloride-based plastics is not a viable option because of the risk that additives such as phthalates and dioxins will migrate into the environment and, in the case of landfill fires, be dispersed into the atmosphere.

Incineration of waste materials is not viable for similar reasons: the release of carbon dioxide, dioxins and furans into the atmosphere, and the production of large quantities of hazardous salt waste in the ash residue.

WHAT TO DO

Recycling is promoted as the best alternative but isn't well catered for. In the case of plastic, each plastic type has a specific performance characteristic, making it necessary to sort the product accurately and reprocess it separately. This is labour intensive and tends to make recycling a marginal exercise.

In New Zealand quantities of the less problematic plastics, such as those used for milk and drink bottles (PET and HDPE), are collected from many households on a regular basis. Most district councils support this and much of the collected lightweight waste is successfully recycled. This is the tip of the plastic iceberg, however. The bulk of waste plastic is dumped in landfills.

Just as pollution is the accumulation of many seemingly trivial actions, small efforts to conserve and recycle by many individuals can reverse this process. The key is to think small.

To practise conservation and recycling it helps to hold to simple principles:

➤ Use less.

➤ Link with others.

➤ Learn from nature.

Less is best

This is our first line of defence. As a society, if we don't make it, we don't have to get rid of it. As householders, if we don't let it in the gate, we don't have to pass it on.

~ *Less packaging*   You can cut your domestic rubbish in half by favouring products which minimise packaging or use biodegradable or recycled packaging (bearing in mind, reduction is more effective than recycling). Standard behaviour in some European countries is to strip products of unnecessary packaging at the counter, and fill your own pre-weighed containers from open bins.

In addition to product packaging, most shoppers return home with a swag of plastic carry bags. Greenpeace, the ecostore and some district councils sell reusable cloth shopping bags modelled on the supermarket bag that slip quickly and neatly over the bag holder at supermarket counters.

You can easily make your own strong, reusable bag using an unbleached fabric such as calico or hemp, though you may encounter resistance from stores who like to use logo-branded plastic bags as advertising. Store security is another obstacle cited by retailers who favour plastic bags. If this is a problem, a see-through string bag or basket may be the answer. Some supermarkets such as 'Pak'n'Save' provide waste cardboard boxes for packing and charge for plastic bags, raising awareness of the true cost of packaging.

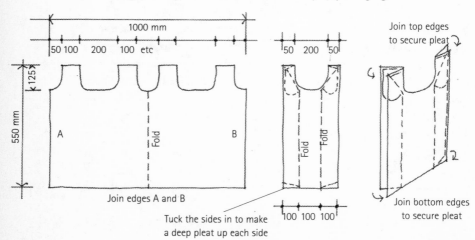

Shopping bag pattern

(In some overseas countries supermarkets charge customers considerably more than the bag is worth, to discourage their use. Discarded bags are responsible for blocked waterways, as happened in the devastating floods in the Bangladesh Delta in 1989 and 1998. They also cause the death of many sea creatures, which either eat the bags or become entangled in them.)

Fewer throwaways

It is an old-fashioned idea to buy quality and buy to last by choosing well-made, well-designed products.

Reusable items are more eco friendly than disposable goods — washable cloths are better than paper towels, handkerchiefs are better than tissues (dry mucus is sterile), cloth nappies are better than disposables (and more comfortable) and reusable utensils and crockery are better than paper, polystyrene or plastic. (It isn't completely cut and dried — energy and water are still required to clean these items.)

~ *Less paper*   You can reduce junk mail with a 'No Circulars' sign on your letterbox. Personalised junk mail can be 'Returned to Sender' at their expense.

Unbleached paper for household hygiene and home office use avoids dioxin contamination; recycled paper conserves forests and energy; and electronic mail eliminates paper altogether.

Paper that's been used on one side only can be reused in computer printers for 'non letter-quality' printing, or cut into quarters and converted into household notepads.

Envelopes can be re-used — just place a sticker over the old address (and cross out any bar-codes, or your letter to Aunt Nellie will go astray).

~ *Fewer pesticides*   You can avoid pesticides by choosing organic food, organic cleansers and organic gardening practices. Most city councils use

---

Controlling weeds

It helps councils control weeds without heavy use of pesticides if individual properties are kept free of invasive weeds. To keep weeds from spreading:

➤ Remove newly classified noxious weeds from flower beds.

➤ Keep machinery and footwear clean.

➤ Target isolated plants (outliers/colonisers) before the main clump.

➤ Remove flower heads and debris that may regrow.

➤ Plant bare ground in desirable plants.

chemical weed control along the road verges but several are experimenting with organic herbicides and weed eating and some are using high-temperature steam weed control. Individual properties can be registered as spray-free zones, although spray drift may negate this, unless others in the street do the same thing (a pamphlet drop is effective).

Link with others

In the past, many households have relied on a single recycling system – the ubiquitous black rubbish bag with a single link via the rubbish truck to the city dump. This is a rapidly vanishing option, as landfills overflow and their toxins leach into waterways. The alternative is for every home to become a recycling hub linked to outside facilities.

The home hub

~ *A recycling hub* Placing recycling bins close to the waste source (but preferably out of sight) encourages recycling in the home. By default, however, the kitchen area often becomes the hub for sorting waste.

To sort waste you will need a:

➤ small covered container for compost that can be emptied each day – out of sight, close to the sink and with easy, dry access to the compost heap (the pull-out, under-sink type bins are practicable)

➤ small covered container in the fridge for storing scraps for pets or livestock

➤ cardboard box or large paper bag for paper

➤ container for shredded paper for the worm farm (small shredders can be cheaply sourced for this purpose)

➤ bin(s) in the kitchen or outdoors – access has to be easy – for plastic, tin and glass

➤ cupboard/basket for disused clothes

➤ corner in the attic, basement, garage or shed for discarded furniture and appliances, while they wait for a new home.

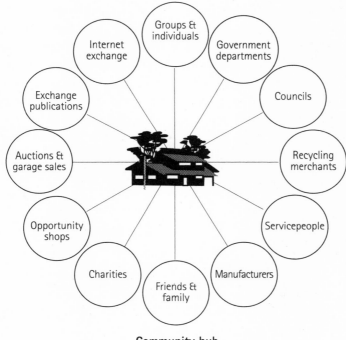

Community hub

~ *Link with like-minded individuals*   There are a number of groups and campaigns that aim at a co-ordinated recycling approach. One broad, bold initiative in New Zealand is the Zero Waste campaign.

(At the end of 2001, close to half of all New Zealand's councils had adopted an aim of zero waste in landfills by the year 2020.) This campaign aims to:

➤ design waste out of the system

➤ change mindsets

➤ raise awareness of the true cost of waste.

This all-encompassing approach addresses the wider issues and philosophies behind waste management – civic and industrial design, economics, employment and health — and looks at the everyday practicalities of running a city and a home. Support systems and advice at all levels are accessible on-line.

~ *Link with council services* Local councils are our primary link to recycling services and information and most have websites and e-mail contacts to provide information. Many councils are experimenting with waste-reduction and recycling schemes. These schemes involve reducing the size of city rubbish bins; levying rubbish bags; collecting glass, plastic, paper and cans (aluminium and steel); composting commercial organic waste; providing disposal bins for invasive weeds; giving out coupons for worm and compost bins and running 'hazmobiles' for hazardous waste. Some schemes don't survive initial trials; others become well established. Public enthusiasm is guaranteed but viable markets for waste products aren't.

To make the waste collector's job more effective, points to note are:

➤ Waxed or food-soiled paper can't be recycled.

➤ Plastic tops on items such as milk bottles are made of a different material to the bottle. They should be discarded and the bottle rinsed, to assist recycling.

➤ Recyclable plastic is numbered with internationally recognised symbols from 1 to 7 (see page 202).

The symbol does not mean that a particular plastic can be recycled, or that the object bearing the symbol is made from recycled plastic; it only identifies the plastic type. Check which grades of plastic your council recycles, as they vary.

Hazardous wastes accepted by hazmobiles include:

➤ paint, solvents and paint strippers
➤ wood preservatives, glues
➤ garden chemicals, pesticides, fertilisers
➤ petrol, oil and other automobile products
➤ toilet and drain cleansers
➤ kitchen and oven cleansers
➤ pool chemicals, bleach and disinfectants
➤ batteries (all kinds)
➤ furniture and shoe polish
➤ smoke alarms
➤ nail polish and remover.

Unacceptable items include:

➤ explosives (contact police, defence forces)
➤ commercial hazardous waste (private companies listed in the Yellow Pages)
➤ asbestos (private asbestos removal companies)
➤ gas cylinders (private companies)
➤ biomedical waste such as syringes, infectious materials (collected by private medical waste companies).

If you are unsure where to take these items, check with your local council. Extreme care must be taken with the containment and transport of hazardous waste.

~ *Link with recyclers* It is possible to buy recycled materials, though some 'recycled' products are simply scrap products from another industry — petroleum by-products 'recycled' to make cleansing agents, bottle glass recycled to make glass-fibre insulation — rather than genuine reuse of consumer items. In some countries such as the United States the 'consumer reuse' content is specified on the container. This is difficult in New Zealand because of the high content of imported materials. However, our 'consumer reuse' ratio is high compared with most developed countries.

~ *Link with manufacturers and repair services* In the Netherlands, appliance retailers are obliged to remove used goods to regional transfer stations. This does not apply here but Fisher and Paykel will recycle your old appliance, regardless of age or make, when you purchase a new one. The company recovers aluminium, stainless steel, copper, steel, packaging, cabling and compressors from dead appliances — almost nothing goes to the tip.

Local appliance dealers will often strip appliances for usable parts.

Local recycling rates

➤ In 1996, 45% of waste disposal in Auckland was recycled or composted rather than dumped.
➤ 70% of our recycled material is paper or metal.
➤ Recovery rates are around 60% for paper, 37% for aluminium and steel cans, 42% for glass and 13% for plastic.

Did you ever wonder what happens to the junk in your recycle bin?
➤ Matta Products produces rubber mats from recycled PVC and rubber.
➤ Pacific Plastic recyclers uses 5 tonnes of milk bottles, ice cream containers, cleaner bottles and plastic bags each day to make 60–70 different products including plastic buckets, plastic pipes, carpet cores and cables.

PLASTICS FOR RECYCLING – THE PLASTIC IDENTIFICATION CODE

Symbol	Types of plastic	Properties
	PET Polyethylene Terephthalate	Clear, tough, solvent resistant, barrier to gas and moisture, softens at 80°C
	PE-HD High-density Polyethylene	Hard to semi-flexible, resistant to chemicals and moisture, waxy surface, opaque, softens at 75°C, easily coloured, processed and formed
	PVC Unplasticised Polyvinyl Chloride PVC-U	Strong, tough, can be clear, can be solvent welded, softens at 80°C
	Plasticised Polyvinyl Chloride PVC-P	Flexible, clear, elastic, can be solvent welded
	PE-LD Low-density Polyethylene	Soft, flexible, waxy surface, translucent, softens at 70°C, scratches easily
	PP Polypropylene	Hard but still flexible, waxy surface, softens at 140°C, translucent, withstands solvents, versatile
	PS Polystyrene	Clear, glassy, rigid, brittle, opaque, semi-tough, softens at 95°C. Affected by fats and solvents
	PS-E Expanded polystyrene EPS	Foamed, lightweight, energy absorbing, heat insulating
	OTHER Letters below indicate ISO code for plastic type e.g. SAN, ABS, PC, Nylon	Includes all other resins and multi-materials, e.g. laminates Properties dependent on plastic or combination of plastics

(Courtesy Plastics New Zealand)

Common uses	Recycled in
Soft drink and water bottles, salad domes, biscuit trays, salad dressing and peanut butter containers	Pillow and sleeping bag filling, clothing, soft drink bottles, carpet
Crinkly shopping bags, freezer bags, milk bottles, ice cream containers, juice bottles, shampoo, chemical and detergent bottles, buckets, rigid agricultural pipe, milk crates	Recycling bins, compost bins, buckets, detergent containers, posts, fencing, pipes
Cosmetic containers, electrical conduit, plumbing pipes and fittings, blister packs, wall cladding, roof sheeting, bottles Garden hose, shoe soles, cable sheathing, blood bags and tubing, watch straps	Flooring, film and sheets, cables, speed bumps, packaging, binders, mud flaps and mats
Glad wrap, garbage bags, squeeze bottles, black irrigation tube, black mulch film, garbage bins	Rubbish bin liners, pallet sheets
Dip pottles and ice cream tubs, potato chip bags, straws, microwave dishes, kettles, garden furniture, lunch boxes, blue packing tape	Pegs, bins, pipes, pallet sheets, oil funnels, car battery cases, trays
CD cases, plastic cutlery, imitation 'crystal glassware', low-cost brittle toys, video cases Foamed polystyrene hot drink cups, hamburger take-away clamshells, foamed meat trays, protective packaging for fragile items	Coat hangers, coasters, whiteware components, stationery trays and accessories
Car parts, appliance parts, computers, electronics, water cooler bottles, packaging	Car parts, concrete aggregate, plastic timber

~ *Link with recycling merchants*   Lead, aluminium, stainless steel, copper, iron and used car oil can be sold or given to recycling merchants. Cars may fetch a few dollars at spare part dealers. Second-hand shops will offer a small price for resaleable goods. (Recycling aluminium uses just 5% of the energy needed to make it from bauxite.)

~ *Link with the community*   You can advertise second-hand goods in the free-advertising sections of newspapers or on-line. Community markets, garage sales and auctions are also a good way of recycling second-hand goods.

~ *Link with friends, charities, family*   The young flatting population are often keen to receive sofas, chairs, tables, utensils and the like in any condition. Church shops will accept reusable household items and clothing. The Salvation Army will pick up large items on request. Fundraising clothing bins are often within easy reach.

LEARN FROM NATURE

For maximum effectiveness we can hitch a ride with nature. Ecosystems have evolved to effect the continual transformation and regeneration of organic life. With understanding, we can work in harmony with these systems.

Nature has its own purification systems. When water makes its way slowly through the earth to the streams, rivers and oceans, contaminants are gradually filtered out by the soil and microbes digest nutrients. Modern stormwater systems bypass this process — 80% of pollution entering the oceans is carried by stormwater.

*TOP TIPS FOR
RECYCLING*

✓ Use less.

✓ Link with others.

✓ Learn from nature.

We can copy nature in simple ways:

➤ Wash the car on the grass rather than on the roadway so the runoff of heavy metals is filtered through the ground rather than fast-tracked to the ocean.

➤ Take outdated medicines and cleansers to a transfer station rather than flushing them down the toilet.

➤ Plant natural waterways, gullies and ditches with vegetation rather than inserting plastic drainage coil.

The key to conservation and recycling is to take small manageable steps, remembering that small actions, when multiplied by New Zealand's four million people, could have large consequences.

Part Four

Resources

Eco organisations

GENERAL UMBRELLA GROUPS AND ORGANISATIONS

Australia and New Zealand Solar Energy Society (ANZSES)
Address: PO Box 54 223, Mana, Porirua
Phone: (04) 237 1170 (Contact: Andrew Pollard)
E-mail: solaraction@paradise.net.nz
Websites: www.anzses.org and www.converge.org.nz/solaraction

Eco-Environment and Conservation Organisations of NZ (ECO)
An umbrella group of environment and conservation organisations in New
Zealand.
Address: PO Box 11 057, Wellington
Fax/Phone: (04) 385 7545
E-mail: Eco@reddfish.co.nz
Website: www.eco.org.nz

Department of Conservation (DOC)
The central government organisation charged with conserving the natural
and historic heritage of New Zealand on behalf of and for the benefit of
present and future New Zealanders.
Phone: For conservation emergencies: 0800 DOCHOTline (0800 36 24 68)
Otherwise, contact regional conservancy offices as listed on website.
Website: www.doc.govt.nz

DOC, MAF, MAG and Ministry for the Environment
Website for biodiversity: www.biodiversity.govt.nz
Draws together efforts by government departments to halt the decline of
New Zealand's native species.

Greenpeace NZ

Address: 113 Valley Road, Mt Eden, Auckland
Postal Address: Private Bag 92 507, Wellesley Street, Auckland
Phone: (09) 630 6317
Free Phone: 0800 22 33 44
Fax: (09) 630 7121
E-mail: greenpeace.new.zealand@nz.greenpeace.org
Website: www.greenpeace.org.nz

Local Councils and Regional Authorities

Local councils and regional authorities provide local, practical information
about eco issues, including building, waste management, conservation.
Listings are in the white pages of telephone directory. Websites also operate.
Waitakere City Council, in particular, provides eco information.

Ministry for the Environment

The government ministry with overall responsibility for environmental
decisions. It publishes a quarterly newspaper, *Envionz*, which is available
free on request or from the website.
Address: PO Box 10 362, Wellington
Phone: (04) 917 7400
Fax: (04) 917 7523
E-mail: info@mfe.govt.nz
Website: www.mfe.govt.nz

Royal Forest and Bird Protection Society of New Zealand

New Zealand's largest national conservation organisation. The Society's
mission is to preserve and protect the native plants and animals and natural
features of New Zealand.
Address: Central Office 172 Taranaki Street, PO Box 631, Wellington
Phone: (04) 385 7374
Membership: 0800 200 064
Fax: (04) 385 7373
E-mail: office@wn.forest-bird.org.nz
Website: www.forest-bird.org.nz

Agriculture/Horticulture/Food

GE Free New Zealand

A non-profit organisation with branches in the Kapiti Coast, Dunedin,
Christchurch, Nelson, Wellington, Hawke's Bay, Taupo and Auckland.
Website: www.gefree.org.nz

New Zealand Earthworm Association Inc.
Website: www.earthworms.co.nz

New Zealand Ecological Restoration Network (NZERN)
NZERN is a non-profit, community-driven, membership-based organisation
dedicated to sharing knowledge and experiences about ecological
restoration.
Address: PO Box 9000, Christchurch
Phone: (03) 338 5451 (8 am to 9 pm, 7 days a week)
E-mail: office@bush.org.nz
Website: www.bush.org.nz

Organic Products Exporters of New Zealand Inc (OPENZ)
OPENZ aims to encourage and support the organic export industry.
Address: PO Box 292, Christchurch
Phone: (03) 344 4081
Fax: (03) 344 4083
E-mail: info@organicsnewzealand.org.nz
Website: www.organicsnewzealand.org.nz

Permaculture in New Zealand (PINZ)
Address: PO Box 56107, Dominion Rd, Auckland
E-mail: info@permaculture.org.nz
Website: www.permaculture.org.nz

Safe Food Campaign
The Safe Food Campaign is a nationwide organisation that campaigns for
safer, healthier food.
Address: PO Box 9206, Wellington
Phone: (04) 476 8607 (Alison) / (04) 920 5961 (Lance)
E-mail: info@safefood.org.nz
Website: www.safefood.org.nz

Soil and Health Association New Zealand Inc
Promotes safe, healthy food, protection of the environment and policies for
sustainable farming and resource use.
Address: PO Box 36 170, Northcote, Auckland
Phone/Fax: (09) 419 4536
Email: info@organicnz.pl.net
Website: www.soil-health.org.nz

The Organic Directory New Zealand (Organic Pathways)
On-line guide to organics in New Zealand. A website listing organic products, businesses and organisations throughout the country. It includes organic producers, retailers, processors and services as well as organic groups and organisations.
Website: www.organicpathways.co.nz

World Wide Opportunities on Organic Farms in New Zealand (WWOOF NZ)
WWOOF provides opportunities for voluntary work on New Zealand organic properties.
Address: PO Box 1172, Nelson
Phone: (03) 544 9890
E-mail: support@wwoof.co.nz
Website: www.wwoof.co.nz

CONSTRUCTION

Building Biology and Ecology Institute of New Zealand (BBE)
Promotes a holistic approach to sustainable architecture and healthy building for architects, builders, house owners, the building industry and building authorities in residential and commercial environments. BBE produces and markets an 'Eco Products and Services List' and 24 booklets on various eco topics.

Head office: Wellington
Address: PO Box 1364, Wellington
Phone: (04) 801 8180
E-mail: bbe@ecoprojects.co.nz

Auckland office
Phone: (09) 479 3161
E-mail: jobern@ihug.co.nz
Website: www.ecoprojects.co.nz

Building Research Association of New Zealand (BRANZ)
BRANZ and its associated companies conduct research, testing, consulting and technology transfer on behalf of the building and construction industry.
The BRANZ Green Homes Scheme promotes sustainable building by

accrediting participating architects and assessing house designs for a range
of environmental, health and safety issues (see website).
Address: Private Bag 50 908, Porirua City
Phone: (04) 237 1170
Fax: (04) 237 1171
E-mail: branz@branz.org.nz
Website: www.branz.org.nz

The Earth Building Association of New Zealand Inc (EBANZ)
Promotes the art and science of earth building.
Address: PO Box 1452, Whangarei
Websites: www.earthbuilding.org.nz and www.earthbuilding.co.nz

Waitakere City Council (WCC)
The WCC's Sustainable Home Guidelines provides a practical guide for good-
practice eco building with up-to-date information about energy, water,
materials, safety, waste and other sustainable building issues.
Website: www.waitakere.govt.nz/abtcit/ec/bldsus/shsummary.asp

ENERGY

Appropriate Technology for Living Association (ATLA)
ATLA is a non-profit organisation which promotes environmentally
sustainable alternative technologies and healthy lifestyles. Interests range
from windfarms to house insulation, passive solar architecture to
biodynamics, organic gardening to Reiki healing, earth building to food
additives.
Address: PO Box 27 475, Marion Square, Wellington
Phone/Fax: (04) 479 0404
E-mail: alopex@actrix.gen.nz
Website: www.converge.org.nz/atla/index.html

Bioenergy Association of New Zealand (BANZ)
The Bioenergy Association represents the commercial bioenergy sector.
Address: PO Box 11 595, Wellington
Phone: (04) 385 3398
Fax: (04) 385 3397
E-mail: info@bioenergy.org.nz
Website: www.bioenergy.org.nz

Canterbury Sustainability Expo

An annual two-day event on sustainable living. The event is based around Renewable Energy, but incorporates sustainable development in terms of energy-efficient building design and housing, energy-efficient appliances, transport, waste minimisation, and organics. Involves a wide range of speakers and many and varied exhibitions.
Venue: Canterbury Horticultural Hall, South Hagley Park, Christchurch
Date: First or second weekend of February
Phone: c/- 027 457 6527
E-mail: john@gosolar.co.nz
Website: www.gosolar.co.nz (Click on EXPO)

Energy Efficiency and Conservation Authority (EECA)

EECA works to bring about voluntary changes in the private and public sectors to implement government strategies for energy efficiency.
Address: PO Box 388, Wellington
Phone: (04) 470 2200
Fax: (04) 499 5330
Website: www.eeca.govt.nz

New Zealand ANZSES; NZ Branch (Solar Action)

Address: PO Box 54 223 Mana, Porirua
Phone: (04) 237 1170 (Andrew Pollard)
E-mail: solaraction@paradise.net.nz
Website: www.converge.org.nz/solaraction

New Zealand Photovoltaic Association (NZPVA)

Promotes and supports the use of solar energy to produce electricity.
Address: PO Box 91 129 AMSC, Auckland
Phone: (09) 379 3022
Fax: (09) 379 5075
E-mail: nzpva@photovoltaics.org.nz
Website: www.photovoltaics.org.nz

New Zealand Wind Energy Association (NZWEA)

Aims to promote the use of wind energy in New Zealand.
Address: PO Box 553, Wellington
Phone: (04) 586 2003
Fax: (04) 586 2004
E-mail: info@windenergy.org.nz
Website: www.windenergy.org.nz
Newsgroup for non-members: nzwea-news-subscribe@yahoogroups.com

Solar Industries Association

Represents the collective interests of manufacturers, importers and installers of solar water-heating systems and provides a single point of contact to the industry. Their website provides information on New Zealand suppliers and installers of solar water-heating systems.
Address: PO Box 11 595, Wellington
Phone: (04) 385 3359
Fax: (04) 385 3397
E-mail: info@solarindustries.org.nz
Website: www.solarindustries.org.nz

Sustainable Energy Forum

Aims to promote and facilitate the transition towards the use of energy in New Zealand in a manner that improves social well-being, while conserving physical resources, maintaining the integrity of ecosystems, and avoiding the transfer of costs onto future generations.
Address: PO Box 11 152, Wellington
Phone: (04) 586 2003
Fax: (04) 586 2004
E-mail: info@sef.org.nz
Website: www.sef.org.nz

WASTE

Enviroline

Free Phone: 0800 80 60 40
E-mail: enviroline@arc.govt.nz

Plastics New Zealand

Contacts given for plastic recycling.
Website: www.plastics.org.nz

Recycling Operators of New Zealand (RONZ)

RONZ represents recycling service providers, operators and educators in the recovered materials and recycling industry.
Website: www.ronz.org.nz

Zero Waste New Zealand Trust

Established in 1997 to support a growing network of groups working on waste minimisation and recycling projects that have an emphasis on employment and local economic development.

Address: PO Box 33 1695, Takapuna, Auckland
Phone: (09) 486 0734
Fax: (09) 489 3232
E-mail: mailbox@zerowaste.co.nz
Website: www.zerowaste.co.nz

Eco certificators

AGRICULTURAL CERTIFICATION

AgriQuality New Zealand Ltd
The AgriQuality Organic Standard is based on the international Codex Alinorm 99/22, EU Regulations and the Australian National Standard. AgriQuality has established a separate certification body called Certenz (see below).
Contact: David Brown
Address: PO Box 307, Pukekohe
Phone: (09) 237 1807
Free Phone: 050 800 1122
Fax: (09) 238 3757
E-mail: brownd@agriquality.co.nz
Website: www.agriquality.co.nz

Bio Dynamic Farming and Gardening Association in New Zealand Inc
The Association licenses the Demeter trademark and promotes biodynamic practices based on the teachings of Rudolf Steiner.
Address: PO Box 39 045, Wellington
Phone: (04) 589 5366
Fax: (04) 589 5365
E-mail: info@biodynamic.org.nz
Website: www.biodynamic.org.nz

Bio-Gro New Zealand
Administers the BIO-GRO certification trademark and is the trading name of the New Zealand Biological Producers and Consumers Council Inc.
Address: PO Box 9693, Marion Square, Wellington

Phone: (04) 801 9741
Fax: (04) 801 9742
E-mail: info@bio-gro.co.nz
Website: www.bio-gro.co.nz

Certenz
Contact: Andrew Baines — Business Manager
Address: The Homestead, Private Bag 3080, Ruakura, Hamilton
Phone: (07) 838 5872
Fax: (07) 838 5846
Mobile: 025 543 064
E-mail: bainesa@certenz.co.nz

INDUSTRIAL CERTIFICATION

Environmental Choice
The New Zealand Ecolabelling Trust is a voluntary, multiple criteria-based
environmental labelling programme for non-foodstuffs, industrial processes
and products such as paints, tissues and carpets, which operate to
international standards and principles.
Address: PO Box 56 533, Dominion Road, Mt Eden, Auckland
Phone: (09) 845 3330
Fax: (09) 845 3331
E-mail: info@enviro-choice.org.nz
Website: www.enviro-choice.org.nz

Eco distributors, producers and outlets

ASBESTOS REMOVAL

Various: Consult your Yellow Pages.

ASBESTOS TESTING

Capital Environmental Services
Address: PO Box 38 328, Wellington
Mail Centre
Phone: (04) 566 3311

Dowell & Associates
Address: 4 Cain Rd, Penrose,
Auckland
PO Box 112 017, Auckland
Phone: (09) 526 0246

CLEANING

Dr. Bronner Magic Soaps
A charismatic, early pioneer of eco
soaps.
Website: www.drbronner.com

ecostore
Manufacturer and retailer of
natural, plant-based, chemical-free
household cleaners, body care, pet
care and organic gardening
products. It supplies health shops,
organic shops and supermarkets
throughout New Zealand.
Address: 1 Scotland Street,
Ponsonby, Auckland
PO Box 91718 AMSC
Phone: (09) 360 8477
Phone for free mail-order
catalogue: 0800 432 678
Fax: (09) 376 8577
E-mail: info@ecostore.co.nz
Website: www.ecostore.co.nz

Ecover Products
Ecover Products manufactures and
researches eco products.
Website: www.ecover.com/products

Natural Blend Ltd
Manufacturer of eco laundry
powder.
Address: PO Box 26157, Auckland
E-mail: david@naturalblend.co.nz

ENERGY

Able Solar Ltd

BP photovoltaic solar modules.
Address: Unit B, 14 Collard Place,
Henderson, Auckland
Phone: (09) 837 2211
Fax: (09) 837 2212
E-mail: sales@able-solar.co.nz
Website: www.able-solar.co.nz

Alternative Power NZ Ltd

Hydro, solar and wind systems, solar
water heating and underfloor home
heating.
Address: 36 Enner Glynn Road,
Stoke, Nelson 7001
Phone: (03) 547 6397
Fax: (03) 547 6305
E-mail: altpower@xtra.co.nz
Website: www.yp.co.nz/for/altpower

Natural Energy

Designers and suppliers of Electric
Power Systems, including solar
systems and New Zealand-made
wind and water turbines.
Address: 33 Linton Crescent, Matua,
Tauranga
Phone: (07) 576 6528
Fax: (07) 576 6523
E-mail: power@naturalenergy.co.nz

Reid Technology

Beasley solar panels and PV modules.
Address: PO Box 33 1690, Takapuna
Phone: (09) 489 8100
Free Phone: 0508 4 SOLAR (476527)
Fax: (09) 489 8585
E-mail: bob@reidtechnology.co.nz
Website: www.reidtechnology.co.nz

Self Power

Address: 9 Puke Road, Paeroa 2951
Phone/Fax: (07) 862 6235
E-mail: selfpower@xtra.co.nz
Website: www.selfpower.co.nz.

Sola 60 NZ Ltd

Sola 60 solar power systems.
Address: Head office: Tauranga
Phone: (07) 578 2754
Fax: (07) 578 2744
Free Phone: Distributors Nationwide
0800 100 849
E-mail: info@sola60.com
Website: www.sola60.co.nz

Solar Electric Specialists Ltd

Agent/consultant for a range of
solar electric (photovoltaic) and
wind-generation systems including
PV panels, deep cycle batteries,
charge controllers, inverters,
energy-efficient appliances and
lights; contract design/projects,
fountain pumps and water-
pumping applications.
Address: PO Box 6302, Christchurch
Phone: 027 457 6527
Website: www.gosolar.co.nz

Solar Energy Solutions

Supply and/or design and
consultancy work for domestic and
commercial applications. Products
include Chromagen Solar Water
Heating Systems, and Unisolar
Photovoltaic panels.
Address: PO Box 25 621, St Heliers,
Auckland
Phone: (09) 367 7412

E-mail: ses@xtra.co.nz
Website: www.solarhotwater.co.nz
Also at:
Address: PO Box 9055, Marion
Square, Wellington
Phone: (04) 939 6977
Fax: (04) 970 0714

Solarmaster Auckland Ltd
Solar Max products.
Address: PO Box 13 317, Onehunga,
Auckland
Phone: (09) 634 0358
Fax: (09) 636 9569
E-mail: solarmasterauckland@
harrisholdings.co.nz
Website: www.solarmax.co.nz

Solar Tech Ltd
Edwards solar products. Agents for
Edwards solar products available
throughout the country.
Address: PO Box 87 282,
Meadowbank, Auckland
Phone: (09) 520 6787
Fax: (09) 520 6781
Free Phone: 0800 765 278
E-mail: netzer@cyberpress.co.nz
Website: www.solaredwards.com.au

Solwind Ltd
Involved in the design and
development of remote-area power
and alternative energy systems.
Address: PO Box 4295, Kamo,
Whangarei
Phone: (09) 433 7213
Fax: (09) 433 7273
E-mail: info@solwind.co.nz

Sunz Ltd
Sunz solar systems.
Address: PO Box 72 642, Papakura,
Auckland
Phone: (09) 296 7070
Fax: (09) 296 1011
E-mail: info@sunz.co.nz
Website: www.sunz.co.nz

Synergex Systems NZ Ltd
Solahart solar power systems and
Heliocol pool heating systems.
Address: PO Box 35 588, Browns
Bay, Auckland
Phone: (09) 415 7652
Fax: (09) 415 7651
Free Phone: 0800 769 377 (POWERS)
E-mail: synergex@xtra.co.nz
Website: www.synergex.co.nz

Wellwind Energy Ltd
Suppliers of Thermomax solar water
systems; PV and wind power systems
for individual or community needs;
low-energy appliances.
Address: PO Box 7016, Wellington
South
Phone: (04) 389 9476
Fax: (04) 389 8922
E-mail: wellwind@paradise.net.nz
Website: www.wellwindenergy.co.nz

FOOD AND DRINK

Ceres Enterprises Ltd
An umbrella organisation
incorporating wholesalers of
biodynamic and organic food,
including fresh produce, household
cleansers, organic gardening
products, homoeopathic medicines,

organic body-care products, books covering eco living, organics and anthroposophy.

Ceres (wholesale) and Ceres Books
Address: PO Box 11 336, Ellerslie, Auckland
Phone: (09) 574 0373

Ceres Organic Retail Shop
Address: 181 Ladies Mile, Ellerslie, Auckland
Phone: (09) 579 7126
E-mail: ceres@ceres.co.nz
Website: www.ceres.co.nz

Commonsense Organics
Retail supplier of wide range of organic produce. On-line orders delivered throughout New Zealand.
Address: 260 Wakefield St, Wellington
37 Waterloo Rd, Lower Hutt.
Coastlands, Paraparaumu.
Phone: (04) 384 3314
E-mail: mail@organicdelivery.co.nz
Website: www.commonsenseorganics.co.nz

Founders Brewery
Manufacturers of organic beer — Bio-Gro certification. Orders available on-line.
Address: 87 Athawhai Drive, Nelson
Phone: 0800 BIOBREW
Fax: (03) 548 4518 (for orders)
E-mail: info@biobrew.co.nz
Website: www.biobrew.co.nz

Eco On-line Shopping Mall
On-line gateway to a number of eco suppliers and retailers.
Website: www.the shop.co.nz

FRENZS
Grower, distributor and exporter of free-range organic eggs and chickens.
Phone: 0800 373 697
E-mail: info@frenzs.co.nz
Website: www.frenzs.com

i.e.produce
Organic produce and non-allergy food specialist; Bio-Gro certified. Home delivery — order on-line.
Address: 1 Barry's Point Rd, Takapuna, Auckland
PO Box 74128, Market Rd, Remuera
Phone: (09) 488 0211
Fax: (09) 488 0221
E-mail: info@organicfresh.co.nz
Website: www.organicfresh.co.nz

Kea Organic Coffee
Blenders and suppliers of organic coffees.
Address: PO Box 8396, Havelock North
Phone: (06) 874 7681
E-mail: jbdaniell@aol.com
Website: www.keacoffee.co.nz

Millton Vineyard
Organically certified grape grower and vintner of a range of organic (and some non-organic) table wines. On-line and fax ordering.
Address: 119 Papatu Rd, Manutuke, Gisborne
Phone: 0800 464 558
Fax: 0800 329 645
E-mail: info@millton.co.nz
Website: www.millton.co.nz

Nature's Abundance
Retailer (retail premises and on-line shopping) offering South Island customers a wide range of organic and natural foods. Fresh organic produce is certified Bio-Gro, Demeter or Certenz.
Address: 5/300 Colombo Street, Christchurch
Phone: (03) 332 3060
E-mail: natures.abundance@xtra.co.nz
Website: www.organicshop.co.nz

New Zealand Bio Grains Ltd
Miller and supplier of wide range of organically grown grains, flours, pulses, nuts and other produce. On-line orders and nationwide deliveries.
Address: Ashburton
Phone: (03) 308 7349
E-mail: enquiries@BioGrains.co.nz
Website: www.biograins.co.nz

Nicola's Organics
Manufacturers of hand-made organic breakfast food. Phone orders available.
Address: 161 Main South Road, Green Island, Dunedin
Phone: (03) 488 3073
Fax: (03) 488 4445
E-mail: harraways@xtra.co.nz
Website: www.nicolasorganics.net.nz

Organic & Natural Food Specialists
Organic produce: order on-line.
Retail Address: 215/9 Rosedale Road, Albany, Auckland
Phone: (09) 914 2026
Free Phone: 0800 567 888

E-mail: info@ naturallyorganicproduce. co.nz
Website: www.naturallyorganicproduce.co.nz

Organik Natural Foods
Bio-Gro certified grower and distributor of organic potato products (chips and wedges) and 10 varieties of fresh potatoes (including Maori potatoes).
Address: 261 Otauto Road, RD 1, Patea
Phone: (06) 273 8780
E-mail: organik@xtra.co.nz
Website: www.organik.co.nz

Phoenix Organics
Beverages include honey-sweetened or organic ginger beer, lemonade and cola, organic juice and sparkling waters with fruit juice.
Phone: (09) 836 2272
Fax: (09) 836 5232
E-mail: roger@phoenixorganics.co.nz
Website: www.phoenixorganics.co.nz

Real Beer Australia & New Zealand
Distributors of organic beers, including Founders range, Mikes Mild Ale and Green Fern Lager. All have on-line beer store available.
Free Phone: 0800 21 BEER (2337)
E-mail: realbeer@realbeer.co.nz
Website: rbes.net/e/realbeernz

Terrace Farm
Producers of organic grains and flours.

Address: RD 12, Rakaia
Phone: (03) 302 8663
Fax: (03) 302 8623
E-mail: terracefarm@actrix.gen.nz

True Blue Organics
Bio-Gro certified organic producers
and processors of tea tree oil
(*Melaleuca alternifolia*) grown and
distilled in Karamea, New Zealand.
True Blue Organics also produces a
range of products using the
antibacterial, antifungal and
antiviral properties of the essential
oil.
Address: Kongahu, RD 1, Westport
Phone: (03) 782 6888
E-mail: macbeth.clan@xtra.co.nz
Website: www.trueblueorganics.co.nz

Yummy Tummy Organics
Home-delivered, fresh organic
produce, throughout the North
Island.
Free Phone: 0508 986 698 / 0508
YUMMY TUMMY
Free Fax: 0508 986 693 / 0508
YUMMY FAX
E-mail: info@yummytummy.co.nz
Website: www.yummytummy.co.nz

FURNITURE AND FABRICS

Futon Ya San
Manufacturer of natural mattresses,
futons, bed frames, furniture and
bedroom accessories.
Address: 582 Karangahape Road,
Newton, Auckland
Phone: (09) 378 1000
Free Phone: 0800 FUTONS

E-mail: futons@xtra.co.nz
Website: www.futons.co.nz

FutonZ
Manufacturer and retailer of
bedding made from natural
materials.
Address: 23 Pollen Street, Grey
Lynn, Auckland
Phone: (09) 361 1088
Fax: (09) 360 5121
E-mail: info@futonz.co.nz
Website: www.futonz.co.nz

**Global Connections Ltd (Real by
design)**
Producers of environmentally
sustainable furniture.
Address: PO Box 74461, Market
Road, Auckland
Phone/Fax: (09) 634 5544
E-mail: talk2us@realbydesign.co.nz
Website: www.realbydesign.co.nz

GARDENING

Betta-Crop Organic
Manufacturer of organic pesticides.
Phone: (07) 824 4881
Fax: (07) 824 4620
E-mail: info@organics.co.nz
Website: www.organics.co.nz

Certified Organics Ltd
Manufacturers of certified organic
herbicides and biocides, including
Organic Interceptor — a pine-based
weed killer.
Address: Ground Floor, Building 5,
666 Great South Road, Penrose,
Auckland

Postal Address: PO Box 74 382, Market Road, Auckland.
Phone: (09) 525 3432
Fax: (09) 525 3462
E-mail: info@certified-organics.com
Website: www.certified-organics.com

Earthwise Direct Ltd
Supplier of natural products for home, garden, personal and pet care. On-line orders available.
Address: PO Box 9128, Hamilton
Phone: (07) 824 4881
Fax: (07) 824 4620
E-mail: info@earthwisedirect.co.nz
Website: www.earthwisedirect.co.nz

Ocean Organics
Manufactures New Zealand liquid seaweed concentrates including products for soil, foliar and animal health, personal body products and seaweed soap. All products use native New Zealand seaweeds or wild herbs and are brewed biodynamically. Bio-Gro certificated.
Address: 4 Fraser Street, Paeroa
Phone: (07) 862 8424
Free Phone: 0800 732 9333
Fax: (07) 862 8404
E-mail: jill@oceanorganics.co.nz
Website: www.oceanorganics.co.nz

Zonda Resources
Suppliers of biological control agents, bumble bees for pollination and sticky traps and pheromone traps.
Phone: (06) 878 6010

Fax: (06) 876 2132
E-mail: zonda@zonda.net.nz

INSULATION

Autex Insulation
Manufactures Greenstuf (thermal) and QuietStuf (acoustic) polyester insulation.
Free phone: 0800 428 839
Fax: (09) 828 4049
E-mail: insulation@autex.co.nz
Website: www.autex.co.nz

Cork Supplies Ltd
Suppliers of cork floor tiles; acoustic underlay; roll and sheet cork.
Address: PO Box 100 148, NSMC, Auckland
Phone: (09) 415 3666
E-mail: sales@corksupplies.co.nz
Website: www.corksupplies.co.nz

Eco Insulation Ltd
Natural wool insulation.
Free Phone: 0800 326 966
Phone: Head Office: (09) 414 2160
Fax: Head Office: (09) 414 2161
E-mail: enquiries@ecoinsulation.co.nz
Website: www.ecoinsulation.co.nz

Eco-Sphere Building Products (Terra Lana Products Ltd)
Wool and polyester insulation.
Address: 23 Cumnor Terrace, Christchurch
Phone: (03) 381 7185
Fax: (03) 381 7186
E-mail: terralana@xtra.co.nz

Wool Bloc Insulation
Address: 29 Bullen Street,
Tahunanui, Nelson
Postal address: PO Box 3158,
Richmond, Nelson
Free Phone: 0800 788 889
Phone sales: (03) 546 4387
Fax: (03) 546 4707
E-mail: lindsay@woolbloc.co.nz
Website: www.woolbloc.co.nz

MOISTURE CONTROL

Domestic Ventilation Systems
Free Phone: 0800 387 387/ 0800
DVS DVS
E-mail: sales@ventilation.co.nz
Website: www.ventilation.co.nz

PAINTS AND FINISHES

Bio Paints Ltd
Manufacturer, importer, wholesaler
and retailer of a wide range of
natural decorative products and
finishes including paints, varnishes,
oils, enamels, waxes, adhesives,
household cleaners.
Address: 106 A Vanguard Street,
Nelson
Postal Address: PO Box 7077, Nelson
7015
Phone: (03) 539 0446
Fax: (03) 539 0442
E-mail: info@biopaints.com
Free Phone: 0800 472 468
Website: www.biopaints.co.nz

Churton Pacific Ltd
Manufacturer and distributor of a
range of products — including

CD 50 Preservative — for preparing,
restoring and protecting timber
surfaces.
Address: 15a Vega Place, Mairangi
Bay, Auckland
Phone: (09) 478 4370
Free Phone: 0800 107 555
E-mail: info@churton.com
Website: www.churton.com

ecostore
Range includes Harlem oil and
vegetable thinners (contact details,
see *Cleaning*)

Equus Industries Ltd
Supplers of Keim-Farben silicate
mineral paint for exterior and
interior surfaces.
Address: Head office: PO Box 601
Blenheim
Phone: (03) 578 0214
Fax: (03) 578 0919
E-mail: admin@equus.co.nz

Murobond
Distributor of environmentally
friendly acrylic, interior and exterior
mineral, cement and limewash
paints that imitate traditional
'washed' finishes. Manufacturer of
mineral paints (waterproof and
breathable).
Address: 23 Schnapper Rock Rd,
Albany, Auckland
Phone: (09) 415 8099
Fax: (09) 415 8036
E-mail: murobond@xtra.co.nz
Website: www.murobond.co.nz

Natural House Company
Address: PO Box 5, Mapua, Nelson
Free Phone: 0800 112 030
E-mail: info@naturalhouseco.com
Website: www.naturalhouseco.com

Natural Oils
Importer and distributor of
environmentally friendly oils, waxes
and paints for the preservation and
finishing of timber.
Address: PO Box 25 352, St Heliers,
Auckland
Phone: (09) 575 9849
Fax: (09) 575 9365
Website: www.natural-oils.co.nz

Natural Paints and Floor Oils
Importer and manufacturer of a
range of interior and exterior
finishes, paints, lime wash, oils,
varnish.
Free Phone: 0800 11 20 30
Website: www.naturalhouseco.com

NVF Oils
Harlem oils.
Address: PO Box 135, Warkworth
Phone: (09) 425 9337
E-mail: nvfoils@wk.planet.gen.nz

Resene Paints
A comprehensive range of New
Zealand Environmental Choice
approved finishing paints, primers,
sealers, undercoats, stains, clear
coatings, waterproofing products
and textured coatings.
Website: www.resene.co.nz

TIMBER

A 1999 list of sawmillers, eco-
timber retailers and the timbers
they stock can be found under the
Good Wood Guide
Website: www.converge.org.nz/gwg/

WASTEWATER AND TOILET SYSTEMS

Bio Systems Ltd
Industrial and residential
composting toilets and greywater
systems.
Address: PO Box 1834, Rotorua
Fax: (07) 346 1015
Free Phone: 0800 246 566 / 0800
BIOLOO
E-mail: tracey.f@clear.net.nz

Eco Toilets
Agents for Aquatron system and
Toatrone urine separating toilets.
Address: PO Box 14 028, Enderly,
Hamilton
Phone: (07) 828 8474
Fax: (07) 828 8212
E-mail: info@ecotoilets.co.nz
Website: www.ecotoilets.co.nz

Jet Waste & Water Systems
Design, manufacture and install
services in NZ and Pacific Islands.
Address: PO Box 302 241, NHPC,
Auckland
Phone: (09) 415 1538
Fax: (09) 415 1438
E-mail: info@jetwaste.co.nz
Website: www.jetwaste.co.nz

Kiwi Bog Company Limited
Compact composting toilets for
baches, cottages, campervans,
boats.
Address: 63 Robinson Road, Nelson
Phone: (03) 546 9769
E-mail: info@kiwibog.com
Website: www.kiwibog.com

Eco journals and magazines

The BBE Eco Products and Services List
A list of suppliers and services (see contact details on page 209, under Eco organisations).

Consumer
Address: Freepost Consumer, Consumers' Institute, Private Bag 6996, Wellington
Free Phone: 0800 CONSUMER; 0800 266 786
Free Fax: 0800 266 766
E-mail: editor@consumer.org.nz
Website: www.consumer.org.nz

Eco Living New Zealand
Bimonthly magazine published by Bedrock Enterprises Ltd.
Address: PO Box 4, Ahipara, Northland
Phone: (09) 409 4585
Fax: (09) 409 4598
E-mail: craig@bedrock.co.nz

Energy Watch
A commentary on sustainable energy published by the Sustainable Energy Forum (see contact details on page 212, under Eco organisations).

Energy Wise News
Bimonthly magazine from EECA.
Address: Free Post 4245, PO Box 388, Wellington
Fax: (04) 499 5330
Website: www.energywise.co.nz

Forest & Bird
Quarterly magazine printed for members of Royal Forest and Bird Protection Society of New Zealand (see contact details on page 207, under Eco organisations).

Organic NZ
Bimonthly magazine of Soil and Health Association New Zealand (see contact details on page 208, under Eco organisations).

Solar Made Easy
Book — available in libraries; reprint
scheduled; accessible also on
website.
Author: Bob Riley
E-mail: solarbob@xtra.co.nz
Website: kiwiingenuity.org.nz

Acronyms

ACQ: ammoniacal copper quaternary

CCA: copper chrome arsenic

CFC: chlorofluorocarbon

CFL: compact fluorescent lamp

CuAz: copper azole

DBE: dibasic ester

DDT: dichloro-diphenyl-trichloroethane

DVS: domestic ventilation system

EMR: electro magnetic radiation

EPS: expanded polystyrene

GAC: granular activated carbon

GM: genetic modification

HEPA: high efficiency particulate arrestor

IIC: impact insulation class

LDPE: low-density polyethylene

LOSP: light organic solvent protection

LIM: land information memorandum

MSG: monosodium glutamate

MTBE: methyl tertiary-butyl ether

NiCad: nickel cadmium

NMP: N-Methylpyrrolidone

PCB: polychlorinated biphenyls

PCP: pentachlorophenol

PE: polyethylene

PERC: perchloroethylene

PET: polyethylene-terephthalate

PFCs: perfluorocarbons

POP: persistent organic pollutant

PP: polypropylene

PS: polystyrene

PV: photovoltaic

PVC: polyvinyl chloride

SAD: seasonal affective disorder

SAPS: stand-alone power systems

STC: sound transmission class

VOCs: volatile organic compounds

WERS: window energy rating scheme

GLOSSARY

Acid rain: Rainfall has a 'normal' pH of 5.6. Acid rain is defined as any form of wet precipitation which has a pH less than 5.6 (on a scale of 0 to 14, with 7 being neutral). The rain becomes acidic when water molecules react with gases, primarily sulphur dioxide and various nitrogen oxides, in the air. Acid rain has a harmful effect on some plants, aquatic organisms, soils and buildings.

Activated carbon: A highly absorbent form of carbon used to remove odours and toxic substances from liquid or gaseous emissions. It is commonly used in water filters to remove dissolved organic matter from drinking water.

Aerobic treatment: Wastewater treatment process by which microbes decompose complex organic compounds in the presence of oxygen and use the liberated energy for reproduction and growth.

Air pollutant: Any airborne substance that could, in high enough concentration, harm humans or other life forms including vegetation. Pollutants may be in the form of solid particles, liquid droplets or gases, and are often grouped in categories for ease of classification, e.g. solids, sulphur compounds, volatile organic compounds, particulate matter, nitrogen compounds, oxygen compounds, halogen compounds, radioactive compounds and odours.

Air pollution: The presence of contaminants or pollutant substances in the air that interfere with human health or welfare, or produce other harmful environmental effects.

Algal bloom: Large, visible, masses of algae that develop in bodies of water during warm weather. Algal blooms may occur in response to additions of plant nutrients (especially nitrogen and/or phosphorus) to the aquatic system, and the subsequent oxygen depletion can kill marine organisms.

Asbestosis: A disease associated with inhalation of asbestos fibres. The disease makes breathing progressively more difficult and can be fatal.

Biodegradable: Capable of decomposing under natural conditions.

Biomass: All of the living material in a given area; often refers to vegetation.

Blackwater: Water that contains animal, human or food waste, usually from toilets.

Carbon monoxide (CO): A colourless, odourless, poisonous gas produced by incomplete fossil fuel combustion.

Carbon tetrachloride: Chemical compound once widely used as an industrial raw material, as a solvent, and in the production of CFCs. Its use as a solvent ended when it was discovered to be carcinogenic.

CCA (copper chrome arsenic): A waterborne timber preservative formulation containing a mixture of metallic salts. Recently withdrawn from use in residential applications in the USA due to concern over a build-up of arsenic in the environment.

Chlordane: A broad spectrum agricultural insecticide, classified as an organochlorine. Also used in timber industry and in manufacture of plywoods, finger-jointed and laminated timbers.

Chlorofluorocarbons (CFCs): A family of inert, non-toxic, and easily liquefied chemicals used in refrigeration, air conditioning, packaging, insulation, or as solvents and aerosol propellants. Because CFCs are not destroyed in the lower atmosphere they drift into the upper atmosphere where their chlorine components destroy ozone.

Chlorosis: Discoloration of normally green plant parts caused by disease, lack of nutrients, or various air pollutants.

Cogeneration: The consecutive generation of useful thermal and electric energy from the same fuel source.

Compact fluorescent lamp (CFL): Small fluorescent lamps used as more efficient alternatives to incandescent lighting. Also called PL, CFL, Twin-Tube, or BIAX lamps.

Crop rotation: Planting a succession of different crops on the same land area as opposed to planting the same crop time after time.

Cryptosporidium: A protozoan microbe associated with the disease cryptosporidiosis in man. The disease can be transmitted through ingestion of drinking water, person-to-person contact, or other pathways, and can cause acute diarrhoea, abdominal pain, vomiting, fever, and can be fatal.

DDT: A persistent organochlorine pesticide (POP). Widely used in New Zealand in the 1950s and '60s as an agricultural and household insect control measure. Frequently mixed with fertiliser or lime and applied to pasture, as well as lawns, market gardens and parks.

Detergent: Synthetic washing agent that helps to remove dirt and oil. Some contain compounds that kill useful bacteria and encourage algae growth (causing eutrophication) when released into waterways.

Dioxin: A persistent organic pollutant (POP), dioxin is the by-product of industrial processes which use chlorine, e.g. bleaching of paper, manufacture of petroleum, manufacture of chlorine-containing pesticides and plastics. Other potential sources include industrial and domestic woodburners, accidental fires, landfills and vehicle emissions. At very low exposure levels, dioxins have been linked to immune system suppression, reproductive disorders, a variety of cancers and endometriosis.

Ecosystem: The interacting system of a biological community and its non-living environmental surroundings.

Eutrophication: The slow ageing process during which a lake, estuary or bay evolves into a bog and eventually disappears. During the later stages of eutrophication the water is choked by abundant plant life due to higher levels of nutritive compounds such as nitrogen and phosphorus. Human activities can accelerate the process.

Fluorocarbons (FCs): Any of a number of organic compounds analogous to hydrocarbons in which one or more hydrogen atoms are replaced by fluorine. Once widely used as a propellant for domestic aerosols, they are now found mainly in coolants and some industrial processes. FCs containing chlorine are called chlorofluorocarbons (CFCs). They are believed to be modifying the ozone layer in the stratosphere, thereby allowing more harmful solar radiation to reach the earth's surface.

Formaldehyde: A colourless, pungent, and irritating gas used chiefly as a disinfectant and preservative and in synthesising other compounds like resins. Classified as a VOC and a suspected carcinogen.

Fungicide: Pesticides which are used to control, deter, or destroy fungi.

Genetic modification (GM): A process of inserting new genetic information into existing cells in order to modify a specific organism for the purpose of changing one of its characteristics. (Also called GE: genetic engineering.)

Giardia lamblia: Protozoan in the faeces of humans and animals that can cause severe gastrointestinal ailments. It is a common contaminant of surface waters.

Global warming: An increase in the near surface temperature of the earth. Global warming has occurred in the distant past as the result of natural influences, but the term is most often used to refer to the warming predicted to occur as a result of increased emissions of greenhouse gases.

Granular activated carbon treatment: A filtering system often used in small water systems and individual homes to remove organics.

Greenhouse gases: Atmospheric gases, mainly water vapour, carbon dioxide, methane, nitrous oxide and ozone, which act somewhat like the glass panels of a greenhouse, trapping and reflecting solar radiation within the earth's atmosphere, and maintaining the earth's average temperature. Evidence suggests that human activities over the last 50 years have altered the chemical composition of the atmosphere, causing an increased greenhouse effect and a small but significant build-up of heat.

Greywater: Household wastewater excepting toilet wastewater. (As opposed to blackwater.)

Hard water: Alkaline water containing dissolved salts that prevent soap from sudsing.

Hazardous air pollutants: Air pollutants which may present a human or environmental health threat. Such pollutants include asbestos, beryllium, mercury, benzene, formaldehyde, radionuclides and vinyl chloride.

Hazardous substance: Any material that poses a threat to human health and/or the environment. Typical hazardous substances are toxic, corrosive, ignitable, explosive, or chemically reactive.

Hazardous waste: Waste products that pose a substantial or potential hazard to human health or the environment when improperly managed. Household hazardous waste includes paints, stains, varnishes, solvents, pesticides, and other materials or products containing volatile chemicals that can catch fire, react or explode, or that are corrosive or toxic.

Heavy metals: Metallic elements with high atomic weights (e.g. mercury, chromium, cadmium, arsenic and lead). Heavy metals can damage living things at low concentrations and tend to accumulate in the food chain.

Herbicide: A chemical pesticide designed to control or destroy plants, weeds or grasses.

Hexachlorophene: An organochlorine compound commonly used in shampoos, antiperspirants and other skin care products as an antibacterial agent. Chronic (long-term) health effects of exposure to hexachlorophene may include brain damage, paralysis, blindness and skin allergy. There is a suspected association between exposure of pregnant women to hexachlorophene and birth defects.

Hydrophilic: Having a strong affinity for water.

Insecticide: A pesticide compound specifically used to kill or prevent the growth of insects.

Irradiation: Exposure to radiation of wavelengths shorter than those of visible light (gamma, X-ray or ultraviolet), for medical purposes or to sterilise foodstuffs.

Legionella: A genus of bacteria, some species of which have caused a type of pneumonia called Legionnaires' disease.

Lindane: A POP pesticide once extensively used in animal husbandry and pasture management, and in vegetable gardens, orchards and households. Causes adverse health effects in domestic water supplies and is toxic to freshwater fish and aquatic life. Use has largely ceased in New Zealand.

LOSP (light organic solvent preservative): A timber preservative consisting of an organic solvent (e.g. white spirits), an insecticide (e.g. Permethrin) and sometimes a fungicide (e.g. Tributyltin).

Methane: A colourless, non-poisonous, flammable gas created by anaerobic decomposition of organic compounds. A major component of natural gas used in the home.

Methyl bromide: Fumigant used mainly to fumigate soil (often for crops such as strawberries and tomatoes). It is also used to fumigate imported goods being held in quarantine, and some export products, such as logs and fruit. Is extremely toxic to humans and is implicated in ozone depletion.

Nitrate: A compound containing nitrogen that can exist in the atmosphere or as a dissolved gas in water and which can have harmful effects on humans and animals. Nitrates in water can cause severe illness in infants and domestic animals. A plant nutrient and inorganic fertiliser, nitrates are found in septic systems, animal feed lots, agricultural fertilisers, manure, industrial wastewaters and rubbish dumps.

Nitric oxide (NO): A gas formed by combustion under high temperature and high pressure in an internal combustion engine; it is converted by sunlight and photochemical processes to nitrogen oxide, which is a precursor of ground-level ozone pollution, or smog.

Organic chemicals/compounds: Naturally occurring (animal or plant-produced or synthetic) substances containing mainly carbon, hydrogen, nitrogen, and oxygen.

Organochlorine compounds: Any chemicals that contain carbon and chlorine. Classified as POPs, organochlorine chemicals are easily dispersed once released to air, land or water. They do not readily break down in the environment but bio-accumulate in the food chain, with animals at the top suffering the worst adverse effects. Dioxins, PCBs, PCP and the pesticides DDT, dieldrin, lindane and chlordane are organochlorine compounds.

Ozone depletion: Destruction of the stratospheric ozone layer which shields the earth from ultraviolet radiation harmful to life. This destruction of ozone is caused by the breakdown of certain chlorine and/or bromine containing compounds (chlorofluorocarbons or halons), which break down when they reach the stratosphere and then catalytically destroy ozone molecules.

Ozone layer: The protective layer in the atmosphere, about 24 km above the ground, that absorbs some of the sun's ultraviolet rays, reducing the amount of potentially harmful radiation that reaches the earth's surface.

PCBs (polychlorinated biphenyls): Synthetic organic chemicals extensively used in electrical transformer fluids, hydraulic fluids, printing inks, plasticisers and paints. Classified as POPs, the use of PCBs has been illegal in New Zealand since 1995.

PCPs (pentachlorophenol): A synthetic organic chemical, PCP was widely used as a pesticide in the New Zealand timber industry until 1988. Also used to a lesser extent in pulp and paper industry, mushroom cultivation, domestic gardens and on roofs to control moss and algae.

PFCs (perfluorocarbons): A family of synthetic organic chemicals which are completely resistant to environmental degradation. Used to create Teflon coatings on cookware, and stain and water-repellent fabrics. PFCs were initially thought to be completely inert and therefore harmless. Recent findings implicate PFCs in the contamination of human blood and wildlife.

Persistent organic pollutants (POPs): Sometimes called persistent pesticides, POPs are a group of organic chemicals that share four essential characteristics: they resist physical, biological and chemical degradation; pose a toxic threat to human health or the environment; build up in the environment; and are semi-volatile, enabling them to move long distances through the atmosphere.

Pesticide: Substances intended for preventing, destroying, repelling, or mitigating any pest. Also, any substance or mixture intended for use as a plant regulator, defoliant, or desiccant.

Phenols: Organic compounds that are by-products of petroleum refining, tanning, and textile, dye and resin manufacturing. Low concentrations cause taste and odour problems in water; higher concentrations can kill aquatic life and humans.

Polymer: A natural or synthetic chemical structure where two or more like molecules are joined to form a more complex molecular structure (e.g. polyethylene in plastic).

Polyvinyl chloride (PVC): A tough, environmentally indestructible plastic that releases hydrochloric acid and dioxins when burned.

Radiation: Transmission of energy through space or any medium. Also known as radiant energy.

Radon: A colourless, naturally occurring, radioactive, inert gas formed by radioactive decay of radium atoms in soil or rocks.

Sick building syndrome (SBS): An acute incidence of indoor air pollution that can occur in closed or poorly ventilated offices and residences. Symptoms may include irritation of eyes, nose and skin, headache, fatigue and difficulty breathing. Symptoms improve when the occupant is away from the building. May be caused by VOC pollutants, fungi or other micro-organisms, radiation, or simply a lack of adequate fresh air.

Surfactant: A detergent compound that lowers the surface tension of water and promotes lathering.

Synthetic organic chemicals (SOCs): Man-made (anthropogenic) organic chemicals. Some SOCs are volatile; others tend to stay dissolved in water instead of evaporating.

Toxic substance: A chemical or mixture that may present an unreasonable risk of injury to health or the environment.

Toxicity: The degree to which a substance or mixture of substances can harm humans or animals. Acute toxicity involves harmful effects in an organism through a single or short-term exposure. Chronic toxicity is the ability of a substance or mixture of substances to cause harmful effects over an extended period, usually upon repeated or continuous exposure sometimes lasting for the entire life of the exposed organism.

Tributyltin (TBT): An organotin compound used as the active ingredient in biocides designed specifically for use in LOSP timber treatment and preservation, antifouling of boats (in marine paints), antifungal action in textiles and industrial water systems. Highly toxic to marine organisms.

Ultraviolet rays: Radiation from the sun that can be useful or potentially harmful. UV rays from one part of the spectrum (UV-A) enhance plant life. UV rays from other parts of the spectrum (UV-B) can cause skin cancer or other tissue damage. The ozone layer in the atmosphere partly shields us from ultraviolet rays reaching the earth's surface.

Volatile organic compounds (VOCs): Any organic compound that evaporates readily to the atmosphere. VOCs are often components in adhesives, solvents, degreasers, cleaning solutions, cosmetics, dry cleaning fluids, toners, components of pesticides and plastics, and are among the by-products of combustion. VOCs contribute significantly to photochemical smog production, groundwater contamination and health problems, including eye and respiratory tract irritation, headache, dizziness, memory impairment, neurotoxicity and cancer.

INDEX